The Road Leading to the Market

Since the reform and opening-up period, the world has witnessed a transformation within China. This transformation has led millions out of poverty within China and has in recent years seen China as an important and vital engine of economic growth for the rest of the world. While China has made great strides in embarking on the road to a market economy, this book emphasizes that the transformation within China to market-driven development is far from over.

In this book, Zhang puts forward the idea that the reform in China has now reached a crossroads. The next steps have a bearing not only on the sustainability of past reform but even on whether China will become a veritable world power in the future. With the reform at this pivotal juncture, this book explores further reform within China and examines how the reform debate will develop. *The Road Leading to the Market* is a highly readable collection of essays which will appeal to researchers and students of China's economy and a globalized economy.

Zhang Weiying holds a Ph.D. in Economics from Oxford University, is a co-founder of the China Center for Economic Research (CCER) at Peking University, a former president of Guanghua School of Management at Peking University, a former vice director of the International Association for Chinese Management Research (IACMR), and is vice chairman of Chinese Economics. He is well known for his contributions to macro-control policy debating, ownership reform debating, and entrepreneurship studies. He has published numerous articles in some of the top international journals such as *Journal of Economic Behavior and Organization* and *Journal of Comparative Economics*. He is also the author of several well-known books such as *Price, Market and Entrepreneurs, The Logic of the Market*, and *What Has Changed China?* He has been the most cited economist in Chinese academic journals since 1995.

Routledge Economic Growth and Development Series

Series Editor: Linda Yueh

Fellow by Special Election in Economics at St Edmund Hall and Director of the China Growth Centre, University of Oxford, UK.

The aim of the series is to publish a series of books that applies rigorous economic analysis to the field of economic growth and development. The scope includes regional and country-specific studies, as well as cross-country comparisons, to examine the evidence surrounding the pressing and interesting questions on the growth prospects of developed and developing countries.

The Road Leading to the Market

Zhang Weiying

LONDON AND NEW YORK

Translated by Gao Qian

First published 2017
by Routledge

2 Park Square, Milton Park, Abingdon, Oxfordshire OX14 4RN
52 Vanderbilt Avenue, New York, NY 10017

Routledge is an imprint of the Taylor

First issued in paperback 2020

British Library Cataloguing in Publication Data
A catalogue record for this book is available from the British Library

Library of Congress Cataloging-in-Publication Data
Names: Zhang, Weiying, 1959– author.
Title: The road leading to the market / Zhang Weiying.
Description: London ; New York : Routledge, 2016. | Series: China
  perspectives series
Identifiers: LCCN 2015044282 | ISBN 9781138810242 (hardback) |
  ISBN 9781315727097 (ebook)
Subjects: LCSH: Economic development—China. | Capitalism—
  China. | China—Economic policy—1949– | China—Commercial
  policy. | China—Foreign economic relations. | China—Politics and
  government—1949–
Classification: LCC HC427.95 .Z435278 2016 | DDC 330.951—dc23
LC record available at http://lccn.loc.gov/2015044282

ISBN: 978-1-138-81024-2 (hbk)
ISBN: 978-0-367-51663-5 (pbk)

Typeset in Bembo
by Apex CoVantage, LLC

Contents

Preface to *The Wide Reading Series*

Two years ago I was commissioned to establish the Institute for Advanced Studies in Humanities and Social Sciences and a "knowing and doing" Pilot Class of Liberal Arts at Beihang University. Although I had a clear idea of how to carry out general education for undergraduates and high-caliber research on humanities and social sciences in a university dominated by science and engineering, I felt it quite challenging to take a step forward. Thanks to the great support of all of my friends of the academic world and inclusion of young talents in my team, we managed to set our exploration on the right path of imparting knowledge and educating people.

I still remember that shortly after the founding of the Institute for Advanced Studies in Humanities and Social Sciences, I along with my young colleagues conceived of editing three series of academic writings entitled *Wide Reading*, *General Knowledge*, and *Knowing and Doing*, respectively. *The Wide Reading Series* aims to include all of the writings by the chair professors and scholars of our institute in a bid to publish their academic researches, social reviews, and sketches of lecture notes for the pilot class and to present the splendor of insights of our teaching staff. *The General Knowledge Series*, as a collection of research reports of the institute, focuses on succinct excerpts and comments concerning general education at home and abroad and manifests our ideas, experience, and practice of general education. *The Knowing and Doing Series* is the academic journal of our institute and centers on a range of topics concerning literature, history, philosophy, politics, economy, and law; for the sake of forging the journal into an ideological banner, we appoint young lecturers as chief editors responsible for carefully selecting the topic of every volume. After over two years of hard work, these three series are basically completed and will be published soon.

Today, writing a preface to *The Wide Reading Series* is for me a lightly heavy burden. In "Farewell to Zhang Hu," Su Shi (an outstanding Chinese poet of the Song Dynasty) said, "Alas, when you arrive in the imperial capital, you must concentrate on study. You'd better read widely and use what you learned cautiously; you'd better be well-prepared so as to succeed with ease. That is what I'd like to advise you to do." Likewise, Zeng Guofan (an eminent Han Chinese official of the late Qing Dynasty) in "Preface to Sun Zhifang's Remarks" wrote,

"Though I differ from Liu Jiaoyun in the amount of writings, yet both of us agree on reading widely and using what we learned cautiously." When holding the nine books of the first volume, the fruit born by our utmost effort, I feel indebted to my friends of the academic world, and, in particular, I think it necessary to reassert the belief our institute holds. As a matter of fact, earlier I wrote about the belief in the name of the dean's speech on the institute's website, which was to open soon. I might as well copy it as follows.

Even though our country has sustained over 110 years of changes from past to present and conflicts between China and the West, we are still in the middle of making arduous efforts to construct a free, democratic, constitutional country. There are plenty of reasons for the rise and fall of a country, but education is supposed to be a crucial factor. A hundred years ago, Liang Qichao (a Chinese scholar and reformist who lived during the late Qing Dynasty and early Republic) advocated a theory of New Citizen and asserted national education and cultivation of talents bore on China's future. Although there has been no consensus on what talents colleges and universities are expected to cultivate, undeniably, for several decades the narrow-minded utilitarianistic view of education has been prevalent, and cultivation of moral qualities has been absent for long. I esteem that general education is, in principle, free education fostering free personality and great mind, which is supposed to be the purpose of running our institute. Therefore, our general education emphasizes classics at all times and in all countries, ranging from records of statecraft of rulers (of the Xia, Shang, and Zhou Dynasties) to ancient and modern researches on Confucian classics, from writings of Athenian democracy to studies of *an Inquiry into the Nature and Causes of the Wealth of Nations*. We aim to take advantage of classical traditions to open a modern chapter and to contrast Chinese culture with Anglo-American cultures. We endeavor to school students to experience the inspiring humanistic spirit of our institute and thus upon graduation throw themselves into social reform. It has been our aspiration to enable our students to manage their lives and to achieve triumphs.

The publication of *The Wide Reading Series* is bound to lead us toward the coast of freedom.

Gao Quanxi
Beijing, March 21, 2012

Author's preface

This book includes my thirty-seven short articles concerning China's reform and development that I published in the past several years.[1] These articles, like other books I have published before, are expressive of my real thoughts. Although many people disagree with my opinions, and I cannot ensure all of them are necessarily right, I feel obligated to voice them publicly. I believe in Thomas Paine's words: "It is necessary to the happiness of man, that he be mentally faithful to himself. Infidelity does not consist in believing, or in disbelieving; it consists in professing to believe what he does not believe." Telling lies publicly is the most severe moral corruption.

Each article of my collection focuses on practical problems confronting China's reform and development. These problems are as follows.

Is China's economic boost in the past thirty years a result of marketization reform and the rise of private enterprises, or a result of government intervention and the leading role of state-owned enterprises (so-called "China Model")? Are problems emerging during the reform process (such as corruption, unfair income distribution, backward medical services, food safety problems, moral corruption, and so on) caused by over-marketization or excessive government regulation? Is the global financial crisis a failure of market or of government? Does it pertain to China's policies? Are Keynesian economic policies the cause of the financial crisis or the effective way of coping with the crisis? Does the transition of economic growth model rely more on market mechanism and entrepreneurship or on government monetary policies and industrial policies? Confronted with new challenges at home and abroad, should we insist on the direction of "the private sector advances, and the state retreats" or take the road back to follow the direction of "the state advances, and the private sector retreats"? How should we look at the role of entrepreneurs in society? Are they the propelling force for social advance and harmony, or the maker of social conflicts? What is the cause of Chinese enterprises' lack of a motivating force for innovation? What system conditions and policy conditions do we need for the sake of fostering enterprises' and entrepreneurs' initiative in innovation? Are the efforts of China's economic reform sustainable, and is China's economic growth sustainable, if we don't start political-system reform after the over-thirty-year economic reform? How should political-system reform be carried out?

These problems have aroused numerous discussions and heated debates in the media and the academic world, but no consensus has been reached, and many popular opinions are no more than catchwords or emotional release. Apparently, personal as my views are, I believe that they, right or wrong, might contribute to helping people consider them rationally.

The gist of my book can be generalized as follows.

A market economy is a system that is most beneficial to human cooperation and social advance. Nothing but a market economy can avoid disasters caused by a combination of ignorance of the majority and shamelessness of the minority. A market economy is based on individual freedom, private property rights, and entrepreneurship. It is owing to marketization that human society has experienced a leaping development over nearly the past two hundred years and that China has created an economic miracle in the recent thirty years. It is time-consuming both for Western society to change from feudal landlord estate economy to market economy and for China to turn from a planned economy into a market economy. In the meantime, anti-market forces (due to resistance of vested interests or wrong ideas) always attempt to hinder the change, and people's superstition about government intervention is looming like a subterranean stream.

Although China has already made great progress in approaching a market economy, the transition toward marketization hasn't accomplished, and we haven't established a solid foundation for a market economy, because our economy is based on the foundation of privileges instead of rights, and private property rights haven't been effectively protected, and entrepreneurship is suffering from various forms of suppression and even destruction. In particular, since the global financial crisis hit the world in 2008, marketization reform has raised public doubt, and relevant government departments have published a quantity of anti-market policies in the name of macroeconomic management and industrial policies. The reform is halted and even begins to retrogress; as government intervention in economy augments, state-owned sectors grow stronger. China's reform is at the crossroads, and how to make the next move determines not only whether achievements our reform has already made are sustainable but also whether China can evolve into a world power or not.

We must acknowledge that government's intensive intervention and domination of state-owned enterprises are not the cause of China's economic miracles but the cause of multiple contradictions and inequalities in China. Huge state-owed sectors have become one of the main obstacles to China's economic growth, to giving play to entrepreneurship and to developing domestic markets. Keynesian economic interference policies not only cannot offer solutions to the global crisis but foreshadow a new crisis, which hinders China's transition of economic growth pattern. We must return to the track of marketization reform and continue to diminish government intervention in economy and the proportion of state-owned enterprises, creating a more favorable environment for private enterprises. Only in this way can Chinese entrepreneurs be motivated to innovate and Chinese enterprises establish real core competitiveness; thus, the transition of China's economic growth pattern can be truly accomplished.

With regard to economic reform, we still have a lot of work to do. But without political-system reform, there will be little room left for further economic reform even if we have wise and resolute political leaders. Therefore, the next stage of reform should focus on political-system reform. Only if we establish a real democratic system under the rule of law will the system foundation be laid for complete economic marketization and will China really evolve into a market economy country.

Some of the articles are based on my speeches delivered at forums and seminars. Special thanks go to my academic assistant Mr. Cen Ke for his help with my writing. Of course, I am fully responsible for any error in my book.

I am indebted to Chief Editor Professor Gao Quanxi. Without his invitation and supervision, the book wouldn't be published.

I am equally grateful to Managing Editor Ms. Chen Lixia for her earnestness and responsibility as well as high-quality editing.

Zhang Weiying
March 6, 2012

Note

1 Academic papers I wrote in the same period are included in *The Logic of Market* (Shanghai People's Publishing House, 2010, 1st edition; 2012, revised edition; its English translation will be published by the Cato Institute in 2015). Media interviews are collected in another book, *What Has Changed China?* (Citic Press, 2012).

Part one

The power of the market

The power of the market[1]

According to the study of Bradford DeLong (an economist of UC–Berkeley, USA), in the history of 2500 thousand years (from the Old Stone Age to 2000 A.D.), human beings spent 99.4% of the whole time obtaining 90-international-dollar (a measurement unit for wealth appraised by the international purchasing power in 1990) world per capita GDP 15,000 years ago; then they spent 0.59% of the time raising the world per capita GDP to 180 international dollars by 1750 A.D. From 1750 to 2000 – namely during 0.01% of the history – the world per capita GDP grew thirty-seven times (to 6,600 international dollars). In other words, 97% of the wealth in the possession of human beings was created in the past 250 years – namely, 0.01% of the time.[2]

If DeLong's study is represented by a curve chart, we can see during 99.99% of the whole period (from 2,500 thousand years ago till now) the curve of world per capita GDP hardly fluctuates, but, in the past 250 years, the curve suddenly ascends almost vertically. So is the case with the major developed countries. It is mainly in the past one or two hundred years that these countries have experienced their economic boost, whether so-called Western European offsprings such as the United States, Canada, and Australia, or Western European countries including Britain, France, Germany, and nine other countries, or the new rising Japan.

Figures cannot be overwhelmingly persuasive. So let us imagine our ancestors, ordinary Chinese people who lived one hundred years ago, consumed the same goods and products as ancient people during the Qing, Han, Sui, and Tang Dynasties, even less and worse ones than people did during the Song Dynasty. So is the case in Europe. In 1800 what a common English person could consume was also accessible to an ancient Roman, or even a Roman could live a better life. However, today what we can consume is beyond the imagination of people that lived a hundred years ago.

It is estimated that according to retailers' measures of the number of types of products, known as stock-keeping units or *SKU*, 250 years ago people could only consume about 10^2 types of goods at most, but now, more than 10^8 types of goods.

Why did human beings' economic boost take place during the past 250 years, but China's economic growth did in the past thirty years? Have human beings become more intelligent and wiser than their ancestors? Of course not, at least not so much. Since the beginning of recorded history, human intelligence and wisdom have hardly improved. I am sure none of today's Chinese people can be intelligent or wise enough to excel Confucius, Mencius, and Lao-tze. It holds true for Westerners. Human intelligence has almost remained the same in the past two or three thousand years.

Is it because our natural resources have multiplied? Also no. Natural resources haven't increased. Instead natural resources related to land are gradually decreasing. So what is the reason? The sole reason is that human beings have developed a new economic system – that is, market economy. Western countries began to carry out the system about two hundred years ago, so their economy started to thrive ever after. In contrast, China started to implement it thirty years ago, so China underwent a giant leap ever after.

Why can market economy create enormous wealth? In *An Inquiry into the Nature and Causes of the Wealth of Nations*, Adam Smith, originator of economics, claims that the market, as an invisible hand, converts each individual's pursuit of self-interest into achievement of the best good of all. That is the mystery of market economy.

So why? In a market economy, everyone who is situated in the chain of social division of labor produces for the sake of exchange; it is up to others instead to value how much contribution an individual makes to society and how much he or she can share. In the market anyone that doesn't create value for others cannot earn personal interests. For this reason, you have to endeavor to benefit others. Prices give us a signal that the market has the final say about what's valuable or what's worthless. For example, you think a product is quite valuable, but, if no one would like to buy it, it is worthless. Moreover, none would pay higher than the value of services he or she is offered. As far as two competing enterprises are concerned, when we think one of them is more advantageous, we mean that it can create more surplus for consumers – namely, so-called "consumer surplus" in economics. In most cases, enterprises compete with each other for creating more consumer surplus value.

Market economy is a synonym of commercial society. In a commercial society, cooperation is often conducted between mutually unfamiliar individuals, while, in a traditional society, cooperation is always conducted between acquaintances or relatives such as siblings or people from the same villages or the same church and cooperation between unfamiliar people is uncommon. However, today human beings' cooperation has transcended inter-regional and international borderlines and gone global. With regard to all the goods we consume, we are unfamiliar with 99% of their producers; when an enterprise sells a product to consumers, the majority of buyers are anonymous to the company. It is the large-scale cooperation that astonishingly accelerates the accumulation of wealth all over the world.

However, to achieve cooperation between unfamiliar people, an essential problem must be solved – that is, trust. If two unfamiliar individuals don't trust each other, their cooperation is impossible; thus, human beings could not share advantages of market economy. In order to comprehend my point of view, we must have a better understanding of enterprise, profit, and entrepreneur.

Enterprises are the basic accounting unit of a market economy. For instance, there are 1.3 billion Chinese people, and, if each of them produces and sells goods in the market, who you will trust? In other words, if all goods' brands are removed, what dare you buy? Perhaps you merely venture to buy some primary goods such as potatoes, rice, and fruit. Will you venture to purchase products whose quality and function are not instantly discernable, such as automobiles, computers, mineral water, and projectors? No, you won't. You won't probably purchase 99% of goods in the market.

Is there any solution? We can divide 1.3 billion people into different groups, say, geographically into thirty groups such as Henaners, Hebeiers, Shandongers, Shanxiers, Beijingers. After the grouping is done, we can discern who is from Shandong and who is from Guangdong and can make certain judgments, even if we are unfamiliar with each of them. Likewise, an enterprise is similar to one group of this kind. Each enterprise has its own name, so if it deceives us, we can sue it or we will stop buying its products and it won't survive eventually. When the society is divided into enterprises, each of them should shoulder the responsibility for its actions; thus, we can establish trust. Without enterprises, every one of us would be engaged in individual production, and no trust would be established.

How can enterprises enable us to trust each other? The answer lies in owner-ship allocation and profit. For instance, if an enterprise consists of ten thousand people, theoretically each of them could be an owner; if its annual profit is 100 million yuan, each could obtain 10,000 yuan. It sounds quite fair, but who will shoulder responsibility if there arises a problem? If everyone is asked to be responsible, probably it turns out to be that none of them would be.

In reality, enterprises adopt another way to distribute responsibilities; in other words, a group of people shoulder negligence liability, and the rest of them do strict liability. The former – that is, employees – earn contract income, and as long as they are punctual at work and don't leave early and don't violate work rules, they ought to be paid at the end of a month. The latter – that is, employers – should assume strict responsibility or residue responsibility. To put it simply, being an employee, if others cannot find your fault, you have no liability; being an employer, if you cannot find others' faults, you will be responsible for all the faults. An employer has no right to claim income before consumers even if he or she doesn't err, while an employee can claim income before his or her employer if he or she doesn't err. This is the difference between being an employee and being an employer.

Employers earn their pay from profits that are not always within their reach. Profit is the residue after cost is deducted, positive or negative, so it is an incentive mechanism. As far as an enterprise is concerned, if I don't know its employees, the reason why I trust it should be that someone shoulders residue responsibil-ity. If you are the boss of a restaurant, you must bear responsibility when some customers suffer from diarrhea and are hospitalized just because your cook didn't wash food ingredients clean. In order to earn profits, an enterprise owner must bear residue or strict liability and be responsible for any mistakes made by any employee, so the owner has to try every means to motivate and supervise employees. Only this way can customers trust and purchase the enterprise's products.

Furthermore, an enterprise is supposed to assume the responsibility for faults made by not only its employees but also its suppliers. For instance, if you buy a brand-name computer and something wrong goes with the computer's parts such as screen, chip, or fan, or its battery explodes, the first one to bear responsibility should be the computer enterprise instead of its part suppliers. In other words, a brand-name enterprise, in fact, makes use of its brand to write a pledge for consumers and to bear responsibility if its products you have bought go wrong. Therefore, a market where we can trust each other comes into being, and cooperation between unfamiliar people can be reached, which promotes social wealth to grow steadily.

Hence, in my view, a market economy is a responsibility system in which profit serves as a testing mode. The market divides accounting units by enterprises and uses profits to prosecute responsibility, thus making everyone be responsible for his or her actions. Only if an enterprise is enable to shoulder responsibility is it qualified to make profits!

Entrepreneurs who earn profits ought to be responsible for organizing and producing for the whole society and supervising others. When we discuss about market economy, we should never forget entrepreneurs. An enterprise is the business of an entrepreneur. We cannot have full understanding of the market economy merely from the perspective of price.

An entrepreneur is the most suitable one to shoulder strict responsibility as the owner of enterprise, because he or she has two fundamental functions. First, the function of coping with uncertainties. According to the idea put forward in 1921 by Frank Hyneman Knight, an American economist, entrepreneurs have to predict the future, for the market is abundant with uncertainties. In *Risk, Uncertainty and Profits*, he proves that profits are the compensation given to entrepreneurs for taking uninsurable risk, and, from the perspective of economics, without uncertainty there is no profit. Second, the function of promoting innovation. Innovation is the responsibility of entrepreneurs instead of technicians who are engaged in invention; innovation turns inventions into what are valuable to consumers. Innovation is creative destruction – for example, MP3s and the iPod have destroyed Sony's Walkman, which had replaced the cassette player. Every new product is the replacement of the older one, which is the significant idea proposed in *The Theory of Economic Development* by Joseph Alois Schumpeter in 1911. Entrepreneurs must bear the responsibility for success or failure of innovation.

We are living in the age of globalization. The so-called economic globalization is the marketization of global economy. Every country, every enterprise, and every person is situated in the chain of global division of labor and linked by market. In the age of globalization, what happens in any place will probably exert influence upon every country, every enterprise, and every individual. The global financial crisis triggered by the US subprime lending crisis is an obvious illustration! The globalization means more intensive competition and more uncertainty! Only if every country, every enterprise, and every individual have a better understanding of changes of global commercial environment and rules of market economy and possess innovative spirit and capability could they survive and develop in intensive competition!

Understanding Business is a unique textbook. It makes use of the global perspective to combine classic theories of economics with management science and applies theory to practical case analyses. The book in a simple and explicit way helps us acquire a better understanding of rules of market economy and managerial practices in the age of globalization. I am sure you will benefit from reading it whether you would like to be an employer or employee in the future. Hence, I would like to highly recommend it to you.

Why do human beings make mistakes?[3]

For several years I have pondered over one question: why do humans commit mistakes, even disastrous ones? The final conclusion I have drawn is that there are two reasons – namely, ignorance and shamelessness. Of course, according to Buddhism, shamelessness is essentially an expression of ignorance, because shameless persons are in ignorance of their fundamental interests.

People with good intentions often make mistakes due to their own ignorance, ignorance of not knowing the consequences of their actions and behaviors. A typical example is tragedies caused by parents' good-intentioned interference into their children's marriage. Besides, there are also plenty of similar examples. Benefiting oneself at the expense of others' interests is a mistake caused by shamelessness, such as the burning of books and burying of scholars ordered by Emperor Qinshihuang more than two thousand years ago.

In reality, of course, many mistakes are caused by a combination of ignorance and shamelessness. For example, the Cultural Revolution is a product of a majority's ignorance and a minority's shamelessness. A minority of people (particularly Mao Zedong) waged a campaign for the sake of authority and power, but out of their ignorance the majority, who regretted their mistakes after it was too late, energetically supported the campaign. Therefore, a tremendous historical tragedy that decimated Chinese culture and humanity took place. What I attempt to remind you of is that there are hundreds or thousands of similar disasters in history for which a huge price was paid.

Another example is the Boxer Rebellion in China in 1900. The boxers were so ignorant as to think they could be invulnerable as long as they received one-hundred-days training and recited some special incantations. Likewise, the rulers of the Qing Dynasty such as Empress Dowager Cixi, Gang Yi (Grand Minister of State), Zailian (Prince Dun), Zaiyi (Prince Duan), Zailan (Burubafen Duke Who Assists the Nation), and Zaixiong (Prince Zhuang) were both ignorant and shameless. They intended to take advantage of the rebellion to struggle for power in order to consolidate their ruling positions. That is shamelessness. There were also some court officials who shamelessly considered the movement as a good opportunity of winning promotion and fortune. Consequently, Chinese people were plunged into an abyss of misery, and the fate of the nation hung in the balance. More aware of these consequences than aforementioned rulers, some leading officials such as Li Hongzhang, Liu Kunyi, Zhang Zhidong, and Yuan Shikai had jointly adopted the strategy of South-East Mutual Protection to prevent the southeast from impact of the rebellion as well as invasion of foreign countries.

Consider another example: the Great Leap Forward Campaign taking place in 1958. The campaign called on people to build backyard furnaces to smelt steel and had everyone "eat from the same big pot", which is a manifestation of ignorance. There were so many exaggerated and false agricultural reports such as wheat yield per mu^4 reaching over ten thousand jin^5 or even a hundred thousand jin, which resulted in tens of hundreds of people dying from starvation. For the sake of retaining their positions, some officials exaggerated and falsified reports and even treated people's lives like dirt. The reason seems to be that they had no choice, but it is because of their shamelessness.

So what was the most severe disaster caused by ignorance in human history? It was the system that was imperatively implemented from top to bottom in countries with more than one-third of world's total population. That is the so-called planned economy.

We can hardly imagine why so many wise scholars, politicians, and government officials were so confident that the central authority was capable of telling the whole society what should be produced, how and for whom products should be produced, and how they should be priced. However, these people had a deep-seated faith in the system at the time. Give it a careful thought, and you'll find those who advocated for the planned economy did so not only out of ignorance but owing to that they were so ignorant of their ignorance. Lao-tze preaches to us that not knowing, yet thinking you know, is sickness. In other words, obviously you are ignorant, but you think you are not. What a tremendous economic and social disaster was caused as a result! What a deplorable and pathetic consequence!

One thing I would like to call your attention is that rationales for a planned economy were provided by both traditional Marxists and Western mainstream economists. Oskar Lange, a Chicago-based Polish economist, adopted a neoclassical economic paradigm to argue that a planned economy was feasible. He regarded assumptions proposed to verify feasibility of the market as the reality per se and claimed planning could imitate a competitive market system and play an effective role of the market in allocating resources effectively. As a result, Lange was considered as the winner of the debate over feasibility of the socialist planned economy and was held in high esteem by many mainstream economists, while other economists including Mises and Hayek who were strong opponents of a planned economy became laughingstocks.

If we give it a careful thought, that sounds quite ridiculous. Is it possible for the central authority to collect a large quantity of data? Besides, since the economy is a dynamic process, assumed data would not exist without the market and enterprises. For instance, how to make a statistical analysis of customers' demands for the iPad before it was produced? Though we have done many things, we are not really aware of what we have done. Even mainstream economists haven't figured out how the market operates, but they think they have.

The above example also tells us how to look at science in perspective. The overall goal of science is to reduce humanity's ignorance, but sometimes scientific research will enhance our ignorance instead. For instance, up to the early nineteenth century, European doctors and botanists were still calling on all the people to cut down trees so as to improve public health. Why? Because scientific researchers then indicated many infections were caused by flies and mosquitos, and diseases would be reduced if trees were cut down to decrease insects. However, people soon discovered their suggestion had caused ecological disasters.

Now have a look at our country; the situation seems to be much graver. There are so many public programs, such as the National Innovation Program, and the Program of Fostering 1000 Steve Jobses in Ningbo City of Zhejiang Province. We assume we can carry out scientific innovation, develop proprietary intellectual technologies, and grow entrepreneurs in the same way engineers design buildings. Considering social problems in an engineer's way as such is a manifestation of ignorance.

Now review my ideas about price reform. When I began to prepare my master's degree thesis in the second half of 1983, I surprisingly found that almost all economists and government officials held that right prices could be calculated by government and that so-called price reform meant how government made adjustments in prices. However, there were divergences of opinions on whether government should fix prices according to the labor value, production price, or equilibrium price and whether adjustments should be accomplished in one leap or step by step. But few people doubted prices could be obtained by calculation.

Government's top decision-makers were also confident of that. Therefore, the government established the Price Center of the State Council in 1981 and summoned about fifty economists and price experts to formulate input-output tables with the help of purchased macro-computers and collected national input-output statistics. Although that sounded inconceivable, everyone had a profound belief in the calculation; even leaders of the central government awaited the final outcome and expected to reset prices accordingly. Of course, we are now aware that right prices remain unobtainable, and, even if they had been calculated, none of us would believe them. This is what I knew of at that time.

From the beginning I took a skeptical attitude toward government's ability to calculate right prices. How could prices be calculated? I have spent much time pondering over this question: how a right price takes form. My fundamental conclusion is that price merely takes form in the market and price cannot be a real one as long as it is fixed by government. In my view, the price fixed by government is like an invar-made thermometer. Even if the initially fixed temperature reading is appropriate, it is meaningless when the thermometer doesn't respond to changes of temperature.

Therefore, Chinese price reform couldn't be accomplished by adjustments in one leap or step by step. We shouldn't put all eggs in the basket of price adjustments. I then proposed my suggestion that the only solution should be to loosen up price control. In what way? By means of a step-by-step dual-track system.

The conception of the dual-track system is actually quite understandable. First of all, once planned targets were fixed in accordance with historical conditions at that time, products within plans should be traded at fixed prices and the prices of products outside plans should be loosened up; thus, the dual-track price system of products of the same kind would take form. The next step is to take various measures (including both adjustments and loosening-up) to gradually change planned prices into market prices, which becomes technical problems.

Why shouldn't we loosen up all prices once for all? There are two reasons. Firstly, we are ignorant; secondly, we have to consider vested interests. If we loosen up all prices, enterprises will be thrown into confusion, because market prices are variable prices and state-owned enterprises then had been accustomed to governmental fixed prices. As I once said, enlivening the market and changing production-oriented enterprises into production-marketing-oriented ones is like forcing a child that used to feed off his parents to live independently, which requires an adaptation process. On the other hand, the raw material and livelihood material supplied at the fixed prices as such are the vested interests of enterprises and urban citizens, so the reform should presuppose vested interests. On the basis of respecting vested interests, the dual-track system is aimed to materialize the market economy gradually.

This is the main content of my paper "Taking Price Reform as the Center of Systemic Economic Reform". The paper was finished on April 21, 1984, over four months earlier than the Moganshan Conference (the first National Academic Seminar of Young and Middle-Aged Economic Science Researchers held in Zhejiang), and it was published in the third issue of *Experts' Suggestions*, an internal publication issued by the Energy Department of the Economic and Technological Center of the State Council. Actually, before the conference, I had already finished the second version of my paper and had it published in the fourth issue in 1984 of *Inner Mongolia Economic Research*, which was a public journal.

What I am telling you is that, if we come to realize that we human beings are ignorant of many things, there may be different approaches to tackling system problems. When we think we are knowledgeable and wise, in fact we will waste much time on what is not contributing to solving problems we are confronted with. As far as price reform is concerned, if we think we know what a reasonable price is and what we should focus on is how to adjust prices accordingly, we are coming to a dead end. But if we admit we are ignorant, we will naturally turn our attention to how to loosen up prices and conceive the dual-track system.

Now we are facing the same problems. For example, according to Keynesian macro-economic theory, many of us think we know relationships between money supply, employment, and inflation and know when we should decrease or increase interest rates. Is that so? Recent history has proven that not only Chinese economists and government officials but also other countries' economists and officials are ignorant of relationships among macro-economic variables.

What is the best policy we should adopt when we are ignorant? It is to counter changes with the same unchanged stance. Stop taking actions blindly. We shouldn't inject money flow whenever an economy slows down, nor should we employ a credit crunch whenever inflation is drawing near. Denial of ignorance has cost us dearly.

Consider industrial policies. Many government departments still hold that government is capable of knowing what will be a core industry and leading industry in the future and how we should develop them. However, historical experience has indicated that we made too many mistakes. As a matter of fact, we are totally ignorant of what on earth will be a core industry and a leading industry and the future hi-tech development direction. Research into these issues should be entrusted to entrepreneurs.

Ningbo Municipal's (Zhejiang Province) ambition to foster one thousand Steve Jobses is another example showing our ignorance. Just as Lao-tze's saying goes, we are sick.

In reality, government's industrial policies often become means of rent-seeking employed by the ignorant and the shameless to conspiratorially appropriate public resources. Sometimes, for the sake of individual interests, some people or enterprises tend to deceive government and blindfold government officials who are in charge of allocating resources, so tens of millions of funds are allocated. At other times, government departments will continue super-adding funds in order to cover up their previous decision-making mistakes made by their ignorance. As a result, ignorance evolves into shamelessness, which is as wrong as wrong can be. The scandal of faking research into computer chips by a professor of Shanghai Jiao Tong University is a typical example. There can be plenty of similar examples.

Why do we need a market economy? Apparently, only a market economy can prevent disasters caused by a combination of a majority's ignorance and a minority's shamelessness. A market economy means decentralized decision-making and decentralized resource allocation. Even if a minority of power holders attempt to expand the scale of actions, they are unable to mobilize a large quantity of resources.

Would there have been the Great Leap Forward Campaign if we had carried out a market economy? Would there have been so many casualties? Definitely no! Of course, even if we had a market economy, we might have the gap between the rich and the poor and casualties in case of natural disasters such as earthquakes and tornados, but there would be no casualties caused by the shortage of food.

A market economy can reduce much ignorance, too. In the market, correct knowledge and accurate prediction of the market determine the amount of profits, which will motivate entrepreneurs to reduce their ignorance as much as possible. Marketing is a process of entrepreneurs' incessantly discovering, creating, and producing information that does not exist under the conditions of the planned economy.

A market economy can prevent our selfish actions from turning into harmful shameless ones. In the market, anyone but producers has the final say. In a competitive market, if you want to seek your interests, you should create value for others – namely, consumers and clients. The market competition is competition of creating value for consumers. In contrast, in a planned economy, the best way of seeking personal interests is to impair others' interests, plunder others' fruits, and profit at others' expense. That is why we need a market economy. If it was out of ignorance that we once carried out a planned economy, it is out of shamelessness that some people now continue doing it.

But how to ensure my sayings above are not a product of my own ignorance or even of my own shamelessness? The only solution is freedom of thought and academic competition. Whenever it occupies a legal monopoly position, any thinking, whether philosophical or religious and no matter how great its creator is or how correct when it is created, will become the thruster for ignorance and the patron saint of shamelessness and thus will breed ignorance and shamelessness that are destined to bring about disasters. Therefore, our hope lies in our future academic environments. If we are able to have academic freedom and if we allow ideas competition, our ignorance and shameless will be reduced, so will human-made disasters.

From Lao-tze to Adam Smith

It took as long as half a month to go with the China Entrepreneur Club to visit the United States from Wall Street in the east to Silicon Valley in the west. What a lengthy journey! Though I have been in high spirits since I stepped on the land of America, I suddenly become quite eager to return home when I am leaving today.

The east differed from the west not only in geography and time but in atmosphere and people's mental attitudes. My overall impression is that the visit to the east seemed "macroscopic", while the visit to the west "microscopic"; in the east everyone looked like a politician, but in the west everyone was a real entrepreneur.

During the beginning several days, in New York we attended several times "The Dialogue between Sino-US Business Leaders", listened to the Luncheon Speech delivered by Albright (former secretary of state of the United States), and had a meeting with Secretary-General of the United Nations Ban Ki-moon; in Washington we met Powell, former secretary of state, in a café and participated in a breakfast seminar held by the Brookings Institution and official meetings with Secretary of Commerce John Bryson and Under Secretary of state Robert Hormats as well as some congressmen. What concerned us were some big issues such as prospects for global economic growth, European countries' debt crises, Sino-US relations, the exchange rate of the *renminbi*, and China's economy and political system reform. When we were discussing, the atmosphere was filled with pessimism, and what I saw on our faces were anxiety, confusion, and lostness. It seemed that as long as politicians regulated economy and took control of the world, it was difficult to be optimistic.

However, when we arrived at Silicon Valley on the west coast, the situation was the opposite. We visited Google; had a face-to-face meeting with Mark Zuckerberg, founder of Facebook; listened to introductions made by senior executives of Oracle; communicated with several legendary pioneers and venture capitalists; and attended a theme luncheon held by the Bay Area Enterprise Society and a symposium of the Stanford Graduate School of Business. Our topics revolved around such "microscopic" concepts as enterprise startup, innovation, risk, knowledge inheritance, merger, and enterprise growth. Only at that time could I find myself among a group of outstanding entrepreneurs. I sensed vitality and vigor. It seemed that as long as there was entrepreneurship, the world never disappointed us!

When discussing big "macroscopic" issues, everyone was an eloquent expert at voicing his or her opinion, but, of course, probably no consensus could be reached. Generally speaking, Americans were more pessimistic than Chinese about the prospects for the US economy, while Chinese were more pessimistic than Americans about the prospects for China's economic growth. Surely, among Chinese entrepreneurs there were also optimists. But I had no idea about whether this optimism was expressive of people's aspiration or was based on facts and reasonable judgment.

As an economist, I used to be an optimist. However, since the global financial crisis took place in 2008, I have become less optimistic just for two reasons. Firstly, after the global financial crisis, the whole world is undergoing a crisis of beliefs, and more and more people begin to doubt market mechanism but believe in government intervention. The United States is the most marketized country, but it has pinned all hopes on anti-market Keynesian quantitative easing monetary policies and on strengthening government regulation as well as trade protectionism. So is the case with China. Some government departments have blind worship in state-owned enterprises and industrial policies and revel in the so-called "China Model", so they keep issuing anti-market policies. Consequently, within several years the country's disposition has altered tremendously, and the economic reform has remained stagnant and even retrograded; state-owned enterprises are triumphantly thriving, while private entrepreneurs are astonishingly plunged into a plight.

The second factor I am concerned about is the crisis of global leadership. Globally, the quality of governmental leaders is decreasing. In the 1980s there were many great politicians such as Deng Xiaoping, Ronald Regan, and

Margaret Thatcher, but today we can hardly find such politicians the world over. The reason why they were great is that they had mission, vision, and passion. Today's world that is abundant with politicians and irresponsible bureaucrats is badly in need of missionary political leaders.

Political leaders serve to lead the populace to recognize their common interests and achieve win-win cooperation between separate groups. In fact, the consistency of interests among different countries and groups is much more than most people think. Regrettably, politicians often deliberately mislead the populace so as to gain political interests, which results in more conflicts of interest. Here is a typical example: US politicians attributed the financial crisis to China, especially the *renminbi*'s exchange rate; therefore, an opinion poll indicated most Americans regarded China's development as a threat to their country. In the interview with Powell, former US secretary of state, I advocated that when discussing the Sino-US relationship, US politicians were too political and Chinese were too emotional; being less political and less emotional will bring about a more harmonious Sino-US relationship. General Powell was quite in favor of my view. Unfortunately, people of his kind tend to think they are not suitable for politics, so they quit the political arena finally.

After Albright delivered a speech at noon on November 9, I addressed a brief speech. I recommended two books to US politicians – namely, *An Inquiry into the Nature and Causes of the Wealth of Nations* by Adam Smith from 235 years ago and *Tao Teh King* by Lao-tze from 2300 years ago, because the former would help them have a better understanding of importance of free trade and the latter would tell them how to be a global leader. The United States is founded by free trade, but trade protectionism is still prevalent there. The US government should recognize that the solution to unemployment lies in a bigger and opener global market, not in protectionism that separates the global market. I think China is not interested in and not capable of challenging US global leadership, which does no harm to China, but America must change the way it leads.

Lao-tze is probably the first liberalist thinker in human history. Although he may not understand the significance of market mechanism, his ideas of governing without interruption and minimal statism are undoubtedly the prerequisite to the effective operation of market, which is in accordance with Smith's liberalism. It is said that Smith was enlightened by French Physiocrats, who were influenced by Lao-tze's thoughts. If today's politicians could believe in Lao-tze and Smith, there would be less conflicts in the world.

In contrast to other countries the world over, the United States is still a paradise for business startup, which was unanimously acknowledged by Chinese entrepreneurs after they had visited Silicon Valley. After the visit, our entrepreneurs felt less pessimistic about the prospects for the US economy than when we first arrived in the west. What they sighed with sadness at is that given the differences between China and the United States in social conditions, the cultural atmosphere, and educational system, it is an arduous task for China to surpass the United States in the future. Without freedom and the rule by law, there will hardly be real innovation and entrepreneurship; without innovation and entrepreneurship, there won't be sustainable development.

Though the visit to the United States is coming to an end, it has inspired our lingering afterthoughts.

Written in Four Seasons Hotel, Silicon Valley,
on November 18, 2011.

How to establish market: from privileges to rights[6]

Recently there has been an influential case arousing our attention – namely, the case of Wu Ying. Wu Ying, a young female entrepreneur from Zhejiang, was convicted of financial fraud and sentenced to death by the Supreme Court of Zhejiang Province, because she illegally raised 700 million yuan from eleven relatives to plunge into businesses. Is there any similar case taking place in the Western market economy? No, there isn't, but there was. For example, during the second half of the seventeenth century (the Age of Louis XIV), the French government executed at a time more than sixteen thousand entrepreneurs because they were convicted of importing and producing textiles, which violated the industrial and trade policies formulated by Minister of Finance Jean-Baptiste Colbert. Thus, how far are we from a market economy? About three hundred years or two hundred years at least! Because our economy is still based on privileges instead of rights. In other words, we haven't set up a real foundation for a market economy.

So what is the foundation of market? I think there are such three foundations: freedom, property rights, and entrepreneurship.

Freedom is a human right rather than a privilege

Freedom is a fundamental human right to pursue happiness and is an innate right just like life, which shouldn't be deprived of without proper and legitimate procedures. We are in need of freedom, because we feel uncomfortable without freedom in the same way we are when not allowed to eat, drink, and use the toilet. The only limitation on freedom is not to infringe others' rights, because everyone is created equal. In a positive sense, freedom means that all citizens can make use of their wisdom, knowledge, skill, and labor to make their own decisions, improve their lives, and realize their dreams; in a negative sense, freedom implies that everyone is free of enslavement by others and has the right to protect their own interests from being infringed.

In a society where everyone enjoys full freedom, only voluntary cooperation can bring about mutual assistance and benefit. In other words, to gain his or her personal profit, everyone must create value for others; to acquire happiness, everyone should bring happiness to others, which I called "the logic of the market". Moreover, freedom can ensure fair competition, and it is fair competition that fosters innovation that can really propel the advance of our society and enhancement of everyone's life. In this regard, freedom is synonymous with market. If a person approves of market but disapproves freedom or vice versa, I think his or her actions seem contradictory. If there is no freedom in a society, a part of the people can coerce and exploit others and acquire their happiness at the cost of others', which is typical of the gangster logic. If a society is deprived of freedom, nothing but injurious fights will remain, let alone real free competition. In the age of planned economy, quantities of fights instead of real competition took place daily and monthly. Fights destroy wealth, while competition creates wealth. Therefore, freedom is also the foundation of social prosperity.

Here I intend to emphasize that freedom is a fundamental right, not a privilege. To put it simply, rights are equally shared by everyone regardless of their blood and status, while privileges are merely granted to a particular group of people owing to their blood and status. Rights are not easily deprivable, but privileges are. In Ancient Greece and Rome there was so-called freedom, which was a privilege instead of a right, so only a group of male people could enjoy it, but slaves and females who accounted for a large portion of the population couldn't.

In a privilege-prevalent society, there won't be a real market economy. Market economy means opportunities are open to everybody and every citizen should be entitled to plunge into the industry he or she likes, to produce what he or she likes, and to set up an organization as he or she likes, including manufacturing enterprises, financial institutions, and non-profit organizations such as charity foundations, universities, clubs, and political communities. All of these ought to be rights everyone can freely enjoy rather than privileges only a particular group can share.

However, we are aware that in China the aforementioned choices are still privileges instead of commoners' rights. For instance, if you attempt to start up an enterprise, you have to sustain many vetting procedures that are controlled by a minority of people. These people have the final say about who are eligible, and only a small portion of people can be approved. That is a privilege. In particular, our industrial policies have set up entry barriers, so only persons in possession of connections are permitted to enter the industry; thus, a large portion of potential entrepreneurs have been discriminately excluded. In fact, each of our industrial policies is a rent-setting policy or one that grants privileges, which leads to many rent-seeking activities and corrupt practices. Recently the State Council has decided to invest 15 billion yuan to sponsor the development of micro-sized enterprises, but suppose our citizens had the right to freely establish financial institutions, would the investment of this kind be necessary? I think it wouldn't. Whoever gains access to the money enjoys a privilege instead of a real right.

Furthermore, getting permitted to start up a non-profit organization is more like a privilege rather than a right. For example, if you intend to set up a charity foundation, whether you are rich or not, first of all you have to turn to a "responsible institution"; a "responsible institution" must be a governmental or government-affiliated institution; it is totally the privilege for them to decide whether they are willing to be your "responsible institution". If you haven't found or even if you have found a responsible institution, the department of civil administration will not necessarily approve of your application; no matter how great the good deeds you are willing to do are, nothing can be done. Therefore, you cannot conduct good deeds whenever you want to. We don't even have the freedom of doing charities. How pathetic it is!

Here what I emphasize is not that any industry should remove its minimum and essential entry threshold but that freedom means any entry threshold shall be minimized and necessitated for the sake of social interests and shall also be impersonal – namely, treating all applicants equally regardless of their family background, blood, or social status. But in China many entry thresholds are personal and based on privileges rather than rights. For example, if you want to establish a financial institution, you will be more likely to be approved when you know or can get acquainted with a leader of the department of financial supervision and regulation; or there is a faint hope you can obtain approval. Thus, this exemplifies a privilege. This privilege-based entry system has fed numerous connections-centered (not knowledge-centered) so-called "consulting companies" whose profits come from the division of spoils in the privilege system, but not from value creation.

Here I must note the significance of the marketplace of ideas. The marketplace of ideas where human beings employ their intelligence and rationality to explore truths is an indispensable part of a market economy, because a market economy is born to propel social advance, and only advance of ideas of sciences and humanity can bring about the technological and systemic innovation that is the source of social development. The marketplace of ideas denotes that exploration of truths is free of any ideological constraint: everyone's free will is acknowledged, and any idea can't occupy legal monopoly.

The main reason why the United States becomes the most innovative country is that its constitution clearly stipulates that the country shall make no law respecting an establishment of religion or abridging the freedom of speech or of the press. However, in China the freedom of speech and of the press are still privileges rather than rights. For example, if you want to initiate a publishing house, a magazine, or a newspaper, you must obtain official permission, which is quite difficult unless you possess connections. Some new rising disciplines in China seldom have a legal platform for academic exchange, so plenty of academic exchange activities cannot be carried out, let alone the establishment of free academic organizations. We are advocating rejuvenation of the cultural industry, but we should be aware that without the freedom of ideas, the cultural industry is nothing but a plastic greenhouse at best. Without the marketplace of ideas, there is no real market economy.

Government's taxation right and state-owned enterprises' privileges shall be constrained in order to protect property rights

The second foundation of a market economy is property rights. In some sense, property rights are a type of human right and guarantee our freedom. If a society is unable to protect private property from infringement, the populace will have no real freedom, even no personal freedom.

Property rights are also the foundation of social order. The reason why our society is orderly is that we mutually respect property rights. If you are doubtful, just imagine how chaotic a supermarket will become if everyone is allowed to enter it and take whatever they like. Thus, in a society where private property rights aren't protected properly, the majority of people will be stuck in anxiety.

Property rights are also the foundation of social morality. The basic requirement of ethics is that it does no harm to others; only if we respect individual rights and earn our incomes by means of creating value for others can we become moral persons. I cannot imagine a society that disrespects private property rights will foster good moral standards. Willful and wanton infringement on property rights will surely breed the moral culture of living off the toil of other people. When local government officials wantonly infringe on interests of the populace, we should never expect the populace to volunteer to do good deeds. One of the main reasons why our country's morality has deteriorated is that individual rights and private property are not well respected and protected.

Property rights are the foundation of social trust. If private property rights cannot be effectively guaranteed, no one would think long-term and no enterprise would have initiative in building a good reputation in the market; thus, we will find ourselves surrounded by large quantities of frauds and fake and shoddy goods, and we can never trust goods we bought in the market.

Property rights are the foundation of innovation, because only when entrepreneurs have confidence in what they acquired by means of wisdom and diligence will they be willing to spend several years or even several decades pursing a new but quite uncertain thing. In this regard, priority should be given to protection of intangible property. We do worse in protecting intangible property than tangible property; moreover, our protection of intangible property is often selective but not universal. For example, if your reputation right is infringed and you report the case to the police, the police will ask if you are a member of the National Committee of CPPCC or a deputy to the National People's Congress or a celebrity; if not, your case won't be placed on file for investigation. In fact, this is a privilege-based law enforcement.

My sayings are, of course, not new ones, because many philosophers and theologians from Aristotle in ancient Greece to Thomas Aquinas in the Middle Ages and such have already had in-depth expositions. Here are two examples. William of Occam, an English Franciscan friar and scholastic philosopher at the end of the thirteenth century and the beginning of the fourteenth century, once said private property rights were a supreme legal right and rulers could not usurp or willfully confiscate property of the ruled. Giles, Archbishop of Bourges in the thirteenth century claimed the main function of government was to protect personal freedom and the private property system: "the function of ecclesiastical government is to uphold justice and protect people's personal safety and property safety from being endangered in a bid to enable every citizen and honest people to enjoy their own property".

One of the significant measures for protecting private property rights is to constrain government's taxation right. Without limitation on government's taxation right, there is no real protection of property rights. Cen Ke, research fellow of China Entrepreneurs Forum once said that unconstrained taxation was tantamount to robbery. I cannot agree more. Back in 1215, John, king of England, was forced to sign the Magna Carta peace treaty, which aimed to constrain the king's taxation right. In other words, from then on, the king couldn't tax the populace willfully, and the lengthy construction of the British constitutional system just kicked off. However, up to now, constraint of government's taxation right hasn't attracted enough attention; we always prefer to regard the government's revenue increase as good news rather than ask where it comes from.

Last but not least, I highlight that privileges possessed by many state-owned enterprises as such are severe infringement on property rights. Some industries are only open to state-owned enterprises, which is a denial of personal rights. In some industries such as coal, steel, and petroleum, a number of state-owned enterprises forcefully acquire private enterprises, which is gangster logic, not a market rule based on property rights.

Any law and any policy against entrepreneurship is against the market

The third foundation of market is entrepreneurship. Entrepreneurs are the spirit of market economy and kings of economic growth. The market per se is the process of entrepreneurs creating and innovating; without entrepreneurs, there might be product exchange or primitive product exchange rather than real market economy and real innovation. Entrepreneurs are sensitive, enterprising, innovative, diligent, and adventurous. They account for a relatively small proportion of the population, so whether their spirits and capabilities can be given full play will determine the pace of social innovation and of social wealth growth.

It can be said that the great achievements human beings have made in the past two hundred years rely on promotion of entrepreneurs' capabilities and spirits. The reason why China has made such great achievements in the past thirty years is that we gave play to the role of entrepreneurs. In the market economy where free competition thrives, entrepreneurs' job is to serve people, so their success depends on how much happiness they create for us and how satisfied we are with their services. Any policy in the way of entrepreneurs' innovation defies market and consumers.

Our planned economy is fundamentally characterized by suppression of entrepreneurship; as a result, we lived for thirty years in a shortage economy. Who is the biggest victim of the obstruction of entrepreneurs' activities? The populace or the common consumers. When we excluded Google from the Chinese market, it was tens of millions of netizens rather than Google Corp. itself that suffered, because they had no access to more accurate and valuable information any more. If, in a society where people have insufficient freedom, their property rights cannot be guaranteed but privileges prevail and the government takes control of abundant resources, then entrepreneurs will turn to rent-seeking activities instead of creating value for consumers.

What I should remind you of is that not all entrepreneurs are creating wealth for the society. In a privilege-prevalent society, there will be plenty of robber-like entrepreneurs who do anything but create wealth. We should also prevent Chinese entrepreneurs including private entrepreneurs from defending their vested interests. There will always be winners in any system, and some of them might have great initiative in maintaining the status quo instead of promoting institutional reforms. Especially those who rely on privileges will often be more motivated to uphold their privileges instead of turning privileges into equal rights.

In summary, a market economy has three foundations: freedom, property rights, and entrepreneurship. Unless citizens can fully enjoy the freedom of speech, action, and business startup; unless private property rights can be effectively protected by law and culture; and unless entrepreneurship can be given free rein, we cannot establish a real market economy! So is the case with democratic politics. The sanctity of freedom and property rights must be acknowledged or so-called democracy will become a tool for some people to exploit others.

In essence, a planned economy is expressive of the gangster logic. China's reform during the past thirty years is a process of gradually changing the gangster logic into the logic of the market. What is the gist of President Deng Xiaoping's speeches during his China's South Tour twenty years ago? Give people more freedom of business startup and earning money, acknowledge the legality of private property, and make entrepreneurs play the leading role in China's economic development. This is the reason why China's economy underwent a great leap after 1992.

On the road leading to the market, we have made great progress, but our economic reform still has a long way to go because our economy is still based on privileges rather than rights. Western progress in the past two hundred years was turning privileges merely shared by a minority of people in a traditional society into rights equally enjoyed by common people. In contrast, privileges rather than rights are still attached more importance to in China to date.

Let's go back to the Wu Ying case. What does the case imply? It implies Chinese citizens have no freedom of fundraising. It is still a privilege instead of a fundamental right to be permitted to raise funds. State-owned enterprises are permitted to do it, while private enterprises are not. In other words, in China, trade of property rights on the basis of voluntariness cannot get protected. In Wu's case, her eleven relatives didn't admit they were deceived, but our court convicted Wu Ying of fraud. After Wu was arrested, her property was mandatorily auctioned without her personal permission, which is disrespect for private property rights. The case also indicates that our entrepreneurs are still being wrecked mentally to varying degrees. Illegal fundraising is a crime defined by a law or rather a bad law, akin to the crime of speculation and profiteering in those days under the planned economy. I remember many years ago there was a concept in banks of China, "extracorporeal capital flow", which denoted capital flows in private sectors. In the past extracorporeal capital flows were not permitted and were to be cracked down on, whereas, thanks to our progress, they are permitted now. However, illegal fundraising is still a severe label that can be stuck on almost any private entrepreneur. In fact, if there is deceit in the market, we have crime of fraud at hand and are in no need of crime of illegal fundraising. The law that per se aims to stipulate people's principles of behavior and punishments for violation shall be suitable enough to clearly define what is legal or what is illegal. But if it stipulates an ill-defined "illegal" crime, that is a protective privilege.

Many years ago Deng Xiaoping offered protection to Nian Guangjiu, a well-known private businessman in the 1980s, but today Deng is gone; we cannot expect another Deng to protect Wu Ying. Therefore, I have to appeal to our entrepreneurs, government officers, scholars, and journalists to pay more attention to the Wu Ying's case, because Wu's death sentence signifies the retrogression of China's reform. To care about the case is to care about China's future and everyone's freedom and life. If Wu Ying is sentenced to death, I wonder how many other people shall be sentenced to death.

The harm of the corruption of language[7]

The word "corruption" is one of the most frequently used catchwords in China. According to a keyword search in Baidu, there are nearly three million pieces of related news. There is a variety of corruption, such as political corruption, official corruption, company corruption, judicial corruption, academic corruption, educational corruption, and even football corruption and the like. However, there is one type of corruption that is more prevalent and more harmful and deserves more attention – that is, corruption of language.

Corruption of language denotes that people – for an economic, political, or ideological reason – willfully change the meanings of words or even add to words new meanings that greatly differ from the original ones so as to hoodwink the populace and manipulate their minds. A simple example of corruption of language is labeling a wrongdoing as a good deed or vice versa. The Chongqing's wide-ranging mafia crackdown is another typical example. "Mafia" literally refers to organized crimes, so in any society no one would disagree that it is rightful to crack down on these crimes. But as far as we know, in the so-called mafia crackdown in Boxilai's Chongqing, "mafia" became a label that could be stuck on any person or any enterprise the power-holders disliked; thus, the crackdown turned out to be political infringement on human rights and private property.

In fact, one of the main reasons why leftism gains popularity and followers is that leftists are adept at corruption of language. In this regard, the Gang of Four reached the zenith. They labeled a campaign that destroyed humanity and culture as "the Cultural Revolution", their political opponents as "the capitalist roaders", persecution as "rectification", illegal custody as "reformation through labor", and protesters as "counter-revolutionists". In particular, they claimed the demo-cratic movement – which was started on April 4, 1976 (China's Tomb-Sweeping Day), to mourn Premier Zhou Enlai and to give vent to people's dissatisfaction – to be "a counter-revolution revolt", claimed persons who died uncleared of false charges to be "alienating from the people", claimed the closed-doorism to be "independence of sovereignty", and claimed learning advanced technologies and cultures from foreign countries to be "worshiping foreign things". Such examples are legion. As a matter of fact, in the dictionary of the Gang of Four, so-called "national interests" refer to their personal interests, so-called "patriot-ism" means blind loyalty to their gang, so-called "the people" denotes a small group of their followers, and so-called "the opposition" is identified with anyone who showed resentment toward them. Just because they were good at corrup-tion of language, their wrongdoings that went against the tide of history lasted as long as ten years. Their political language still has so much impact on our lives that their spirit has revived under the banner of "singing red songs and cracking down on mafias" after their downfall over thirty years ago.

The phrase "corruption of language" is not my coinage. It was first coined by George Orwell in an article in 1946 and now has become a classic term of political philosophy. There had been phenomena of corruption of language since ancient times, but only after the twentieth century, especially after Hitler and Stalin, these phenomena became a social hazard. Orwell's novel *1984* offers us many classic examples. For instance, a ministry that is responsible for falsifica-tion of news is named Ministry of Truth; secret police that serves to supervise, arrest, and persecute dissidents is entitled Ministry of Love; a ministry that is in charge of waging wars is called Ministry of Peace. In other words, truth is fallacy, peace is war, and ignorance is power. Of course, this is fictional in a novel but is not far from reality. The full name of North Korea is Democratic People's Republic of Korea; East Germany was formerly named the German Democratic Republic; the party led by former Egyptian President Mobārakeh is called "The National Democratic Party"; the ruling party of former Tunisian President Ben Ali is entitled "Rassemblement Constitutionnel Democratique" (RCD). How ridiculous they are!

In today's China corruption of language is severe to the utmost. Whoever has a sound mind, as long as he or she closes his or her eyes, can pick up plenty of examples such as "truth", "fact", "rumor", "morality", "democracy", "rule by law", "freedom", "human rights", "constitution", "election", "representative of the people", "national interest", "patriotism", "harmonious society", "reform", "macroeconomic regulation", "modern enterprise system", "board of directors". These words have been corrupted to some extent; even the word "corruption" in and of itself has also been corrupted. When an official says he or she is a public servant, he or she implies that he or she holds power and you must obey him or her. The "Representative of the people" originally referred to the persons who are elected from among the people and entrusted to speak for and serve them. Even if a person actually speaks for and serves the people, if not entrusted by the people through a proper procedure, he or she cannot be entitled "representative of the people", because that will be labelled as infringement. However, today, "representatives of the people" are, in fact, officially designated. Of course, they have passed through voting procedures apparently. Originally, voting is expressive of voters' free will and consciousness, but our voters vote merely with hands rather than with minds, let alone free will, so the word "voting" has also been corrupted. Take "reform" for example. It originally denotes measures taken to abolish the planned economic system and to establish a market economy; besides, it means the government shall relax control over the economy and give people more freedom of undertaking economic activities. But in recent years, some government departments have labeled anti-reform policies that strengthen governmental control over economy and restrict freedom of trade as "reform", even as "measures to deepen reform". Likewise, macroeconomic policies literally refer to broadly slackening or tightening monetary or fiscal policies, but our so-called "macro-policy" is often identified with micro-economic intervention, including entry restriction and price control. State-controlled enterprises claim they have established modern enterprise systems, but, as a matter of fact, their boards of directors have no right to appoint a vice CEO. So what is meant by "modern enterprise systems"?

What harmful consequences can corruption of language bring about? There are at least three hazards.

Firstly, corruption of language strikingly damages the communicative function of language and leads to the degradation of human intelligence. Humans create languages to communicate, and all of the progress humans have made is based on this function. For the sake of communication, words must possess widely acknowledged meanings, but corruption of language means the same word has different meanings in the minds of different people and, moreover, languages become wordplays, making it difficult for people to communicate with each other. Corruption of language gradually deprives us of rationality and logical thinking, so our brains seem to be shrinking; our articles are loaded with catchwords, and we are more used to exerting authority over others or to be passively obedient instead of convincing others by reasoning and discussing with others on equal terms. For instance, when we say "keep the public ownership economy dominant and strive to develop other forms of ownership economy", we don't bother thinking that it is impossible to develop other forms of ownership economy when the public ownership economy is dominant. When official documents tell us to give play to the leading role of X and to keep Y dominant on the basis of Z, none of us can discern the relations among X, Y, and Z. The longer our articles grow, the less they inform us. We can easily write a work report in ten or twenty thousand words and work out a guidance material in tens of thousands of words, which is still confusing. This is double waste of human intelligence and material resources. In China there are thousands of high-intelligent talents living by doing such wordplays full-time and millions of people part-time. A great deal of word-waste has not only sullied people's minds and wasted precious material resources but polluted our living environment.

Secondly, corruption of language causes degradation of morality. The bottom line of human morality is honesty, but essentially corruption of language is dishonesty. As far as humanity is concerned, telling lies is more challenging than doing wrongs. In China the statement that "the criminal confessed his or her crime" is always written on a court verdict, which means we still believe the criminal could tell the truth even though he or she dares to do wrongs. In Western countries when a witness testifies in court, his or her testimony will not be accepted if the lawyer of the other party can prove that the witness is a frequent liar. According to this standard, we can hardly find a qualified witness in our society any more.

As Thomas Paine, a US thinker during the War of Independence, said in *The Age of Reason*:

> It is necessary to the happiness of man, that he be mentally faithful to himself. Infidelity does not consist in believing, or in disbelieving; it consists in professing to believe what he does not believe.
>
> It is impossible to calculate the oral mischief, if I may so express it, that mental lying has produced in society. When a man has so far corrupted and prostituted the chastity of his mind, as to subscribe his professional belief to things he does not believe, he has prepared himself for the commission of every other crime. He takes up the trade of a priest for the sake of gain, and, in order to qualify himself for that trade, he begins with a perjury. Can we conceive anything more destructive to morality than this?

In a word, it is really challenging, if not impossible, to make a shameless liar blush even when doing wrongs. Given that our language is so corrupted, it is not surprising that our government corruption is so severe, our market is abundant in fake and shoddy goods, and our social morality is so degraded. A government official, who keeps telling lies all day long, won't be morally obliged to restrain himself or herself from accepting bribes and abusing power for personal gains. Some corrupted officials may feel regret or unlucky, but never feel shame in court once they are arrested. When government officials' language and behavior are corrupted, the producers who produce fake and shoddy goods will also hardly feel guilty. And it is even nearly impossible to make the people who are educated in lies and grow up in lies possess social morality.

Hidden rules have become a main form of today's social corruption; it is an open secret that a commission must be paid to services an official renders. One of the main reasons why hidden rules are so prevalent in our society is corruption of language. They make written rules as useless as a piece of wastepaper.

Thirdly, corruption of language leads society to intensive uncertainty and unpredictability. One of the significant functions of language is to convey the signal of the operation state of society. When corruption of language becomes extremely severe, the signal will be strikingly distorted; as a result, when society is crisis-ridden, we might mistakenly think everything goes well and are unaware of approaching disasters. Any thunderbolt will probably cause sudden collapse of the whole system. The fall of the Soviet Union twenty years ago and the recent upheaval in the Middle East are two typical examples.

China's future reform and development as well as social stability, to a large extent, rely on how we can tackle corruption of language. As Confucius said over two thousand years ago, "If names be not correct, language is not in accordance with the truth of things. If language be not in accordance with the truth of things, affairs cannot be carried on to success". To combat language corruption is to rectify names and to resume original meanings of words. For example, so-called "representatives of the people" shall be elected from among people and the election shall be open, transparent, and competitive and shall really reflect people's will but not be manipulated by relevant departments. If we cannot ensure that, we should use other new words such as "Seat of Government Officials", "Seat of Celebrities", "Seat of Mass Organizations" to replace it.

Throughout history and around the world, the extent of corruption of language has been closely related to the freedom of speech and of the press. I am sure, if we can exactly put into force the thirty-fifth clause of our constitution – namely, exercising the freedom of speech and of the press – we can eliminate at least 50% of language corruption, which is the most harmful. The remaining 50% is the least harmful. If we can eliminate the most harmful part of language corruption, we will most likely eliminate 80% of government corruption; thus, our government will become honest and clean, and our morality will improve.

It's high time to wage war against corruption of language!

Social capital and culture[8]

We are aware that humans have many shortcomings, one of which is that we tend to fix our eyes on what is easily observable, but turn a blind eye to what is not. For example, when you look for a mate, many people will advise that whether your marriage is happy doesn't rely on the looks of your mate but on his or her moral quality and personality, because his or her looks are not a crucial consideration. But as a matter of fact, every one of us has a bias toward a good-looking mate. Besides, whether a person is satisfied with his or her job or whether the job is a good choice doesn't merely depend on how much he or she gets paid. A high-paying job is not necessarily satisfactory. Sometimes, you probably feel satisfied with some jobs that can offer you a good humanistic environment and enable you to work with good colleagues, even if they pay somewhat less. However, everyone still cares first how much he or she can get paid when hunting for a job.

The common characteristic or shortcoming we humans share is equally embodied in our opinions about social development. For example, what did we emphasize when we considered social development and national prosperity in the past? It was national economic growth. In particular, we used to identify economic growth with growth of the GDP – namely, the growth of material wealth. It seemed our country would grow strong, and our people would become happy as long as material wealth increased. Actually we know that was not the case. Studies carried out by plenty of scholars have proven that not all of the regions and the countries where their people enjoy high income are ones where their people feel happy, and, likewise, not all of the people who get high pay feel happy.

It is of overriding importance for us to propose bringing moderate prosperity to China in an all-round way. In other words, we should not only value increase of material wealth or the GDP but draw attention to all the considerations contributing to human happiness, many of which cannot be measured by some hard indicators. Of course, anyway, we are still supposed to recognize economic growth plays a crucial role in achieving human happiness. We have noticed in many countries, especially in the third-world countries where the people are suffering a shortage of food and clothes, it is possibly more difficult for them to discuss happiness. Even in our country there are still plenty of people living below the poverty line. Therefore, it remains a significant topic how to advance our economic growth.

The problem is what on earth determines the economic growth of a country. In this regard, opinions of economic circles and social science circles have been changing. I am an economist, so I value views of economic circles. Generally speaking, before the 1960s or 1970s, it was commonly believed that increase of material capital or capital accumulation was the major or even the only contributing factor to national economic growth. People thought the more they accumulated and invested, the faster national economy would grow. Thus, after World War II, many developing countries including China adopted an accumulation-oriented development strategy. In other words, we made use of government's authority, by carrying out a planned economy, to concentrate on investment programs. However, experience of many countries including China has proven that accumulation of national material capital is not tantamount to national economic growth, because the productivity of the same machine varies in different hands and in different countries. Therefore, since the 1960s and 1970s economists have begun to draw attention to human capital and realized that without excellent human capital, the national economy will not grow well even if we possess material capital, because material capital eventually has to be managed by humans, and, if a country's national education level and the quality of labor force remain quite low, its economy won't develop fast.

After the 1980s and especially after the 1990s, economists started to think over another question: why some countries accumulated human capital faster than other countries. One of the main findings was that economic growth depended on not only material capital and human capital but social capital, which was also a crucial factor. So-called social capital refers to a cooperative capability possessed by the people in a country. The key to achieving a cooperative result is not only whether we can create value by means of cooperation but also whether the other party is worthy of our trust. Take buying a product, for example: if a product's manufacturing cost is 10 yuan and its value to a buyer is 20 yuan, the trade will bring value to society and do good to both sides. But if the buyer doesn't trust the seller and has doubts that the product is fake, he or she will probably not be willing to complete the deal; likewise, if the seller doesn't believe the buyer is capable of paying for the deal as scheduled, the seller wouldn't like to sell the product. If there is no mutual trust among people, division of labor will be impossible and economic development will be impossible. A great deal of research has indicated that people in developed countries tend to have a higher degree of mutual trust, compared to developing countries in the world. I have also done research on China and drawn a similar conclusion. Among China's thirty-one provinces, municipalities, and autonomous regions, whichever has a higher degree of mutual trust has witnessed faster economic growth.

From a microscopic perspective, a country's economic development hinges on enterprises and expansion of enterprises. The overriding consideration in expanding enterprises is whether mutual trust among people can be established. Take starting up an enterprise for example. When an enterprise develops to a certain extent, it is impossible to merely rely on your personal effort to expand it, and you have to employ external personnel. If you don't have enough trust in employed personnel, you will not venture to hire them, and thus your enterprise will not possibly expand. We are aware that this is the most severe problem Chinese enterprises are confronted with. One of the major reasons why lots of private enterprises cannot expand is that entrepreneurs lack confidence in external personnel. Although some of them are well skilled and well educated, they are not necessarily the managers worthy of trust, and their bosses are unwilling to employ them. This is the most important problem confronting our country.

This is not only a problem confronting an individual enterprise but a problem confronting the whole society. How high is the degree of trust in our society? Or to what extent can our social capital support our sustainable economic development? A survey of developed countries has shown that in the past twenty years two thirds of their economic growth came from expansion of current enterprises and one third derived from entry of new enterprises. But the situation in China is probably the opposite. Our economic growth largely depends on entry of new enterprises instead of expansion of existing enterprises. It is believed in the world that China's economic growth is bound to encounter a bottleneck: too little accumulation of social capital. Francis Fukuyama, a US sociologist and political philosopher, wrote a book entitled *Trust* and proposed that in China, which had a low degree of trust, enterprises were unlikely to expand and it would be challenging to achieve sustainable economic growth.

We must admit that our degree of trust is extremely low. We are skeptical about everything we are engaged in. For example, we even become cautious about ordering a dish. We dare not eat what we used to enjoy, such as soft-shell turtles, because they are probably bred artificially. We introduce high technologies, but they are destroying traditional industries. Now we daren't buy lots of building materials, just because they probably contain radioactive elements.

A question we may ask is whether China's low degree of trust is caused by Chinese people's nature or China's institutional problems. In this regard, I have some personal reflections. In my view, at present Chinese society is a society with a low degree of trust, and our social capital or our cooperative capability and the trust among our people are relatively low. But that doesn't mean that Chinese society is naturally characterized by a low degree of trust. Once I wrote an article titled "A Big Country and Small Enterprises" and put forward a question: "if Chinese lack mutual trust, we cannot expand enterprises, but why could we develop our country into a large one in China's history?" China used to be an unparalleled large country with an unprecedented long history. Without mutual trust, that would not have been that case.

Historically there are two considerations in establishing mutual trust. First, a good system, a legal system, as well as social norms; second, good culture. Without a good system, it will be arduous to achieve cooperation in society. But an official system is insufficient, because we cannot use written legal provisions to solve all of the arising problems and nor can we make everyone be responsible for their actions. Over two thousand years ago, Confucius created Confucianism, which has played a significant role in promoting stability and development of Chinese society and in maintaining social order. Confucianism expounds how to reach mutual cooperation effectively and how to maintain social order. It can be said that the reason why our social trust is low today is most probably that Chinese traditional culture, especially Confucian culture, has been remarkably ruined. Therefore, I think the key to reestablishing our social trust and promoting fast economic development lies in reestablishment of Chinese culture. Although in Chinese culture there is a lot of junk, Confucianism is of great value.

The requirement for establishing mutual trust is that everyone's actions should be constrained and everyone should bear the responsibility for his or her actions. By what means? By law as well as consideration of reputation. In a society some people enjoy higher positions and good reputations, and the reason why they behave well is not necessarily that they intend to gain material interests but that they care about their reputations. For the sake of their good reputations, they cannot do wrongs at the cost of others' interests but do good deeds beneficial to the whole society. In other words, in our society people of moral integrity are necessary; without them, it will be much more difficult to maintain social order. As Confucians advocates, "Punishment will not apply to senior state officials and rites will not apply to the common people". In my understanding, Confucians don't mean people are unequal before the law. Instead they highlight that as for people of moral integrity as well as excellent social citizens, their behaviors won't cross the boundary of law. As we all know, law is the bottom line for constraining people's actions. I also believe all of us present here won't cross the boundary of law. Why? Because we care about our personal reputations, we ought to behave ourselves and be ready to help others, but not at the expense of society and others' interests. But only for those who disobey social norms (namely, rites) and disregard their reputations do we need criminal law, real punishment to constrain their actions.

At least in Chinese history our society wasn't a society with a low degree of trust. One of the major reasons why our trust degree is low is that Chinese culture or traditional culture is destroyed during the planned economy. Thus, the mission of our next generation is to rejuvenate Chinese culture, especially of traditional culture, which is excellent and contributive to constructing a moderately prosperous society. What should every one of us strive for? We should strive to be persons of moral integrity instead of despicable persons. As a saying goes: "Although gentlemen are keen on wealth, they acquire it in a proper way". Here "a proper way" means creating social values and common interests. Many of our social norms need, actually, to be created and defended by generations of people. Our youths are supposed to assume a greater responsibility. It is difficult for senior people to turn evil or to turn good after they become bad, whereas it is easy for young people to turn evil or to turn good after they grow bad. When I was in the countryside, I found a great deal of agricultural equipment was mainly damaged by youths. When I was small, old peasants were honest, but the young were more cunning. Why were old peasants honest? Because before the collective system they got into the habit of getting down to doing farm work, but young people grew up under the collective system and didn't have time to get into such a good habit. So, we have cunning young foxes rather than cunning old foxes. Therefore, I think young people should assume the great responsibility for establishing good social order. In other words, we ought to reflect on our actions all the time and to strive to be people of moral integrity when we experience primary education, secondary education, and higher education and start to work.

I work in Guanghua School of Management of Peking University, and our school invites senior management personnel from enterprises to teach. In our school our students can not only acquire knowledge but receive moral education. We can say since you come to be a student of Peking University, you have to accept its constraint; you are not probably allowed to do what you used to do or what violates social norms, because you stand for Peking University. We have strict requirements for our students. Our students should be not only outstanding professional managers and entrepreneurs but good examples of morality. We attach importance to their moral quality when enrolling new students. I told all of the students to "be honest, courteous, well-educated and true to their word and possess a moral sense and a sense of responsibility". As a student, you go to school for the sake of studying. Chinese ancestors emphasized learning and courtesy and advocated the purpose of learning was to acquire courtesy. We hope Peking University's graduates all possess a sense of social responsibility. Only more and more talents with a sense of social responsibility can contribute to building our moderately prosperous society.

Three essential factors for a harmonious society[9]

Harmonious society is the ultimate goal humans have been pursuing ever since the start of their existence. In my view, a harmonious society consists of three essential factors: first, some core values that are accepted by the majority of people; second, game rules or behavioral norms in accordance with core values; third, a guarantee given by societal organizational forms. For example, in the ancient Confucian harmonious society, benevolence and righteousness are the core values, rites (*Li*) are its core behavioral norms, and family is its organizational form. Confucianism employs family to ensure the implementation of its core values and uphold its behavioral norms. So Confucianism strikingly emphasizes the important role played by family in maintaining social order.

Core values accepted by the majority of people

First of all, social core values are of significance to establishment of a harmonious society. If there are no core values that are acknowledged by the majority, there is no criterion for judging what is right and what is wrong; as a result, no consensus will be achieved on the same issue and harmony will be a castle in the air. For instance, harmony cannot be achieved in the circle of mathematics unless mathematicians take for granted some fundamental axioms. To put it simply, if some of them deny the assumption that one plus one equals two but believe that one plus one equals three, there is no way to discuss mathematical issues.

If we want to establish a harmonious society, we must set up some fundamental core values first. One of the important ones is respect for individuals' fundamental rights and, more specifically, respect for property rights. As a matter of fact, property rights are not only individuals' fundamental rights but the foundation of freedom. If in a society individuals' property rights cannot be well protected by laws and respected by culture and people are keen on contending for and partitioning others' property, more conflicts rather than harmony will be brought about. We can hardly imagine a society that disrespects property rights can maintain harmony.

The further extension of respect for property rights is respect for entrepreneurs' role. In reality, some economic activities are filled with uncertainties and risks, so entrepreneurs deserve compensation for dealing with such uncertainties and risks. If we deny the role of and payment for entrepreneurs, what we are doing is disrespect for property rights. If people pay more attention to how to create wealth than they do to how to distribute and contend for wealth, the society thus cannot be harmonious.

Entrepreneurs' activities are often risky, and perhaps only a few of them can have a chance to succeed even if many people undertake the same activity. People are willing to take risk under the condition that winners can obtain payment that exceeds the gross cost all adventurers have to pay. For example, ten people each invest 1 million yuan, but only two of them succeed, so everyone has a 20% chance of success, and the payment required by winners is at least 5 million yuan. Furthermore, considering people's natural aversive attitude toward risks, the payment should exceed 5 million, probably 6 million or 7 million yuan. In hindsight, the distribution is probably unfair; some people earn nothing, but some people win several million yuan. In foresight, however, it is quite fair because everyone has an equal chance to take risks. If the unequal distribution under the condition of equal chances cannot be acknowledged, our respect for equal chances is, in fact, denied.

The core values should also include acceptation of Pareto Improvement. In other words, if we carry out a reform that benefits at least a group of people but not at the expense of anyone's interests, we should admit it is reasonable. If we don't even admit that, any reform is unlikely to take place and our society can never make progress. Moreover, we must acknowledge the right to willingly, freely trade and conclude agreements; people have the right to willingly, freely trade and conclude agreements. If we do not acknowledge this right, that means some people are allowed to impose their will on others.

The core values for a harmonious society are often formulated by some thinkers and scholars. Confucian core values are advocated by Confucius and his disciples, and the core values of modern Western society are advocated by scholars of the Renaissance and the Enlightenment. Today's Chinese scholars are also confronted with the same mission.

Reasonable behavioral norms

Since core values guide us to deal with plenty of conflicts of interests and coordinate large quantities of activities, rules of the game seem to be quite crucial. As our ancestors advocated, "there is government, when the prince is prince and the minister is minister; when the father is father and the son is son". This is a behavioral norm. Without definite game rules, we won't know how to tackle arising problems, and the whole society won't be harmonious.

Game rules of such kind are divided into two types: respectively, laws and social norms or culture in a narrow sense. We have no doubt about importance of laws but pay less attention to significance of social norms. Because social life is so complicated that we cannot change all social norms into laws, we need some unwritten but socially accepted rules to guide our behaviors. Moreover, moral norms also deserve much attention.

Here what I intend to highlight is that laws cannot play an active role unless laws per se are reasonable. Their rationality stems from the aforementioned value judgment. If laws per se are not in accordance with well-accepted value judgment, they are "evil laws". If there are too many "evil laws" in a society, the society won't be possibly harmonious.

In an ideal society, the reasonable should be legal, but the legal must be reasonable. However, now in our society there are plenty of illegal but reasonable, or legal but unreasonable, phenomena that need to be corrected by means of institutional reforms. If we don't remedy these phenomena, we will be at a loss about what to do when encountering them.

If you are required to do what is reasonable but illegal, should you do it or not? Considering an individual's social responsibility, you should do it; but considering personal risks, you should not. Likewise, in the face of what is legal but unreasonable, if you carry out it, you don't need to undertake legal liability, but, if you really do, that will bring great damage to the whole society. Hence, we ought to coordinate rationality and legality to the greatest extent by means of modifying game rules. This is a major task we are confronted with when building a harmonious society.

A guarantee given by societal organizational forms

As I mentioned above, familial organization plays a crucial role in Confucian values of harmony. Through use of joint liability and its members' behavioral norms, family exerts influence upon the country and thus helps to maintain the order of traditional society.

In a modern society, family is still a significant organization, but I think there is a more significant organization – namely, business enterprise.

Modern enterprise organization plays a crucial role in maintaining social trust and social order. For example, if we buy a product from an unfamiliar person, we probably distrust the quality of the product and fear being cheated. But if there is an enterprise selling products that cherishes its reputation and long-term interests, we can rest assured if we buy its product.

As a matter of fact, the order of the modern market relies on, to a large extent, large and brand-name enterprises. Behind large enterprises there are many small enterprises. This is not only a chain of value but a chain of fiduciary duties. For instance, a large supermarket is backed up by thousands of suppliers; and consumers cannot supervise every supplier, so the responsibility of supervising suppliers and upstream enterprises is delegated to the supermarket. Much value of the supermarket comes from helping consumers monitor its suppliers. Without large enterprises, the market will be in chaos.

However, without real owners, enterprise organizations cannot bear the responsibility for maintaining market order. Owners are, in fact, beneficiaries of enterprises' reputations, and they must bear the responsibility for consumers and undertake the joint liability for employers in enterprises in the same way the head of family bears the joint liability for members of family in a traditional society. If an enterprise doesn't have a real owner, no one will take care of the enterprise's reputation, and the order of market won't be established. In order to draw owners' attention to enterprises' reputations, legal protection of intangible property such as brand and goodwill seems to be fatal. Therefore, again we reach an agreement that without effective protection of property rights there is no harmonious society.

Apart from enterprises, there is another type of important organization – namely, non-governmental organizations and non-profit organizations. At times, there are some things that cannot be well done by profit organizations, or government departments, but it is more appropriate for non-governmental organizations and non-profit organizations to do them. Non-governmental organizations are also the effective forms of people's offering the compassion; and so for the sake of building of a harmonious society, it is quite significant to tremendously propel the establishment of non-governmental organizations and non-profit organizations.

All of these are the three aspects I intend to highlight.

Questions and answers section

Q: Do we need to consider other factors when thinking about core values? What is the relation between core values of other disciplines and economics? (Your core values are basically proposed from the perspective of economics, so they center on science and benefit. Are societal core values related to national and ethnic cultural tradition, international status, and orientation? If so, what are these core values?)

A: Core values per se are relatively stable, but don't remain unchangeable. For example, when tackling inter-country relations, we cannot adopt the predatory values that were prevalent several decades or hundred years ago. Now it is well acknowledged that voluntary trade between individuals, organizations, or countries are win-win games. Take globalization, for example, we can work together to make a larger pie of the international market. If we think that inter-country relations are simple matters of wealth distribution, it will be totally wrong. As far as protection of property rights is concerned, we can consider it from the perspective of core values. Why shall we protect Americans' intellectual property rights? Because if we don't, we can hardly encourage Chinese to innovate; once Chinese have no initiative, it will be nearly impossible for us to establish our status in international competitions.

To some degree, the values of economics can also be applied to other fields, but, in fact, I believe although different disciplines have distinctive research methods, we are confronted with the same problems and have the same goals – namely, to make humans live more happily and harmoniously.

Q: Are there any old core values that need to be changed? (As you mention, today there are no fundamental core values that are accepted by the majority in our society. You also point out that lack of core values would result in a division of society. Why are there no well-accepted core values? You don't elaborate the underlying reason, though you enumerate people's discordant opinions on related core values. If we used to have core values, why we don't have them anymore?

You have listed four main types of new core values: respect for property rights, acknowledgement of Pareto Improvement, equality of opportunity, and idea of right and wrong respectively. Since you mention "new", what are old values?)

A: We need to change some old ideas. Twenty years ago I said there were some old ideas that need changing. Under the old economic conditions, wealth was measured by land, but the limitation of land per se determined that the more land you took, the less land others were left. However, in the modern market economy, wealth is always in the process of being created. That some people get more wealth doesn't mean less wealth is left to others. But some old ideas such as a sense of sympathy and a sense of right and wrong advocated by Mencius are still important today.

Q: Why should scholars and thinkers play a guiding role in the process of establishing core values? Is knowledge also touched with subjectivity?

(You pointed out, we used to employ imperative authority to impose certain values upon people in a short time, which is superficial harmony; and when everyone has opportunities to voice his or her opinions, well-accepted core values in mind will become more significant. But how to be well accepted? You advocate that the establishment of new core values isn't a totally spontaneous process and needs guidance. Scholars and thinkers should bear this responsibility. Obviously, you advocate guidance of knowledge and of ideas and oppose imposition of authority. I have two questions, if I may ask. Is knowledge objective? Is knowledge free of influence of authority?)

A: Over two thousand years ago, Mencius once said "the people that possess fixed assets have morality". However, he also argued that those who possessed morality instead of fixed assets were so-called "literati" (*shi*) – namely, today's scholars or public intellectuals. The reason is that learned persons are supposed to have a broader horizon of interests than ordinary people, and pay more attention to national and ethnic long-term trends of development. Ordinary people are busy with daily life, while knowledgeable persons are relatively unworldly and should play a guiding role in forging the development direction of history. The formation of core values is not a simple natural process. In fact, our Confucian literati played a crucial role in establishing Chinese core values with a history of over two thousand years. The American Constitution was not voted by all Americans but formulated by a small group of elites, so we cannot deny the significance of elites in guiding social changes.

Of course, knowledge is partly subjective, but we can solve this problem through contention of schools of thought. For example, during the Spring and Autumn and the Warring States Periods, there were various schools of thought advocating different core values and game rules. Through contention, Confucianism became the leading one. Surely, it is inadvisable that Emperor Wu of Han abused political authority "to Pay Supreme Tribute to Confucianism but Ban All Other Schools of Thought". It holds true for today's circumstances. Although different disciplines vie with each other, we are obligated to guide the society toward a right direction.

Q: What is the relationship between the moral bottom line and core values?

(You have mentioned that in a harmonious society people must have a fundamental requirement for humanity or moral bottom line. Therefore, you borrow four manifestations of human nature from Mencius [4S for short] –

namely, a sense of sympathy, a sense of shame, a sense of modesty, and a sense of right and wrong. Is the fundamental requirement for humanity or moral bottom line identical to the core values you proposed? So what on earth is meant by core values? Do they refer to the moral bottom line?)

A: What Mencius called "four senses" may be human's innate nature, or the moral bottom line of humanity, but they still need our promotion. I think the idea of right and wrong must be based on the foundation of core values; otherwise we cannot reach a consensus and even cannot have the common ground for discussion. Besides, as Confucius said, "do not impose on others what you yourself do not desire". This is also the value that should be accepted in society. We should put ourselves in others' shoes. Let me quote a popular saying from thirty years ago: don't impose Marxism-Leninism on others, while you believe in Liberalism! We ought to aim at helping others out of good will rather than treat them out of bad will!

Q: What is the attitude of the masses and of mass media toward knowledge elites?

(You mentioned that mass media do damage to academic research, despise scientific thoughts, and humiliate scholars' personalities; and these are unforgivable crimes in our society. I think all of these are your temporary reflections. In my view, the receptors of mass media are the populace, and if their contents cannot gain popularity among the populace, they cannot survive. On the other hand, the attitude of mass media reflects the attitude of Chinese populace. So why do Chinese mass media or specifically the populace treat scholars, academic research, and scientific thoughts in such a way? Do they hate elites? But in traditional China, scholars were held in highest esteem! Do the populace mistake elites, the relation between knowledge elites and authority, as well as the relation between knowledge elites and wealth?)

A: The populace need guidance. Without the guidance of scientific knowledge and rationality, they will be a group of mobs. The society cannot be guided by them.

Actually, not only now but in history the populace cast doubt upon elites. But I believe rational thinking can endure the test of time. Maybe just because the populace tend to be emotionally impulsive and behave irrationally, science and knowledge seem more important. So I think, only under such circumstances, do rational thinking and serious scholars seem to be a must. Suppose everyone at all times can make right judgments about public affairs, scholars won't be needed any more.

Indeed there are varieties of scholars, but I advocate that "a scholar" should meet two requirements. First he or she must have a strict scientific mindset, and his or her wisdom and logic can enable him or her to see further than others. Second, he or she must possess high professional ethics; he or she cannot be an opportunist and must adhere to what he or she thinks is right, instead of changing his or her views according to his or her personal interests or becoming all things to all people in order to win applause.

Q: You just mentioned it was within the following twenty years that Chinese new core values would come into being. What do you mean by twenty years?

A: In fact, it is not specific time; maybe it will take a longer time. Since the Opium War, we have been losing faith in traditional values and been looking for a new type of values but in vain all the time. After more than one hundred years, we think it is high time we establish our own values and make a common judgment about the long-term future of our country. We must be well aware what we should do and shouldn't do. We can say the reform in the past twenty years has laid a good foundation for establishment of our new values. However, more and more problems are exposed, and I assume when conflicts of ideas grow bigger and bigger in a society, it is also high time to come to a convergence. Of course, this cannot naturally happen, and it requires our combined efforts. I think a nation's fundamental soul shall not be divided. If it is divided, it will pose us a challenge.

Notes

1 A preface written on June 16, 2009, to the Chinese translation of *Understanding Business* (by William Nickels, James McHugh and Susan McHugh).
2 Quoted from Eric D. Beinhocker, *The Origin of Wealth*, pages 9–11, Harvard Business School Press, 2006.
3 A speech I delivered at the China Economist Forum 2010 & China Economic Theory Innovation Awarding Ceremony on December 26, 2011.
4 Chinese area unit.
5 Chinese mass unit.
6 Based on a keynote speech I gave at the twelve Yabuli China Entrepreneurs Forum on February 2, 2012.
7 A speech addressed at the Annual Summit of China Green Companies on April 21, 2012. An abridged version was published in *The Economic Observer* on April 28, 2012.
8 Based on a speech I delivered at the Youth Civilization Forum.
9 A speech I delivered at a seminar of Tsinghua University in 2005.

Part two
The logic of reform

How to understand China's economic reform[1]

The Chinese economic reform initiated by Deng Xiaoping has been witnessed for thirty years. Looking back, we didn't anticipate at least two things when we started it.

First, we didn't expect the path of reform would be so lengthy. Originally our reformers conceived it would take around five to ten years to accomplish the reform; even in the mid-1980s many reformers still optimistically anticipated the reform would be finished by 1990 or at the latest by 1995 (that's why the Five-Year Midterm Economic Reform Plan and the Ten-Year Long-Term Reform Plan were designed in 1986). However, after thirty years China is still in the process of reforming, and we still have no idea about when the reform will come to an end.

Second, we didn't expect China's economy would gallop so fast and its achievements would be so tremendous. In the early 1980s Deng Xiaoping set a goal that by 2000 the GDP would quadruple. At that time many people were skeptical about it and thought it seemed somewhat "hasty". But it has been proven that China's economy grew much faster than Deng anticipated. During the past thirty years China's GDP per capita doubled every less than ten years and had reached 2,500 US dollars by 2007. The ranking of China's economic aggregate in the world rose from thirteenth in 1978 to fourth in 2007; the proportion of China's imports and exports in world trade ranked twenty-third in 1978 and third in 2007 respectively. At the beginning, we were unlikely to anticipate that after thirty years the exchange rate of China's currency, the *renminbi* (RMB or CNY), would become an international economic issue; we were also unaware that in 2007, of the largest listed companies by market value in the world, five would be Chinese companies.

As far as I am concerned, the common reason why the path of China's reform is so long and its achievements are so great is that within the past thirty years China embarked on a marketization-oriented reform. At the beginning, we failed to realize that it would be an arduous task to establish a market economy; we were also unaware it had such great power to create wealth!

I believe understanding China's economic reform and achievements of the past thirty years requires us to grasp the following five aspects.

First, quantitative planned targets have been replaced by market prices in resource allocation.

The basic fact of economy is that social resources are scarce. So how can a society utilize limited resources to create maximum value? In the planned economy there was no reasonable criterion for resources allocation but "social needs" presumed by government officials. For example, prior to the reform and opening-up, China was in critical need of light industry products. However, economic planning officials assumed heavy industry was essential for China's economic development, and thus they invested a large quantity of resources in heavy industry. As a result, China's consumption goods were constantly in short supply, and ordinary people, without ration tickets, couldn't purchase daily necessities.

In a market economy, prices serve not only as signals for coordinating economic activities but as a mechanism for motivating people to make optimal choices. Prices are determined by the social value of and production costs of goods, indicative of demand and supply relationships. After the reform and opening-up, markets and a price signal system were introduced; therefore, demand directed supply, and resources flowed to production of products that were valued highly by consumers. Prices direct resources allocation not only among different products but also among enterprises of different forms of ownership. In the early 1980s some essential resources (such as steel and raw materials) were mainly allocated by the government to state-owned enterprises. Later, township and village enterprises (TVEs) and private enterprises emerged. These non-state enterprises were more willing to pay higher prices for, by all means, obtaining the resources that were originally at the disposal of state-owned enterprises. They produced products that consumers were in want of. Gradually the shortage of consumption goods vanished, and supplies became abundant in the market. It has been proven that using prices as signals for guiding resource allocation is more beneficial to the creation of social wealth and improvement of people's living standards than government planning.

One of the major features of China's economic reform is that the price mechanism was introduced by the dual-track system step by step. The dual-track system ensured a steady transition from governmental control of prices to market-determined price system and prevented drastic oscillations of economy, contributing to carrying out reform and development concurrently. The dual-track system equally alleviated conflicts of interest arising during the reform and made China's reform become a more or less Pareto improvement instead of a revolution that deprived people of vested interests.

In the present, price signals play a role in not only most product markets but production factor markets. China's labor market is the most developed one in all of the factor markets. Market salaries and wages have become main signals for adjusting human resource allocation. Without a well-developed labor market, there won't be a great deal of rural labor force pouring into industry, nor will there be development of private enterprises and foreign-funded enterprises that belong to the most vigorous sector of China's economy. However, China's capital market and land market are still heavily regulated by government administration, and there arise most of the problems. Therefore, China's next reform should focus on how to reduce government's intervention in the capital market and the land market and how to liberalize factor prices (including interest rate and land price) in order to revitalize dead capital. Government ought to avoid excessive intervention in the labor market by the labor contract law; otherwise we may destroy hard-won reform achievements.

Second, entrepreneurs replace government officials as decision-makers.

In reality, any resource allocation is done by human beings; an enterprise or a government per se is unable to make any decision, because it is merely an organization. It is individual human beings who have a decision-making capability. Under different systems decision-makers vary. For example, in a planned economy government officials are policy-makers, while in a market economy entrepreneurs are. One of the main changes during the thirty-year Chinese reform and opening-up is the emergence of entrepreneurs who are gradually replacing government officials as economic decision-makers.

When entrepreneurs make decisions, they must use prices as signals for predicting the future, giving top priority to earning profits. In other words, they must balance the value created by their investment against the cost. If they lose money, they will go bankrupt. Therefore, their decisions, in most cases, accord with the demand of creating social wealth. The more accurate their predictions are, the more profits their companies will earn; likewise, resource allocation will be more rational and more social value will be created. In contrast, when government officials make decisions, they prefer "political sake" and "social sake" rather than economic interests. That is to say, they often turn a blind eye to market demands, costs, and profits. Because even if they make wrong decisions and invest in unprofitable programs, that won't stop them from getting promoted. Consequently, a great deal of government investment turned out to be invalid and wasteful. As a matter of fact, in the planned economy so-called "political sake" and "social sake" that were echoed by government officials were no more than cover-ups of their decision-making mistakes.

At present both government officials and entrepreneurs play the role of decision-maker. The reason why there are a number of problems with our economy is that entrepreneurs haven't utterly replaced officials as economic decision-makers. Many industries are dominated by a large amount of government investment; and enterprise's investments still need the government's approvals. Policies published by the government are changeable, and some of them are directly harmful to enterprises' operation freedom. Moreover, there are plenty of contradictory policies resulting from conflicting departmental interests, so entrepreneurs are engaged in dealing with the uncertainty of policies. All of these have suggested our marketization reform isn't fulfilled. If we give more freedom to entrepreneurs and enable prices to serve as signals well, resource allocation efficiency will improve, technological advance will speed up, and corruption will be reduced.

Thirdly, property-based interests replace position-based interests as the foundation of our economic system.

In a planned economy, a person's personal interests rely only on his or her governmental position; his or her control of and share of social resource allocation are also determined by his or her "official position" and "status". The higher position he or she occupies, the more control and enjoyment he or she has. Under such circumstances, a person must first acquire an official position in order to obtain the domination of wealth and the right to use wealth. How to earn a position and what position you can earn hinge not on how much wealth you create for the society but on other considerations (such as one's revolutionary career and social connections) or a certain process of pan-politicization and pan-bureaucratization. Hence, the process of seeking a position and pursuing happiness is not the process of wealth creation but the one of wealth redistribution and power-based rent-seeking. Abundant social resources and personal talents are spent in internal struggles and in-fighting, which often result in damage to and destruction of wealth rather than an increase in wealth.

In a market economy, personal interests are defined and guaranteed by the property an individual possesses rather than by his or her official position. When property rights are effectively protected, for the sake of earning wealth and income, a person must, first of all, create value for others. Thus, the process of an individual pursuing happiness is tantamount to that of wealth creation. Market competition means that only if a person can more efficiently make use of social resources – for example, using the same amount of resources to create more market value or using less resources to create the same market value – can he or she survive. Market competition and pursuit of wealth propel specialization and technological advance and thus promote the economic development and accumulation of national wealth.

China's economic development in the past thirty years owes much to that more and more people tend to seek private property instead of official positions. However, our marketization reform hasn't been accomplished, and position-based interests coexist with property-based interests. As a result, government officials are still endowed with the unlimited power of allocating resources, and power-for-money deals are prevalent, arousing public indignation. In the future, only if we found our economic system on property-based interests instead of position-based interests can we eradicate corruption as much as possible and narrow the income disparity that leads to inefficiency, stimulating Chinese people's enthusiasm and wisdom for creating wealth.

Fourthly, fiscal centralization is replaced by fiscal decentralization.

In China's planned economy, economic development strategies were often made by the state, and resources were mobilized by the central government. One of the main characteristics of China's reform is introducing inter-regional competition by means of decentralization reforms. That was brought about by China's Big Fiscal Contract System (or so-called "eating from different pots") as well as a series of decentralization reforms in the 1980s. Decentralization as one of the major forces propelling China's reform and development played an influential role in China's economic marketization.

Decentralization motivated local government officials' initiative in developing the economy. The Fiscal Contract System was first introduced in 1980, partially adjusted in 1984 and completely institutionalized in 1988. In accordance with this system, lower-level governments turned fixed proportion of fiscal revenue over to a higher level and kept the remaining part. The rest kept by governments at various levels and government departments at the same level couldn't be transferred by the central government freely. As a matter of fact, this policy defined property rights of governments at various levels. In other words, it divided the whole Chinese economy into many small public-owned economies, and every part of them became a "quasi-company", making local governments at different levels become real owners of economies they administrated; whichever local government had a faster economy would obtain greater financial resources, thus giving more rights and interests to its officials. In such a system developing its economy became the primary goal of each of the local governments, which induced inter-regional competition for developing economy and stimulated the development of township and village enterprises and private enterprises.

Inter-regional competition advanced the marketization of the whole economy. Though local governments might employ administrative planning means to control local enterprises, in the face of other governments they had to appeal to bargaining. The haggles between local governments made it more difficult for a centralized planned system to operate as supposed and forced enterprises and regions to barter with each other in the market, leading to the dual-track system and gradual destruction of the centralized planned system. Although decentralization accompanied local protectionism, it was also the major force that terminated market fragmentations. The region whose economy was more efficient would produce products that were able to enter marketplaces in other areas and to develop its economy by making use of nation-wide product markets and factor markets. Interregional competition urged local governments to improve market environments and to appeal to external investors.

Competition between different regions also triggered the wave of privatization after the 1990s. The reason is that owing to extremely intensive interregional competition in product markets, every area had to reduce production cost in order to maintain a minimum market share necessary for surviving; without markets, fiscal revenue would be impossible. In a bid to motivate enterprises to reduce production cost, local governments must transfer all of or a portion of shares to managerial personnel. That is the main reason why enterprises in Southern Jiangsu were privatized in the 1990s and so is the case with enterprises in other areas.

Till now we can still see most local governments are engaged with developing economy, but a majority of Chinese central ministries and commissions are engaged in "vetting procedures". Though actions of our local governments are often under criticism, we cannot forget the important role of local governments and of inter-regional competition. Without decentralization that triggered inter-regional competition, the privatization pace would hardly be so fast, nor would China's economic reform be so successful. Of course, it should be the major topic of further reforms how to transfer to inter-enterprise competition dominance from interregional competition and how to let entrepreneurs instead of local government officials make decisions in allocating resources.

Fifthly, the Chinese economic operating system changed from closedness to openness.

When it comes to China's opening-up policy, the common people will consider it as utilizing the international market, international capital, international technologies, and the like. Indeed, as early as more than two hundred years ago, Adam Smith once said economic development relied on the division of labor that was subject to the extent of markets. In other words, the bigger the markets are, the deeper the division of labor will be, product exchanges will be more developed, and the economy will develop faster. The reform and opening-up carried out in the 1980s expanded markets and enabled China to more efficiently take advantage of the international market, international capital, advanced technologies, and managerial systems that were accumulated by developed countries. It equally enabled China to give play to its comparative advantages in a bid to create national wealth and evolve into a world power of manufacturing. That is a crucial foundation for China's high-speed economic growth.

In my view, more importantly, the reason why the opening-up played a crucial role is that it had introduced institutional competition and promoted domestic reform. In a closed economy, because of no comparison and no competition from alternative systems, a system with low efficiency can exist for long. However, in an open economy, efficiency becomes the criterion for judging whether a system is advantageous; thus, the shortcomings of a planned economy and state-owned enterprises will be exposed thoroughly, and a market economy and non-state-owned enterprises will be accepted by more and more people. As a matter of fact, it is the low efficiency of state-owned enterprises (in contrast to foreign-funded enterprises as well as private enterprises) that led to the transformation of state-owned enterprises and their gradual disappearance from competitive fields. In an open market, consumers use the money they possess to vote against state-owned enterprises. When state-owned enterprises lose the market, their existence won't be justifiable.

Besides, the opening-up introduced new thoughts, new ideas, and new game rules. For example, several years ago what we did in terms of standardizing government's conduct, diminishing government's power, and annulling vetting systems were closely related to China's accession to WTO. When we entered WTO, it was to bring us in line with the international community and those unreasonable rules and regulations that don't comply with what WTO promises should be eliminated one after another. Therefore, the opening-up is the influential factor advancing reforms, and, without the opening-up, there won't be today's reform achievements.

The five changes above are the keys to understanding the achievements and problems of China's marketization reform. It has been thirty years since the reform and opening-up was carried out, but, unfortunately, some opinions emerging in our society and some policies published by our governments run counter to these changes: people's trust in price mechanism is decreasing instead of increasing; various forms of intervention in prices are published under the support of public opinion; government's control of social resources are strengthening instead of weakening; the environments for running enterprises and conditions for starting up business are deteriorating instead of improving; enterprises are more constrained in recruiting and employing workers, and a new type of "iron bowl" becomes the direction of social employment; the institutional innovation of local governments are criticized instead of being encouraged, and media and public opinion blame most economic problems on local governments and marketization; the opening-up policy is under doubt, and populism and narrow nationalism are prevailing; some government departments are closing their opened doors. All of these have indicated the prospects for China's marketization reform are not promising and China's reform has a long way to go!

It is extremely difficult for China to establish a market economy. During the period of planned economy, we totally denied the role of markets; after the reform and opening-up, we partly acknowledged markets; after Deng Xiaoping's Speeches during his China's South Tour in 1992, we totally accepted markets, after the painstaking efforts of several generations and even paying blood prices. But nowadays an anti-market wave begins to prevail in society. If such a wave evolves into government policies and laws, China's reform and development will be fatally harmed. At the moment economists are expected to stand out to summarize and clarify some fundamental problems.

China's reform has sustained for thirty years, yet its prospect is still tinted with uncertainty. During a social system reform, it is political leaders' personal choices that play a critical role in a short time, but in the long run it is ideas and the value orientation of common people that play a fateful role. The destiny of China's reform and development relies on what we believe in and what we don't believe in. We ardently anticipate the efforts of Chinese economists will contribute to building good ideas of common people and propelling China's reform to march toward the direction of marketization.

From a position-based economy to a property-based economy[2]

What should our society fear most? It's not that government intervenes in economy too little but that government does too much. With regard to industrial policies, I would like to share my personal views that differ from mainstream ones.

Many ideas concerning industrial policies are based on the hypothesis that in contrast with entrepreneurs, government officials are more farsighted and abler to predict future, and have a better understanding of the technological development direction and market rules. But we know the hypothesis is false, and it has been proven that most of our industrial policies failed. The comment "failed" is not mine but is quoted from some retired government officials who used to be responsible for formulating industrial policies. In their view, our industrial policies failed. Take policies of the automobile industry for example. Suppose at the beginning we had allowed China's automobile industry to develop freely; China's domestic brands would be stronger.

Some of our industrial policies are made "thanks to" institutional obstacles set up intentionally by the government agent. This reminds me of an example of riding a bike in the 1980s. At that time, there was an incident that you usually came across. When you rode a bike in the neighborhood of a bike repair shop, your tire was often punctured by a sharp tack. As a matter of fact, it is the repairer who dropped sharp tacks on the road on purpose – because he wanted to create a job opportunity. If your tire is punctured near his shop, you will surely come to his shop and have you bike repaired. What I intend to say is that government often creates jobs for their own interests by restricting entrepreneurial activities. If we permit the market to freely play its role and motivate entrepreneurs to predict the future, especially to think long-term, many mistakes can be avoided. However, we must admit that under current circumstances, because of constraints of various institutional arrangements, many Chinese entrepreneurs think short-term. They probably merely pay attention to the planning of industry and the market trend of the next one or two years instead of the next ten or twenty years, which hinders our structural adjustment. Many entrepreneurs are trying to fathom some national industrial policies. But what do most of the industrial polices turn out to be? As far as I am concerned, they become a mechanism of interest distribution, or, more specifically, rent-seeking activities. It holds true for new energy policies. The government encourages new energy, so some people manage to apply for many funds in the name of new energy programs and then appropriate money for other programs. It reminds me of that, in order to ensure the healthy development of our society, what is important is to motivate people to create wealth instead of allocating wealth.

Every country has its own development path, but humanity has remained the same till now, no matter which country you come from. How can a good system turn human impulse of pursuing happiness and joy into that of creating value for others and bringing happiness to others? I attempted to answer this question in my latest book *The Logic of the Market*. Many people discuss the "Chinese Economic Model", but what is the main characteristic of China's economy? They may say that China is unlike Eastern European countries and the former Soviet Union, which implement privatization, and we adhere to many public ownership economies, and our economy grows faster than theirs. In my view, this is a big misunderstanding, which indicates we haven't got in-depth understanding of what is private ownership and what is public ownership.

It is usually but wrongly believed that in a state-owned economy or public ownership economy, all rights belong to all people or the collectivity, while in a private ownership economy, rights belong to individuals. In any society, whether public or private ownership, all rights belong to individuals and the subject to exercise rights must be individuals; only a living human being who has soul and thought can exercise rights, and a country or an enterprise cannot. What is the main difference between state-owned or public ownership economy and private ownership economy? It is that in a public ownership economy, rights are attached to official positions, so I call it "position-based economy". For example, do you have the right to invest? It depends on whether you have an official position or not; moreover, not all positions have the right to invest. We are aware that the higher position you occupy, the more resources you can control, and the lower position, the less resources. In our planned economy, not only allocation of resources but also allocation of living material depend on positions. Take our riding on a train when on business for example. It had been well stipulated who could enjoy a cushioned berth or an ordinary berth or an ordinary seat. Only cadres of departmental directorship could enjoy cushioned berths; mid-level cadres, ordinary berths; and cadres of section-level and under, ordinary seats. Moreover, it all depended on the level of your position whether you could install an in-house telephone or whether you could have a special car or how big the house you could live in. Even what news or what newspaper you could read was also determined by your position. Senior cadres could read full versions of *Reference News*, while ordinary people only had access to abridged versions. All rights depended on positions, let alone channels for acquiring information. So in the system of this kind, in order to obtain rights, even the right to survive, what will you first strive to do? First of all, you must enter the government, then find the most powerful department and gradually climb the authority ladder step by step. The higher you climb, the more authority you have. This is a fundamental characteristic of our public ownership system.

What about a private ownership economy? In a private ownership economy, rights depend on property that people are in possession of. To put it simply, the universal criterion for property is money; as long as you have money, you have rights to consume and invest. If you have money, you can invest, buy stocks, and even start up a bank. You can purchase a car however big you like it to be; you can buy a big house, choose a good hospital when you are hospitalized, and enjoy better food. All of these are based on the foundation of property.

In a position-based economy, the best way to earn a position is not to create more wealth for society, but to strive to win over political rivals. Though in a public ownership system people make use of competition to achieve their goals, their competition is always destructive; maybe another word "battle" would be more pertinent, which means people will try every means to use others like a steppingstone. We are too busy with these battles instead of creating wealth. In a private ownership system, if you want to earn money, you must produce and sell goods; who will determine whether you can sell out or how much you can earn? It's up to consumers. Consumers use money to vote for your destiny. Competition among enterprises is, in fact, the one that creates surplus value for clients. Whichever enterprise leaves more surplus value will survive in the market. Therefore, we can see that competition in the private ownership system is the one that creates wealth and brings happiness and joy to others, which brings about many new inventions and technological advances. In order to win rights, entrepreneurs have to create, and their creations will succeed only if their prediction of the future is more accurate than others'.

What will China's entrepreneurs discuss most when they assemble together? Of course, policies. Because whether they can earn money, to a great extent, depends on their judgment about polices rather than about the market. If a policy per se can bring much money, they will make efforts to win favorable conditions the policy permits even if they know it is wrong. Because as long as they gain advantages, they gain wealth. Therefore, the difference between a public ownership system and a private ownership system is not humanity but human behaviors or whether people create value for society and others.

In this regard, it is understandable that China's reform during the past thirty years focused on, in fact, how to change from a position-based economy to a property-based economy. In the past only if we had an official position could we exercise rights; now if we have money or wealth, even without an official position, we can exercise rights. The change first started from the countryside. At the beginning peasants couldn't enter the government and even couldn't live from hand to mouth. After the reform and opening-up, even if peasants still couldn't enter the government, they were given freedom of speculation and profiteering, so there were a lot of 10,000 yuan households (Wan Yuan Hu),[3] and peasants were getting rich. Then the change took place in cities. Many urban citizens used to be excluded from the government and state-owned enterprises and to live a tough life. Now rich citizens can live a good life whose living standard is more or less equivalent to that of a secretary of the Party committee of a county and even exceeds that of a secretary of a municipal committee of the CPC; they can buy luxury cars and live in grander houses. To some extent, rich people can enjoy the same life as that of power-holders. As Si-ma Qian said over two thousand years ago, "A family of wealth is tantamount to a king of a kingdom; billionaires live the same life as monarchs". In other words, wise people don't need to enter the government to allocate resources and to enjoy a better life; by means of starting up enterprises and bringing happiness to and creating value for consumers, they can also improve their lives. Thus, our country can obtain thrust for economic development. So is the case with all countries over the world. Only if we make wise people create wealth for others and value for consumers can our economy develop. If a system makes some people try every means to gain happiness through robbing others' wealth rather than creating wealth for others, the economy will surely halt.

Today, there are a lot of problems in China, and one of those is corruption. What is the cause of corruption? It is easily understandable that we have both a position-based economy and a property-based economy at the same time;

thus, some people including entrepreneurs acquire resources through bribing power-holders or buying rights from those that take control of resources, not necessarily through creating wealth. For example, if I get a piece of land at a very low price through contacts, I can earn a fortune after selling it out. It is much easier to make money in such a way than many people engaged in manufacturing. This is a severe problem; as a result, more and more people quit manufacturing and plunge into real estates or other industries. Is the outcome good or bad for China's future? I don't think it is good.

So what's the next step of China's economic reform? To put it simply, it is to narrow the scope of the position-based economy as usual – namely, to reduce resources under the control of government. If we cannot solve this problem, we cannot find a solution to corruption. What is worse, under such circumstances, many excellent entrepreneurs spend energy and time making use of connections with officials and government policies instead of creating value for society and others, in a bid to accumulate wealth. If so, our economy might be confronted with troubles.

Of course, we can see we are drawing lessons from the past after this financial crisis. As a saying goes, a fall into the pit, a gain in your wit. But if we draw a wrong lesson, we probably obtain no gain in our wit. After this crisis, plenty of people pondered over why it happened. Their conclusion turned out to be malfunction of market; therefore, they advocated further increasing government's authority. As a matter of fact, our policies in the recent two years including investment policies and industry policies incline to continually enhance government's authority. We can imagine what consequence will be brought about. Consequently, allocation of current resources will be distorted, and what's worse, great changes will take place in entrepreneurs' ability allocation and their behavior pattern. It will be a great waste of entrepreneur resources – China's most precious resources – if our entrepreneurs spend their time and energy fawning over powerful government officials and making them happy and joyful instead of satisfying consumers and making them happy.

We should think over where our achievements on earth came and what path we should follow in the future. If we think our achievements owed much to mighty government's intervention and our large state-owned enterprises, I think we have drawn a totally wrong lesson. Drawing a lesson per se is nothing wrong, but a wrong lesson will lead us to a disappointing direction or even a direction toward destruction in the future.

How to correctly handle the relation between government and market?[4]

It is a crucial question how to understand the relation between government and market during the transition from a planned economy to a market economy. In this regard, opinions from Chinese academic circles and government officials have undergone several stages. The first stage is the period of planned economy before the reform and opening-up, and they unanimously thought "government is almighty and market is useless". They applied such an idea to policies and concentrated on planning instead of market. The second stage is from the early period of the reform and opening-up till 1984. They realized "government is not almighty and supplementation of market is necessary", which brought about the official guideline of "relying on planning and giving play to the supplementary role of market". According to the guideline, the government would do what it could do and would allow the market to work for it when it couldn't. Although their understanding sounded progressive, it still put the cart before the horse. In 1985 economic circles reached a consensus that we should allow the market to do what it could do and should turn to government only if the market was incapable; or in other words, government was the supplementation of the market. As a matter of fact, that is what we have learned from microeconomics textbooks. During the same period I proposed a view that even when the market did not work perfectly, we needn't necessarily turn to government because government would likely do worse than the market. It was commonly believed that the market was not perfect, but many people didn't realize that government could probably do worse than the market. Unfortunately, my view hadn't won support among the people yet and nor had it become the leading idea for formulating policies. Actually many government departments still adhere to the idea of "relying on the leading role of government and giving play to the supplementary role of market".

The idea of the government-leading and market-supplementing can be expressed in various forms. It is popularly believed in a market economy that government isn't supposed to be a participant or, for example, a player but a referee and a rule-maker. It is correct to say government shouldn't be a participant or a player, but it will overestimate the role of government to regard government as a referee and a rule-maker of the market economy. Now my speech focuses on refuting this popular view.

First of all, it isn't in accordance with actual conditions to claim government to be a referee and a rule-maker of a market economy. In reality, the order of a market economy is largely controlled by "an invisible hand", so in most cases the outcome of competition needn't be judged by a referee. For example, after we sign a contract, is it because I fear being punished by government that I honor my promise? Not necessarily. The reason why I am willing to honor my promise is that I am afraid nobody would like to do business with me any more if I cannot keep my word. Only on occasion will we turn to government. For instance, it is quite rare in a market economy that we need government to supervise us to implement the contract after we sign a contract. Here I would like to put forward a new concept – actually not new. When Adam Smith advocates market economy is an invisible hand, he actually denies government is a rule-maker and referee; otherwise, market economy is not directed by an invisible hand. If we give a closer look to Adam Smith's book, we will find the market not only is an invisible hand but also has an invisible eye – namely, reputation mechanism. The reason why market economy operates well is not that a government is supervising what you are doing but that the invisible eye or reputation mechanism is watching over everyone.

Second, it isn't also in accordance with the development history of market economy to regard government as a referee and a rule-maker. Before the appearance of government people had already begun to trade with each other. International trade is a good example. In the eleventh century, commerce started to revive in the Mediterranean. Since Mediterranean commerce is international commerce, how can it emerge without a unified government? It depended on merchants themselves, because they had a private legal system (Law Merchant) instead of an official legal system. Till now this legal system remains the fundamental framework for international commercial arbitration. Even in the United States, which has the most developed legal system, most of commercial disputes are solved not by courts but by private arbitration institutions. Therefore, whether historically or currently, we cannot think that in a market economy the government is the only judge and rule-maker. Of course, some rules need to be formulated by government and some disputes depend on government judgments, but the major rule-maker of a market economy is not government but merchants themselves.

Third, if government is the sole rule-maker, a series of problems will arise. Hereby I propose the following three propositions. The first proposition is that the more energy its government spends tackling business problems and the more energy enterprises will spend tackling their relationships to government, the more backward a country will be. How much energy do foreign ventures spend dealing with government after they come to China? Our government officials often proudly claim they care about foreign ventures because all day long they are busy meeting foreign investors and employers. We can almost see such shots on TV every day, which is extremely abnormal. If we start up an enterprise in America, do we need to meet the US president, governors, or mayors? No. The president of Konka Group Co., Ltd., at Shenzhen proudly said he hadn't been to the municipal government for half a year. That sounds good, but ten years would be better. In developed countries, public relations originally refer to relationships to media, but in China they denote relationships to government. Any large enterprise that enters China is supposed to establish a department responsible for dealing with relations to government. Now there has appeared a huge industry that aims at arranging for foreign investors meetings with Chinese government officials. Some of these companies are owned by foreigners, and others are run by Chinese; they get high pay, and their businesses thrive. Such a problem deserves our deep deliberation. It is expressive of backwardness if government officials keep claiming how much time they spend on enterprises.

The underlying reason is our vetting procedures. In other words, whatever we do must get approved by relevant government departments. I insist vetting systems for starting up enterprises be abolished. Take China's Western Development Strategy. I think whether the western region is advantageous for attracting investment hinges on whether its system is advantageous, and vetting systems must be annulled. For example, one of my friends registered a company in America, Hong Kong, and Shenzhen respectively, and, as far as registration is concerned, it cost several minutes in America, half a day in Hong Kong, and over two weeks in Shenzhen. I believe it takes at least two months in Beijing and probably four months in Xi'an. When you register a company, you must get the approval of Ministry of Information Industry as long as your company name contains a word "网" (literally, network or web). Besides, industrial and commercial bureaus are entitled to decide your business feasibility report is not feasible under the excuse of your bad prospects for earning profits. That sounds like a marriage registration clerk refusing their request and telling them to go home just under the pretext that their relation is not good enough for marriage when a couple registers for marriage. That is an extremely severe problem; just look at how much energy people of enterprise circles in our country have to spend dealing with these procedures. We must realize that starting up enterprises belong to an individual right instead of government's discretional power or something the state monopolizes. Thus, relevant vetting systems must be abolished.

In Western countries the spirit of legislation and of government administration are assuming you are good people and allowing you to start up business freely; only if you do wrongs will you be punished. Whereas in China, we will, first of all, assume you are bad people and watch over you; we won't give you opportunities to start up business unless you can prove you are not bad. That's the idea of our vetting systems. Some people may say, since there are lots of swindlers, what if we abolish vetting systems? But my question is, why are swindlers still rampant in China, even if China has the strictest vetting systems and is one of the few countries that impose vetting systems on all industries?

My second proposition: the more government controls, the more swindlers appear in the market. Why are there so many swindlers in China? Because the government controls too much. In a market economy we should rely on reputation mechanism. So-called "reputation" means sacrificing today's interests to trade for tomorrow's profits. The reason why I don't cheat you today is that I won't have a chance to do business tomorrow if I do. It is just like borrowing money; as a saying goes: "return what you have borrowed promptly and you will have no difficulty borrowing again". To have initiative in establishing reputation, people must have stable anticipation for the future. In a society the more stable their anticipation is, the more people tend to be true to their reputation. However, the more government controls and the more variable government policies are, the less stable people's anticipation for the future becomes; as a result, they incline to do one-shot deals. For example, if I manage to start up an enterprise today but if tomorrow the government might tell me I am illegal and compel me to move away, why wouldn't I do a one-shot deal? That's why swindlers are rampant. Why are private enterprises instead of state-owned enterprises willing to be swindlers? Because government departments create too much uncertainty and impose intervention freely, people have no confidence in the future.

There is a major problem with our government departments – that is, almost every department is granted unrestricted legislative power. While what they legislate are probably called policies, all of the policies have legal effect. It was in the name of "for the sake of safeguarding national interests" or "for the sake of maintaining market order" that relevant departments made all of these policies. If we give a second thought to that, we will find they are 90% for the sake of strengthening departmental power instead of national interests. In Beijing we have personally experienced too many such instances. For example, in Beijing automobiles are charged parking space fees and the Foreign Trade & Economic Relation Commission contends with the Ministry of Information Industry for regulatory power over the information industry.

Another problem is that these policies or rules are too vague. Since government controls too much, it is surely difficult to clarify every rule. The reason why government officials make vague rules is quite understandable; the more vague policies are, the more discretional power they have, because they hold control of the final explanatory power for disputes. For if you are confused about policies, government departments have reason to set up various consulting companies that offer paid consulting services. For example, if you have no idea of relevant policies, you can go to a consulting company nearby and figure them out at the cost of several hundred yuan. To settle this problem, we must abolish legislative power possessed by government departments; legislative power shall be taken back to the National People's Congress and merely enforcement power is granted to government departments.

The third proposition is if government plays the role of referee, it will most likely disregard reputation. We ought to learn from British practice and experience after the Glorious Revolution. At that time the British government claimed it would turn from an unlimited government into a limited one. From then on, its capability of issuing bonds had increased several times, which enabled the United Kingdom to defeat France finally. The reason is that when a government is unlimited, people won't trust in it and will be unwilling to lend money to it, but, after the government becomes limited, the populace will believe it can keep its promise and be willing to buy bonds.

So is the case with state-owned enterprises. On the one hand, unless their problems are solved, the function of government cannot be changed. And on the other hand, only if the function of government is changed can the problems of the state-owned enterprises be settled. For what reason? Because when government runs state-owned enterprises, it will automatically turn into a player from a referee. Most of our laws are aimed at state-owned enterprises. For example, Company Law stipulates the equity that intangible assets account for should not exceed 20%. How absurd is this?! Government attaches importance to state-owned enterprises and fears loss of assets of state-owned enterprises. It is totally for the sake of state-owned enterprises that government formulates various protective policies and then applies them to the whole society.

Besides, these days I am thinking over a question: what government officials should learn. Actually it is quite simple. I suggest every official should have a copy of *An Inquiry into the Nature and Causes of the Wealth of Nations* by Adam Smith written over two hundred years ago and spend three months reading and writing down the whole text from memory. That will be more effective than learning anything else. Why? Because *An Inquiry into the Nature and Causes of the Wealth of Nations* was directed against the British government's intervention in the economy then, and it is still applicable to many of our so-called vetting systems.

Harmony presupposes development[5]

Lately I proposed to think rationally about arising problems during China's reform. In my opinion, rational thinking connotes four meanings. First, we must transcend our positions and interests and put ourselves in others' shoes. The poor shouldn't think from the perspective of the poor, nor should the rich think from the perspective of the rich. It is difficult to do that, but we should try to do it; at least scholars should. Second, we must think and make choices within feasible sets and cannot desire what is ideal but unfeasible. Third, discussion must be based on logic and facts. Many of our judgments are easily misleading, because they are often based on direct perception and lack rational analyses. Fourth, just as successful experience of various countries has indicated, we should "look ahead" rather than "look back" when coping with problems arising in our reform. We aim at living better instead of seeking psychological balance.

Establishing a harmonious society is the goal that human beings have been pursuing thorough history. But the problem is, what harmonious society do you desire? Whenever everyone talks of a harmonious society, income distribution seems paramount. But as matter of fact, so-called "harmonious society" that many netizens discuss means egalitarian income distribution. I think what we should establish is a development-based harmonious society, in accordance with Deng Xiaoping's saying: "Development is the absolute principle". Harmony presupposes development; without development, there is no harmony.

Recently I have made some researches on the economic development of thirty-one provinces, municipalities, as well as autonomous regions. Research has shown it is a fundamental fact that during the past twenty-six years, on average, the areas with a fast economic growth or relatively high per capita income exactly had a low Gini coefficient. In particular, China's absolute poverty population dropped from 250 million (accounting for 25% of the total population) in 1978 to 26 million (accounting for 2% of the total population) in 2005. That would have been impossible without development, particularly without the development of private enterprises. A research made by Professor Xavier Sala-i-Martin of Columbia University, USA, indicated, from 1980 to 1998, the global income distribution disparity reduced, which owed much to Chinese income increase. This exemplifies development is an absolute principle, and development is the only solution to income distribution. We must develop a development-based harmonious society.

Many people regard state-owned enterprises as a means of accomplishing income distribution policies, but I figure that in China's urban areas, on average, the more proportion the working-age population employed by state-owned enterprises, the higher the Gini coefficient will be. Therefore, we cannot rely on state-owned enterprises to solve the problem of income distribution as well as of poverty.

If we count on government spending to solve the income distribution problem, we are in need of more effective methods. We shouldn't take it for granted that as government spends more, income disparity will necessarily be reduced. In fact, I discover transfer expenditure hasn't be used to tackle the income distribution problem; on average, the higher the governmental expenditure-GDP ratio is, the higher its Gini coefficient will be.

The increase of nationwide income disparity is closely related to regional differences. According to the World Bank scholars' calculation, the increase of China's national Gini coefficient is 30% to 50%, caused by regional differences – namely, regional differences in economic development. Provincial Gini coefficient is mostly below 0.4, even 0.35, but national Gini coefficient exceeds 0.4, which indicates a big problem. We must recognize that since some regions have much higher income than others, the added-up national Gini coefficient will become high even if every region implements egalitarian income distribution. If so, we should focus on narrowing regional differences. Why are there so many regional differences in China? Besides historical reasons (including the reason of planned economy), all regions differ from each other in the institutional reform pace, entrepreneurship, and proportion of state-owned enterprises. Less-developed regions tend to have a slower institutional reform pace and a bigger proportion of state-owned enterprises and lack entrepreneurship or have an unfavorable environment for starting up business. In this sense, for the sake of solving regional differences, these regions must create a better institutional and policy environment for free business.

What I intend to note is that we must consider China's problems from the perspective of globalization. To put it simply, the Chinese nation's global competitiveness is a prerequisite for our consideration. We cannot close our door to discuss China's problems. In other words, if any of our policies such as the policy of narrowing disparity between the rich and the poor imparts Chinese enterprises' global competitiveness, it will actually impart the Chinese nation's global competitiveness and China's future competitiveness, and the last victims will be hundreds of thousands of common people, because their employment opportunities will be reduced. Our income distribution disparity is partially caused by globalization. In China the annual salary of senior white-collars can reach a million yuan or even higher, while that of an ordinary manufacturing worker is less than 10,000 yuan; the former is one hundred times as much as the latter, which rarely happened in other countries during the process of development. This also indicates the expansion of income disparity in China.

Why is there so much wage disparity after globalization? Because high-skilled professionals are internationally movable and earn a globally average salary in the international market, but low-skilled workers are localized and less movable and only earn a locally average salary. The salary of China's high-skilled and high-caliber workers ranges from a third to a half as much as American workers, or even higher, but China's manufacturing workers only earn a fortieth as much as American counterparts. Given such inevitable difference between China and the United States, what should we do? If we reduce the salary of high-skilled people through taxation, they will move away because they can emigrate. If we, through legislation, raise the minimum wage from 10,000 yuan a year to a high level (for example, 100,000 or 200,000 yuan a year), Chinese enterprises will collapse and foreign-funded enterprises will move to other countries. Private entrepreneurs as well as high-caliber professionals can emigrate, but Chinese peasants cannot. Who will be the biggest sufferer at last? Low-skilled workers. Therefore, we must take a global view to look at China's problems.

Yesterday I discussed with a professor from South Korea about China's problems. He said, it was for the sake of survival and development of their country that Koreans endured about forty years before they got down to tackling problems of this kind. He thought that if we got involved in these internal problems too early but failed to solve them, we would soon end up losing out and China would be at stake.

Considering income distribution and other social problems, if we can carry out a closed economy behind closed doors, egalitarianism may be applicable as long as the majority of people are satisfied. But we cannot even distribute fortune equally, because of international competition. So is the case with Britain. Why did the socialism of the British Labor Party fail? Without participation of Japanese in competition, British people could have lived a sluggish life very well; but with participation of Japanese in competition, there was no way out. Ms. Thatcher said they had no choice but to reform. Though Thatcher's reform widened British income disparity, it drastically increased British employment opportunities and raised absolute income level. Hence, we ought to understand China's reform from an in-depth perspective. What direction we should take is not a simple matter of how to distribute income among Tom, Dick, and Harry, but involves the future development of our nation and country.

It often makes us puzzled about what to say when we discuss reform problems, which has something to do with leadership. I once worked in two companies as independent director. I think there was a big distinction between both companies. One company's leaders had strong leadership. In this company, you, as independent director, were well aware of the future direction of CEO; what you should do was to propose suggestions as critical as you could, and the CEO would weigh whether your suggestions were applicable or not. However, the situation with the other company was the opposite. It was in need of a good leader who knew which direction they would take, so you should be cautious about suggestions, because probably the more suggestions you proposed, the less confident the leader would become and the more trouble the company would suffer. The reason why I give this example is that I think reform leadership is paramount. We have bothered discussing so much; do we know where they want to go? No. If we know the general direction, we can talk over what problem will be brought about if we do it this way. Or else, we really have no idea about how to express ourselves and how to discuss this problem.

If we debate the problems arising in reform including new exposed medical or educational problems, on the one hand, this will embarrass the government; on the other hand, actually some government departments will be pleased because it is a good opportunity for them to seize power. It fits in exactly with their wishes to attribute all problems to marketization. That is relatively dangerous, because at the beginning we could see the dawn of victory, but now it has been totally curtained.

Several years ago I once said the reform in the 1980s was largely helped by the existence of State Commission for Restructuring Economic System (SCRES). Because SCRES had no independent interest from a planned economy, it endeavored to propel reform and then became a force of countervailing other conservative departments. When other departments put forward reform proposals, it would send its own experts to research on them; when top leaders assembled meetings, SCRES would always submit its independent views. Now SCRES is dissolved, and, without SCRES, every department freely snatches its own interests. Therefore, it is difficult to conceive an overall reform plan. No authority is in charge of reform; everyone might as well do as he or she likes. I also suggest if reform leadership is really desired, there should be a quite competent leading team responsible for reform programs. There must arise plenty of problems if the responsible institution has been shut down before the goal of reform is achieved. Finally, people will blame you for what you have done.

China's stock market: regulation and reputation[6]

It is paramount that two years ago, relevant departments of China Securities Regulatory Commission began to strengthen protection of investors and regulation of listed companies. If managers of listed companies don't have initiative in establishing a good reputation, however, we cannot fundamentally protect investors.

Understanding the problem, first of all, involves the conception of financing. In the West, the conception is remarkably different from that in China. According to the description of Western economic textbooks, enterprise financing denotes that if you suppose you have a profitable investment project, how can you raise funds for it, through issuing stocks or bonds? What does financing mean in China? It means if you are permitted to issue stocks, what will you use the money for? In China the first thing you must do is to make up a project and make use of it to obtain the government's permission to issue stocks in the stock market. But because the project per se is fake, it is natural that you may change investment as soon as you manage to raise money. This is the difference of financing between China's enterprises and foreign enterprises.

Strict regulation and frauds

China's capital market has five basic characteristics. First, fast growth. Second, the proportion of listed companies' tradable stocks is quite low. Most listed companies have merely 30% tradable stocks; in other words, only about a third of stocks are being traded, and the remaining two thirds are untradeable legal-person shares and state-owned shares. Third, these tradable stocks have a high frequency of trading. Fourth, stocks' market price exceeds the true value of enterprises and has nothing to do with performances of listed companies. Fifth, government exerts quite strict regulation on listed companies. Government plays a dominant role in the whole process involving approval of listing applications, accomplishing vetting procedures and final pricing. It can be said since the beginning our capital market has been strictly manipulated by government, but as a matter of fact, the whole stock market is abundant with frauds.

There are plenty of fraud examples. For instance, the ¥1 billion fund of KMK Co., Ltd., was used by its parent company. The ¥2.5 billion fund – namely 90% of net assets of 999 Medical & Pharmaceutical Co., Ltd. – was appropriated by its parent company. With regard to the recent "Guangxia Event", all accounting reports of Guangxia Industry Co., Ltd., were found false, and all the statistics were fake.

China's stock market is faced with two questions: first, since our government implements such complicated and bureaucratic regulatory procedures, why is the market still filled with frauds? Second, why do stock prices in the stock market continue being overestimated for a decade?

According to standard economic theory, if all information is symmetric in a market, the market can function effectively by its own, but if all information is asymmetric, for example, the operating status of listed companies is only open to their operators instead of investors, or investors cannot judge or know which listed company is promising or unpromising, which will result in malfunction of the market.

In order to avoid malfunction, government must regulate the market by means of laws and policies. In case that listed companies deceive investors, all the vetting procedures for listing are supposed to aim at ensuring accounts of listed companies are true and what they disclose is true. No doubt, regulation plays a vital role in this regard. However, we should also realize that, when people need to know true information, there is a pair of invisible eyes – namely, reputation functioning. If enterprises intend to ensure their sustainable development, they must pay attention to this pair of invisible eyes watching over them.

What is the difference between regulation and reputation? Who shall be responsible for exerting regulation? A government department or law court? Is government regulation or judgment already sufficient to guarantee contracts between investors and enterprises? How can reputation be embodied?

I have two judgments concerning regulation. First, where there is much regulation, there are many swindlers. Why? Because regulation destroys reputation mechanism the market should have had. Second, the more regulation there is, the more incentives swindlers have in bribing government officials. Swindlers often tend to pay small bribes for their entry into market. As swindlers increase, government will feel there is not too much but too little regulation. As a result, regulation is further strengthened and aggravated repeatedly till there is no place for market competition, which fosters reputation mechanism, let alone enterprises' reputation.

If a court or government department exerts regulation on a certain listed company, first of all it should obtain information of the company; and a court, as the third party, shall pay a high price for verifying or authenticating the information. The cost of employing regulation to solve problems is quite high, but the cost of employing reputation is low. If two persons trust each other, it will be much easier to solve problems, but if they don't, they have to sign a complicated contract that costs a high price, in a bid to provide reasonable and legal rationales.

Thereby have risen plenty of relevant stock market problems. Take information disclosure for example. Information disclosure is legally mandatory. Mandatory discourse is a legal means, but, as a matter of fact, if enterprises cherish their reputations, they will voluntarily disclose their information without legal compulsion. When we go to a shop and buy clothes, although law doesn't stipulate customers shall try on clothes, all shops permit customers to do, and some of them even allow customers to return and exchange clothes. These shops volunteer instead of being forced to offer their information owing to that they attach importance to their reputations. Now, mandatory information disclosure is prevalent in society, including China's financial institutions. However, current research hasn't proven that mandatory information disclosure can be advantageous. What I intend to say is that in the stock market, if enterprises value their reputations, one legal provision will be enough – that is, that you have the right to refuse to disclose your information, but you must be responsible for authenticity of the information you have disclosed. Just like we see in movies, a Western policeman often says to a suspect, "You have the right to remain silent and refuse to answer questions, but anything you do say may be used against you in a court of law".

We cannot force all enterprises to disclose their information – because every enterprise is different. Some of them cannot disclose information, say, since once their business secrets are disclosed, they will lose their business value.

There are four main requirements for reputation formation. First, the game is repeated. Only under such condition can interested parties – namely, enterprises possibly have long-term vision – think of the future and have enough patience to await future profits. All frauds are caused by short-term vision and opportunism. Secondly, a stable environment. When the environment is unstable – namely, today there is an opportunity of earning money, but tomorrow is unknown – the interested parties will become opportunists and be eager for quick success and instant profits. Thirdly, frauds can be discovered in time – that is, the speed of information communication is paramount. Fourth, victims must have incentives for and possibility of punishing swindlers. In China's market, many swindlers are lucky, because victims don't have initiative in and possibility of punishing them. For example, if you are a real estate developer and sell houses to government or state-owned enterprises, though you commit frauds, the buyers will be unlikely to punish you. Because you have bribed them personally with two houses, you can sell them one hundred houses next. When the victims of this kind don't care about their loss, the swindlers won't, of course, care for their reputations.

Enterprises as carriers of information and reputation

In modern society, an enterprise, or an organization, in fact, is also an agency that serves as a carrier of information. In all deals we cannot know everybody, but deals often involve a lot of people. It is quite difficult and costly for us to recognize each of them, so frauds easily take place. However, if an organization or an enterprise commits frauds, it can be easily convicted. For example, international enterprises like McDonald's have tens of thousands of employees; if we want to know which employee sells an expired hamburger, it is quite hard to investigate it and publish the information even if you have found it. But with the brand "McDonald's", consumers needn't know who the specific doer is and "McDonald's" makes it easier to maintain the communication of reputation and turns the enterprise into a carrier of reputation. Of course, it is the job of McDonald's to find the specific doer and make a punishment, which is the value of McDonald's to customers.

An enterprise is compared to a temple, and its managers and employees are akin to monks. Modern market society constrains conduct of monks by means of the temple's reputation. If Shaolin Temple's reputation is ruined, that will directly affect the amount of alms monks will receive. To maintain temple's reputation has two requirements: first, monks can benefit from the temple's good reputation; if their interests have nothing to do with the temple's reputation, they will not care. Second, the right to build a temple cannot be monopolized. When the right to build a temple is monopolized – that is, monks of this temple aren't allowed to build a temple and receive alms – they will pay no attention to its reputation.

Therefore, we can see that the reason why enterprises lack reputation mechanism is that "monks" of these "temples" (enterprises) are all "itinerant monks" or "visiting scholars" who merely stay in one temple for one night. Therefore, they attach no importance to their temples' reputation.

In China many organizations such as accounting associations and lawyers' associations are monopolistic. Their monopoly encourages them to carry out rent-seeking regardless of their reputations and the privileges government gives to them justify their neglect of reputation. That explains a typical phenomenon taking place in China: people are more motivated to grow grass than to grow trees. Establishing a reputation is like growing trees rather than planting grass.

Relation between the regulation on our stock market and reputation

If we draw a coordinate diagram to show the relation between the regulation on our stock market and reputation, in which the x-axis stands for regulation and the y-axis for reputation, we can have two curves. One is a demand curve, indicating that the higher people's reputations are, the less the demand for government regulation people; and the lower people's reputations, the more government regulation will be needed. If there is no reputation – namely, everyone has no incentive in building reputation at all – we have to turn to rely on government regulation for all. Another curve can be called "supply curve". Unlike the demand curve, the supply curve is not monotonous. At the beginning when government adopts regulatory measures, people highlight reputations; as regulation is strengthened, reputations increase but have a critical point. When they reach the critical point, people cease to cherish reputations; the more regulation, the lower people's reputations will be. Why does it happen? Why can governmental regulation ruin people's reputations?

First, the more regulation there is, the more discretion government officials will have, thus the more uncertain the future environment is and the more unpredictable the outcome will become. Consequently, people are inclined to seek short-term interests regardless of long-term interests.

Second, government's regulation often leads to monopoly, which brings about "rents". For example, when your enterprise instead of other enterprises can only be allowed to get listed, you have an opportunity to enjoy these rents. When you can enjoy privileges, you don't care for your reputation. Because investors can share rents guaranteed by monopoly, they needn't worry about performances of your enterprise and your enterprise won't be punished for a bad reputation.

Third, more regulation allows more opportunities of corruption. For instance, if a real estate developer attempts to sell houses to two hundred individual households, he or she must satisfy all of them. But if he or she intends to sell two hundred houses to government- or state-owned enterprises, he or she needs to bribe only one person or a few persons in charge of purchase – namely, the head of the real estate management department. It costs much less to bribe a government department than to satisfy customers. Therefore, in spite of governmental regulation, the accreditation made by government itself deserves no trust.

In addition, the authorities are rarely efficient in exerting regulation. As a result, the more regulation there is beyond a certain point, the lower people's reputations become. As people pay less attention to their reputations, government continues strengthening regulation. Eventually, nothing but regulation is left.

This is what we have seen today. Despite so much government's regulation, frauds are prevalent. If a listed company passes through inspections made by so many official departments and is exposed that its account is false, do investors seem too silly? Why didn't they notice it until ten years later?

In fact, in China's stock market, the situation is not that a person deceives another person or that big investors deceive small investors. China's stock market is a rent-seeking market, and all investors, big or small, share this rent. The deal between the deceiver and deceived is obvious: if I cheat you out of 100 yuan, I will compensate you 120 yuan by means of cheating others. Why wouldn't you like to be deceived by me if you can earn a net profit of 20 yuan? The deceiver believes the deceived will be motivated to make the deal, just like paying 100 yuan for a fake invoice can be reimbursed 200 yuan, because both parties can benefit from the deal.

A main function of China's stock market is to help state-owned enterprises tide over difficulties. As far as a state-owned enterprise on the verge of bankruptcy is concerned, the best way of saving it is to get it listed and, first of all, to raise money from investors. The investors are still willing to buy its stocks, though they are well aware the enterprise isn't promising. The reason is that they know buying its stocks is tantamount to buying a promise made by government; once the enterprise is at stake, government will surely abuse its monopoly privilege to save and shelter it. The investors have already anticipated their investment will be secured.

"Rents" of our stock market stem from government's monopoly of resources as well as of listing qualification, so the monopoly of this kind makes the shell of every listed company quite valuable. Loss-making listed companies have no intrinsic value, but because of their precious shell (that is, entitlement for listing), they still have selling points even on the brink of bankruptcy. When investors buy stocks of these enterprises, they anticipate increase of stocks because of enterprises' selling points. No wonder after some listed companies are given special treatment for bad performance, their stocks are on the rise instead.

Property rights as the foundation of reputation

In the past two years, huge changes have taken place in China's stock market. Especially after Zhou Xiaochuan assumed Chairman of China Securities Regulatory Commission (CSRC), the department of securities regulation began to have a right thinking pattern and vision. In order to achieve sustainable development of China's stock market, we must propel standardization including information disclosure, marketization of listing qualification, and annulment of approval systems. Any eligible and qualified enterprise that has been filed on record shall be permitted to get listed freely.

If so, all the rents of the whole stock market will be eliminated. When enterprises are free to get listed, there is no rent. That's one of the main reasons why stock prices decreased during the past two years. This coincides with reduction of state-owned shares. As a result, people mistakenly think it is reduction of state-owned shares that causes the decline of stocks. As a matter of fact, it is a natural response when, in the face of standardization of the stock market, people are forced to anticipate the rents of the stock market will disappear. This is good news that China's stock market has embarked on healthy development.

However, the disappearance of stock market rents will conflict with many short-term interests of relevant government departments, so some people make an appeal to "maintain stock prices". Today maintaining the stock market price, glorified as "protecting the interests of investors", becomes a top priority. The circles of Chinese economists as well as relevant government departments have vulgar understanding of how to protect investors: for them, protecting investors means protecting investors from losing money. It is a quite wrong view; if all the stock buyers cannot lose money, they will not care whether the performances of stock-issuing enterprises are good or bad, nor will they care whether information of the companies is true or false. Without these considerations, will listed companies care about their performances and reputations? No! As a result, we will surely deviate from the standardized and healthy development of stock market.

It is well known to us, even to officials of CSRC, that the some listed companies' information that was audited and exposed by accounting firms was false. Of course, details we have known vary from one another, but none has cared, especially nor have final investors cared. Why? Because everyone knows in the market the rents brought about by government's regulation are guaranteed by government. Now we have seen that hardly was the false financial information of listed companies exposed when accounting firms were the first ones to blame. Give it a second thought: who should demand them to expose real information, or who should be their real clients? Not listed companies, but stock buyers. If stock buyers don't need real information, accounting firms will tend to produce a great deal of false information.

We cannot ask accounting firms to solve all the problems overnight, even if we intend to standardize the stock market. I am afraid the contradiction still remains covered and government continues to make use of state-owned assets to inject a cardiac stimulant to the stock market for the sake of appeasing investors. If so, the prospects for the stock market will be quite worrisome. From now on, we must make institutional changes to ensure that China's enterprises value their reputations; or else, merely government's regulation, independent directors, and mandatory information disclosure cannot work at all.

I think property rights system reform is the only key to making enterprises value reputations. We must link interests of monks with the reputation of their temple. If monks cannot benefit from the reputation of their temple, why should they value it? If the market value of an enterprise has nothing to do with interests of its management team, why should they value the reputation of their enterprise? The fundamental function of a property rights system is to offer a stable and anticipative rule for repeated games and seeking long-term interests. Property rights are the foundation of reputation, and clear property rights are the impetus to pursuing long-term interests. Only the seekers of long-term interests will cherish reputation. Mencius once said, "The people that possess fixed assets have morality". Likewise, we can say, the people that don't possess fixed assets disregard reputation. Ruining property rights is, in fact, a behavior of disturbing anticipation and destroying morality. In order to obtain good market order, we are obligated to change property rights system essentially.

Reputation of a society relies on patience of the whole society. When people lose patience, the society loses reputation. Likewise, the processes of establishing a reputation and of standardizing the stock market require us to be patient enough. I worry leaders of government departments are keen on growing grass instead of trees, and on short-term stableness rather than future long-term healthy development. If so, stock market problems and societal problems will accumulate rather than decrease.

What has China's accession to the WTO brought to us?[7]

Think with the logic of the market

We should consider the WTO from a historical perspective. Over ten thousand years ago, all over the world, human beings occupied every place that was suitable for their survival. At that time, because of thaw of glaciers, the world was divided into three separate parts – namely, the Euro-Asian-African continent, American continent, and Australian continent respectively. After then many human cultures came into being. However, in the past five hundred years, tremendous changes have taken place. Humans living in these three continents have been reconnected together, and we call the reconnection "globalization". Now we are undoubtedly amid one of the phases of globalization.

During the past five hundred years, there have been two types of logic that define international relations. One is called "gangster logic" to the effect that one country, one nation, or one person pursues happiness at the expense of other countries', other nations', or other persons' happiness. The other is "the logic of the market", which denotes that one country, one nation, or one person pursues happiness by means of making other countries, other nations, or others happy. Generally it is these two types of logic that have functioned in the past five hundred years.

What I am satisfied with is that the logic of the market or so called "multi-win" or "win-win" becomes prevalent, although the gangster logic still exists and is sometimes overwhelmingly but gradually decaying. The gangster logic plays a role amid the emergence of Western countries, but the role of the logic of the market is more significant. Trade exemplifies the logic of the market. During World War II, Japan and Germany were doomed to failure because they worshiped the gangster logic. But why did they reemerge as economic powers shortly after the war? Because they relied on the logic of the market. Generally speaking, the WTO values the logic of the market that benefits all participants.

Today there are still some countries all over the world that are fond of the gangster logic. Though only great powers can follow the gangster logic, some backward countries incline to thinking with the gangster logic. For example, our Chinese people often tend to think with the gangster logic instead of the logic of the market. We are not powerful, so we will not analyze whether we ourselves and others can earn benefits but assume we are probably conned by others. The difference between the gangster logic and market logic can be exemplified by the difference in the way of thinking business between a Shaanxier and a Guangdonger. The former only cares about how much he or she can earn, and will become upset if others earn too much; whereas the latter always pays more attention to how much others can profit. This difference embodies two typical thinking patterns of handling international relations.

If we think with the gangster logic, we always consider what industrial sectors will be impaired if we enter WTO and think that granting foreigners access to markets will not necessarily bring advanced technologies. But if we think with the logic of the market, we are likely to weigh up what advantages we can earn and what our development during the next ten years and future development will be without the WTO.

What I intend to say is that as far as industrial policies are concerned, we shall concentrate not on industries but on essential factors. What essential factors is China in need of? Land or natural resources. If we think from the perspective of China's national interests, why won't it be beneficial if we enter the WTO and can make use of foreign land to feed Chinese and take advantage of foreign resources to develop our country? Now China has managed to use 7% of the world's arable land to feed 20% of the world population, but if half of China's population can rely on foreign land through trade, it will not be a failure but a tremendous achievement.

It is also an achievement that China's oil import exceeds more than half of oil consumption. We cannot say it is a failure to depend too much on others. If Westerners had thought the same way, Western countries would not have developed at all. Why could Europe emerge? One of the reasons is that the discovery of the American continent solved European land shortage. Europeans used to grow crops through deforestation and later began to utilize Americans' land to produce food for them. That's how today's Europe developed.

So is the case with energy resources. Energy resources play an important role in economic development, but in general China is a country lacking in energy resources. The oil of the Middle East, Russia, and the Central Asia is utilized by either Americans or Japanese. If Chinese heavily rely on import of oil from these countries, it will be a greater achievement. Therefore, the advantages the WTO has brought to us lie not in industries but in essential factors. The rare resources we are short of or what we cannot produce can be replaced by resources of other countries.

Let's consider aforementioned technological advances. We cannot deny that today technologies are accelerating and are characterized by the fact that technological diffusion is even faster than technological advance. Several hundred years or several thousand years ago, technological advance was slow but technological diffusion much slower. For example, paper-making technology was invented by Chinese in around 100 A.D., but it took 650 years to reach the Middle East in 751A.D. Today, as long as any new technology is invented in the United States and European countries, it will soon appear in other parts of the world, if without government prohibition.

So I think we should think of technological advance from a different perspective. The conception of independent technological innovation is probably not universally applicable. Because if technologies of every country belong to so-called independent innovation, globalization might not be quite meaningful. Globalization denotes making use of wisdom of all human beings, which is what differs humans from animals. Humans have a learning ability, and everyone can obtain knowledge accumulated by others and knowledge that was historically accumulated, while animals cannot. Hence, from the perspective of "the logic of the market", we might have different understanding of many problems we are confronted with.

As far as China is concerned, we aren't aware of what are good and what are bad. Of course, we think we are. I don't think we can easily make judgment of the WTO's effect on a certain industry. Professor Lu Feng just concluded that what matters most is not whether we are open or not, but what policies we carry out. In my opinion, we shall give play to the role of enterprises and entrust entrepreneurs instead of government departments the duty of judging whether policies are good. I am sure that without the WTO, there would be no success of Huawei Corporation, because more than half of its sales revenue comes from foreign market. Without the WTO, Huawei couldn't go so smoothly in the world. If Huawei imprisoned all of its most intelligent talents, it would die not long before. All human technological advances including European countries' technological advances have absorbed knowledge from other parts of the world. Openness is paramount.

On the whole, in China, either ordinary people, scholars, or officials shall learn to think with the logic of the market, because our society will be prospective if humans think with the logic of the market instead of the gangster logic. The conflicts of interest between countries and enterprises, many of which stem from our subjective understanding, are far smaller than we think. Indeed, we can suppose that if these conflicts are unsolvable, we humans are hopeless; either you kill me, or I kill you. It is because we want to solve these conflicts that we shall try other means. It has been as short as ten years since we entered the WTO. We must consider the world history of the past five hundred years and China's history of the past two hundred years and should not merely fix our eyes on these thirty years. Only this way can we look further and can China have an opportunity to become a powerful country that has a say in making game rules.

Market structure is highly unstable

If we discuss the market, we ought to take consumer's sovereignty into consideration, but many trade protectionists highlight the interests of producers and never care about consumers. From consumers' point of view, whoever creates more value for them will survive. Why can China's products go global? Because they are attractive to American and European consumers for low prices.

Professor Lu Feng said market structure was stable, but actually it is quite unstable. Let's quote the example Lu Feng just mentioned. Ten years ago, when compared with Alcatel-Lucent and Motorola, Huawei and ZTE paled into insignificance, but what status do they occupy today? A decade ago Sony looked down upon Samsung, but today Samsung belittles Sony. Therefore,

I think market structure is highly unstable and so is international structure; or else, Japan, Germany, and the United States as well as China would not have emerged.

In my opinion, instability assumption of market structure stems from ignorance of technology roadmaps. Except that entrepreneurs grope for them, no government officials and scholars can clearly see technology roadmaps. Although Sony used to take a lead in its industry, it failed to see recent technology roadmaps and gradually fell behind. Because of such uncertainty, I advocate thinking with the logic of the market.

I admit that knowledge accumulation is one of the most important facets of globalization. It has already been so, even if we think of the Silk Road or even two thousand years ago, let alone in the past five hundred years. However, during that process, we cannot separate knowledge dissemination and learning from trade, because a lot of intangible knowledge is embedded intangible technologies. As we all know, Chinese people are noted for their great learning ability. However, given that Chinese population accounts for 20% of world population, in terms of the proportion of great contribution to the world innovation, how much have we made? Little. The reason is our closedness. I think Lu Feng doesn't oppose openness. What I intend to say is that after entering the WTO, China's enterprises learn faster than before entering the WTO. To a great extent, today's protectionism is owing to political reasons, or, in my view, owing to those "shameless interest groups" who invent various interest-based theories instead of really making scientific analyses.

Competition fosters advantages

I think adjustment of the exchange rate of the *renminbi* might be contributive to upgrading China's industries. No enterprises will feel pressure when they can sell goods at low prices because of undervaluation of the *renminbi*. I agree with Professor Yu Yongding on the idea that China's enterprises have tremendous endurance. I don't think the pressure test calculated by the Ministry of Commerce is all right. It is a totally wrong assumption that given that the profit margin of many export enterprises is only 2–3%, they will go bankrupt if the exchange rate rises by 2–3%. The market doesn't operate that way. Even if the exchange rate devalued to 10 yuan, China's enterprises would still earn 2–3%. The reason is that their products are fully competitive in international markets and the competition they are faced with has already been sufficient. When the rate is reduced, they would reduce prices accordingly; and when it is increased, their profit rate may not be affected very much and will remain 2–3%. For example, when Americans are willing to pay 8 yuan for a product, competition makes us sell it at a price of 4 yuan at the current exchange rate; if our exchange rate is increased, the price of 5 or 6 yuan is still attractive for American consumers. In other words, every consumer will pay more. Under such circumstances, only profits of multi-national brand-name companies will duck. China's enterprises can remain competitive to the end, although they have to struggle for survival as they are already. To put it simply, I think increase of the exchange rate will help raise the proportion of China's enterprises' revenue in overall increased amount of value.

However, many economists believe that they are cleverer than the market and factitiously propose many hypotheses including calculating dynamic and static comparative advantages, but I am sure comparative advantages, either static or dynamic, are, in fact, products of market competition. I oppose trade protectionism and all industrial policies. Can we see how many of them are beneficial? Industrial policies always turn out to be matters concerning income distribution among the vested interests, and many so-called policies of new energy resources industry are reduced to be a means of applying for governmental subsidies. We must trust the market. Though the market sounds abstract, Chinese people are intelligent, and, as long as they are placed in market competition, they will gain advantages eventually. Perhaps, what we think now is that our disadvantages will become our advantages in the future, which is only dependent on efforts of entrepreneurs. It is extremely absurd that we allow a thirty-year-old mid-level cadre to determine whether we should invest in any particular industry, because we mistakenly think entrepreneurs who stake all they have on investment are more ignorant than these government officials.

Let's consider the problem of leadership. Any reform requires leadership. If a leader doesn't like to reform, there is no use even if all the subordinates intend to. When Deng Xiaoping decided to resume the National College Entrance Examination in 1977, the minister of Ministry of Education once reported to Deng that it was too complicated to resume the examination and they couldn't and were not ready to. But Deng Xiaoping briefly replied, "do it if you can, or I will entrust it to a more capable one". As a result, the minister carried out the resumption at once.

China's accession to the WTO is a milestone, and it has also contributed to preventing institutional reforms from retrogressing in the past years. I am certain, without entering the WTO, reform retrogression would be much more severe than now.

Notes

1 This article was written on April 3, 2008, for the Forum of the Thirtieth Anniversary of Reform.
2 A keynote speech I made at the 2014 Observer Forum.
3 Refers to those families who are able to earn RMB 10,000 annually. It appeared in the 1980s.
4 A speech I delivered at a seminar of Chinese Economists 50 Forum.
5 Based on a speech I made at the 2006 summer seminar held by China Society of Economic Reform.
6 Written in 2003.
7 Based on a speech I delivered at the Tenth Anniversary of China's Accession to the WTO Seminar held by *International Economic Review* on August 4 and 5, 2011. The original version was published in the ninth and tenth issues of *International Economic Review* in 2011.

Part three
Transition of growth patterns

Economic reflection on the financial crisis[1]

It is a crucial phenomenon of financial crises that almost every one of business-people including the most intelligent ones makes the same mistake at the same time. The responsibility of entrepreneurs is to predict the future – namely, judge what they should do or should not. If most of the entrepreneurs simultaneously make mistakes with judgments, what is the reason?

The financial crisis is also a crisis of macroeconomics

There is a simplest assumption in macroeconomics textbooks – that is, economy consists of the sole product of one thing, the so-called GDP. The assumption can sometimes lead to a quite an absurd conclusion. For example, a person spends a million yuan building a house; another person spends a million yuan making a cannon and uses it to shell the house into pieces. As a result, social wealth reduces by 2 million, but statistically our GDP rises by 2 million. This is the fault of macroeconomic analysis.

The first fundamental problem of macroeconomic theory is to focus on the sum total of economic activities regardless of economic structures. According to macroeconomics, GDP is the sum of consumption (C), investment (I), and net exports (NE), the so-called "troika". For example, suppose in an economy, $C = 60$, $I = 35$, and $NE = 5$; and in another economy, $C = 80$, $I = 20$, and $NE = 0$; both of them are assumed to be replaceable. In fact, the first economy greatly differs from the second economy, though they are equal in sum total. It is a big mistake that when investment drops by 15 and net exports decrease to 0, if government can increase domestic consumption from 60 to 80 through expanding domestic demands, the first will soon recover as the second one. If we spend more money on food and clothes, will China's steel overproduction be solved? Will cement overproduction be solved? Whether other countries or China, what they are confronted with are not problems concerning consumption, investment, and net exports but structural problems. What we export to foreign countries are not necessarily what Chinese want to consume. For example, China is a country that produces the most wigs, but how many people can consume these wigs?

Macroeconomics assumes money merely has influence upon the sum total rather than structures including relative prices, industrial structure, and income distribution. In fact, money is not structurally neutral; whoever first possesses newly issued money gets the upper hand, and whoever lastly possesses it loses out. If the total supply of money doubles and all increased amount is in my hands, that means that not simply all prices double but that I deprive each of you of half of the wealth. Furthermore, because my structure of demand is different from yours, the price structure changes. As a matter of fact, through altering relative prices, changes in money supply exert impact on economy. Because macroeconomics is oblivious of this, it is dead wrong that one of the goals of macroeconomic policies is to keep CPI stable. Before the Wall Street Stock Market Crash of 1929 occurred eighty years ago and before this global financial crisis, the CPI remained more or less unchangeable, but why did the economy still go wrong? Because stable CPI doesn't ensure that macro-economy is normal and efficient.

When analyzing macroeconomic problems, we must understand national economy consists of different components and each of them fluctuates variably. Let's see some examples. The growth rate of industrial added value from October 2007 to February 2009 was characterized by the fact that when the economy was on the rise, heavy industry grew faster than light industry; when the economy was in decline, light industry grew faster than heavy industry. Can we say consumption deficiency leads to an economic decline? Of course not. According to changes of several price indexes from 1999 to 2009, including ex-factory prices of production materials, of industrial products, as well as prices of consumer products, when the economy flourished, prices of upstream production materials increased fastest, and prices of consumer products remained nearly the same; when the economy declined, prices of upstream production materials reduced fastest and prices of consumer products still hardly changed. In brief, prices of production materials changed more greatly than prices of living materials. This was indicative of a major problem with macro economy – that is, when prices of upstream production materials soared, the economy would go wrong, though the CPI and consumer goods prices remained stable. If we judge whether our economy goes wrong merely according to the CPI, we will make a mistake the same way as Greenspan justified his judgment that macro-economy was all right because the CPI was stable; and he paid no attention to the sharp increase of capital prices and of raw material prices. We must understand that we cannot regard money as neutral and cannot highlight the overall amount rather than structures.

The decrease of price indexes is thought to be terrible, because it is always mistaken for depression. Throughout history, deflation, however, is not necessarily related to economic depression. From 1873 to 1896, the annual price level of many Western countries dropped by about 2% on average, but no depression took place, and on the contrary, the average annual industrial production level increased by 2–3%. During the ten years from 1870 to 1879, US price levels dropped by 1.8% on average, but the period was the golden age of US economic development on record. Today we are used to inflation but in fear of deflation. When we see prices drop, we become upset and eager to inject money to raise prices. What is the normal status of economy? It is natural that as technology advances and productivity increases, product prices will drop slightly, which can enable everyone to enjoy advantages brought by economic growth. However, to refrain prices from decreasing, government tends to produce more money to raise them, so that whoever can obtain newly supplied money will monopolize advantages brought by economic development.

The damage done by the manipulation of money to economy lies in destruction of structures; when government tries to stabilize prices, actually it has injected too many currencies, so distortion of structure has begun and it has been too late to discern the problem.

There is another fault of macroeconomics – namely, it mistakes saving for a sin rather than a virtue. If saving is a sin, why did the US economy still go wrong even if Americans spent too much? All of our technological advances stem from investment and investment from saving. At the beginning, economists used to regard saving as a virtue, but, after Keynes, saving became a sin. Now many people think China's economy declines because our savings rate is too high. But how high is it? In 1996 China's household savings accounted for 20% of the GDP and 16% in 2006 (in contrast to 22% in India). During the same period, enterprise savings in total saving increased from 13% in 1996 to 20% in 2006. Therefore, we ought to analyze how much of enterprises' savings, especially state-owned enterprises' savings, is good and how much is bad. In fact, enterprise savings are investment. If investment isn't efficient and productive, overcapacity will occur, which will result in economic crises and economic declines.

Before this global financial crisis, Americans didn't save or they even dissaved. Now what should the US government encourage, saving or consumption? The US government cannot answer it, because there is something wrong with their theoretical rationales. In macroeconomics, government spending has a multiplier effect; namely, if you earn 1 yuan and save 0.2 yuan after spending 0.8 yuan on consumption, and if government invests 1 yuan, the GDP will go up by 5 yuan. It is quite ridiculous. That implies that if you spend 0.99 yuan and government invests 1 yuan, the GDP will rise by 100 yuan; and if you spend all your income, one yuan of government spending would lead to infinite increase in GDP.

Macroeconomics puts the cart before the horse. The formula of GDP – GDP = Consumption + Investment + Net Exports – does not mean a cause-and-effect relationship. My income is equal to expenditure on cars, on houses, and the like, but it doesn't mean that if I buy more cars, my income will increase by tens of thousands of yuan. Originally, the GDP is merely our means, and our end is to live better and continually promote the increase of consumption. Now the order of means and ends has been reversed: in order to maintain the increase of the GDP, we appeal to everyone to raise consumption.

Let's consider investment. The goal of investment is to increase future consumption – namely, I spend 1 yuan on investment today for the sake of consuming 2 yuan or 3 yuan later. How do today's economic policies and theories understand investment? Investment is aimed at increasing today's GDP. If we invest for the sake of increasing future consumption, every piece of investments must bring about sufficient gains; but if investment is aimed at raising this year's GDP, we need not care where investments are but make sure money is spent.

Thus, you can have a better understanding of how chaotic and disorderly our macroeconomic policies are, because the order of means and ends is reversed. How could we ensure efficient investments if we are assumed to consume for the purpose of raising GDP instead of creating GDP as means of consumption and to invest for the sake of this year's GDP instead of future consumption and wealth? We are aware of the thinking pattern of the US government, the Chinese government, and local governments at various levels: when I invest 1 yuan today, I will not care whether investment is efficient or not, but care only about this year's GDP. If we don't aim at investing for tomorrow, we cannot ensure efficient investment.

How should government deal with crises?

I think that this global financial crisis was caused by not too little money but too much money. There is too much credit, too much investment, and too much consumption! When the problem arose, we inclined to continue injecting money – namely, to increase consumption if investment decreased or to raise investment if consumption declined. In fact, this cannot address the root cause of the problem. We need to seek more effective methods and to improve our enterprises in the market that abounds in free competition.

I quite agree with Professor Li Yining's point of view that China's economic problems are the ones concerning not total but structural problems. Without structural problems, there are no problems of sum total. In my view, structural problems involve industrial structure, regional structure, and ownership structure. Where does so much redundant overcapacity stem from? It stems from the government and state sector. When a state-owned enterprise makes profits, it cannot distribute all the profits as dividends or bonuses. How does it do with its profits? The only solution is to invest them and spend them blindly.

Marketization is the best way to address structural problems. We shall make our rigid price system, salary system, and employment system more flexible. It would have been easier to make adjustments if we hadn't passed Labor Contract Law last year in which some provisions did damage to China's economy. Originally many private enterprises abided by humanistic management, but now the relation between employers and employees deteriorates because we are on guard against each other. As the employment system becomes rigid, our adjustments will slow down. When enterprises are on the verge of bankruptcy, they should be allowed to cut down employees if necessary. Only by means of marketization can we create new employment opportunities and effectively solve unemployment.

I also agree that private economies should be vigorously developed. Our state-owned enterprises have monopolized many sectors. Most investments are still at the discretion of government's approval. Not only small vendors but big businesspeople are under constraint. Only if everyone has the right to participate in free competition can the economy really recover.

I advocate reducing taxes. In difficult times, government should take into consideration overall economic conditions, become more generous and far-sighted, and think long-term. Everyone should share plight when there is a tough go. Either the world or China cannot rely on expanding consumption to solve economic problems. If we begin to distribute consumption coupons that expire after three months, in place of monetary income, we will spend all the money on consumption; but can we solve all China's problems this way? No.

In addition, there is also something wrong with revitalization plans. Revitalization plans are not always applicable. For example, if the overcapacity of a certain sector has exceeded 20% or 30% already and if we continue to revitalize this sector, its overcapacity will probably be beyond 50% or even 100% three years later, which will surely result in terrible consequences.

How should enterprises deal with crises?

First, entrepreneurs must adhere to their original nature. Their original nature is to discover markets. As long as we notice overproduction, there must be an unsatisfied market somewhere. What they should do is make a careful observation, study it, and find it.

In difficult times, entrepreneurs should travel around the world. How can some people become entrepreneurs? Originally by traveling. When they find a certain place is short of food and clothes but abundant with plenty of resources, they discover a market. Some enterprises are export-oriented; when you are in a plight and are in want of production orders, don't stay at home and you'd better go outdoors to find out what goes wrong with middlepersons or other parts of your business. You must return to the original nature of entrepreneurs: seeking for markets.

Second, make full use of price mechanism. Cut prices if necessary; don't maintain prices reluctantly. Frankly speaking, Vanke Chairman Wang Shi is a good example. When he determined to reduce house prices, many people criticized him so much as to upset him. Now his determination has been proven justified. He managed to recycle money through cutting prices in advance. Every enterprise should take price reduction into consideration, especially in difficult times. In order to set prices, you ought to envision the future and consider marginal and opportunity cost.

Third, make institutional innovation. The reason why we have survived many setbacks during the past thirty years is that Chinese entrepreneurs are expert in institutional innovation. Government may make a lot of policies, not all of which are correct. In the face of incorrect ones, we need to make use of institutional innovation to remedy them. For instance, when a financial crisis happened in 1989 and the economic growth dropped to 3.8% in 1990, how did private enterprises and township and village enterprises tide it over? A major solution they adopted is to cease distributing salaries to employees and to turn their salaries into shares. As a result, these enterprises managed to survive the crisis eventually. This is an institutional innovation; our entrepreneurs are obligated to rack their brains in this regard.

Fourth, technological innovation. If you can reduce cost through technological innovation, you can have a market. When the economy thrives, nobody cares about cost; but when the crisis comes and everyone's budget becomes tight, what you do in terms of cost reduction becomes important. According to the field research I made in Xi'an, an automobile gear enterprise set a good example. Because it succeeded in reducing cost by means of technological innovation, it recovered its market.

Fifth, build an independent brand. Any enterprise that possesses an independent brand will encounter fewer setbacks than an OEM company. China's enterprises used to emphasize OEM, but in time of financial crises, when your previous clients stop placing orders, you may create an independent brand and sell products under your own brand.

Sixth, restructure industries. The concentration ratio of China's industries is extremely low. This financial crisis exactly offers us an opportunity to raise the concentration ratio, and we must take merger and acquisition as an important business strategy. We should not think that when an enterprise is gone, its assets will be gone. Actually after an enterprise is merged, its best assets are just taken away by another enterprise for more efficient use rather than burnt out. This is a process of ownership reform that will raise utilization efficiency of existing resources.

Lastly, our entrepreneurs must draw lessons from crises. Especially, new rising entrepreneurs, unlike their predecessors, haven't undergone tough days. Through learning from crises, they can be less hot-headed. Make your analyses by observing several important curves of economy: as long as some prices are extremely high, whether in the real estate market or stock market, there must be something wrong.

We shouldn't be pessimistic. I anticipate that within thirty years or less, some of China's enterprises will surely be on a par with some major international companies. Free market economy is the key. You will be sure about that if you make a study of the history of US enterprises. History of human beings has clearly shown that no countries can rely on government to make a good job of economy. We must rely on the role of entrepreneurs and spontaneous evolution of the market. I wish that in time of crises, China could make plenty of reforms instead of spending money to stimulate the economy. If our entrepreneurs shoulder more responsibilities of discovering and creating markets, our economy will recover faster.

Watch out for the next crisis[2]

One year ago, we were at a loss in the face of the impact of the global financial crisis. Today, on knowing the GDP last year grew by more than the targeted 8%, we feel relieved and even cheerful. However, at the moment an ancient saying occurred to me: "extreme joy begets sorrow". What I am concerned about is how to prevent the next financial crisis. It isn't a false alarm. In fact, the real problem doesn't lie in whether there is a next crisis but when it will occur and how severe it will be.

I disagree with others that China is the root cause of this financial crisis, but I admit that without China, the crisis would be very different. To put it simply, after going global, China's economy has changed international production cost, economic structure, and policy effect. But China's influence has not been fully realized by foreign governments as well as the Chinese government itself. The impact of China on the world economy is like adding a locomotive to a train unexpectedly: though the train's speed has increased from 120 km to 200 km, all of our signal systems including the driver's conception still indicate the train is running at a speed of 120 km. If so, there will be a problem sooner or later.

Specifically, the crisis was caused by credit expansion and low interest policies. After 2001, the US Federal Reserve and Greenspan thought there would probably be a depression, so they took measures to relax credit and reduce interest rate. But their policies can be justified only if no inflation happens. In fact, just because of China's accession to the WTO, huge changes have taken place in global economic production cost and the inflation that should have occurred didn't emerge, which indulged the implementation of low interest-rate policies.

Moreover, the measures that countries all over the world took to deal with financial crises are exactly the cause of this crisis. Many countries carried out low interest-rate policies and even the zero interest-rate policy and large-scale credit expansion. China was no exception. China carried out the largest recorded experiment in the history of world currency.

During the past thirty years, China's credit expanded fastest in 2009 (1989 was an exception). Within these years, the annual growth rate of China's credit remained between 10–20%, but from January till November in 2009, the growth rate reached 33%. As far as investment is concerned, except 1985, 1992, and 1993, the investment growth rate of 2009 was second to none – namely, over 30%.

Let's consider the proportion of social fixed assets in the GDP. It was only 26% in the early 1990s and later mostly on the rise; especially it rose to over 40% in 2004 and reached 67% in 2009, which is a record that no country ever has had. Besides, the ratio of credit to GDP during the past thirty years was mostly between 0.8 and 1.2, and at most 1.17, but it rose to 1.19 in 2009. That's why I say China is carrying out the largest recorded experiment in the history of world currency.

What long-term consequences can these polices bring about? Just like a drastic remedy will surely beget adverse side effects, there are two possibilities of inducing macroeconomic problems. The first possibility is that when injection of too much money leads to inflation expectations, government will definitely adopt anti-inflation policies, which will result in another round of depression; the second is that when excessive investment causes accumulation of non-performing loans, bad loans in the financial sector will trigger an economic crisis. There's no such thing as a free lunch. In this sense, if the GDP growth rate of 2009 had been 6% rather than 8%, our future should probably be more promising.

Besides, our economic growth relied too much on export, so it is challenging to maintain such growth. In 2007, among all major economies all over the world, only Germany's ratio of export to GDP (39.9%) slightly exceeded China's (37.5%). Other countries including the United States, Japan, Britain, France, Italy, Spain, and Canada greatly fell behind China.

China's foreign exchange reserves also indicated the severity of China's problem. Take Japan and Germany, for example. In the stage of industrialization from 1955 to 1975, the ratio of their foreign currency reserves to US GDP never exceeded 2%; in contrast, after 2001 China's ratio continued rising and reached 12%. As far as the proportion of foreign currency reserves in its own GDP is concerned, Germany's and Japan's proportion rarely exceeded 5% during the period of rapid growth, but now China's has surpassed 50% of its GDP, ten times as many as Germany's and Japan's during the period of rapid growth.

External situations and internal situations indicate that there is no way to go on with an export-oriented growth pattern. Our way out is to open up the domestic market.

China's domestic market is highly potential. If we regard each of China's thirty-one provinces, municipalities, and autonomous regions as an independent country, as far as the GDP is concerned, Guangdong ranking the first place in China will occupy eighteenth in the world followed by Poland, Indonesia, Belgium, Sweden, and Saudi Arab, respectively; Shandong and Jiangsu, the second-place holder and the third-place holder in China, respectively, will rank before Norway, Austria, Iran, Greece, Denmark, and Argentina; Zhejiang, domestically ranking fourth, will internationally surpass Venezuela and South Africa; Henan with the fifth-highest GDP will overwhelm Finland, Thailand, and Portugal; and even our smallest economy, Tibet, will exceed Mongolia. The total population of all developed countries accounts for 18% of the world population, while China's population alone reaches 20%. Two hundred years ago, Adam Smith said China's market was much bigger than markets of all Western countries together, but unfortunately we haven't done well in exploiting our market.

After this financial crisis, whether we can prevent the next crisis or reduce its severity depends on how we can exploit our domestic market and absorb these oversupplied money and excessive investments.

What hinders us from developing a domestic market on earth? Why do China's entrepreneurs have more initiative in developing foreign markets rather than a domestic market? I think there are five reasons. First, China's ownership structure is unreasonable; second, the institution of property rights is vulnerable; third, the Chinese urban market is separated from its rural market; fourth, China's administration dominates its economy; fifth, there is a problem with the exchange rate of the *renminbi*. Let us explain one by one.

First, China's ownership structure is unreasonable. State-owned enterprises occupy a large proportion and take control of too many resources. As a result, the source of household income is very unitary. Household income is mostly labor income and rarely asset income. Therefore, the proportion of household income in the GDP is quite low. Originally, supply creates demand, but because our supply and most of our income stem from the government sector and state-owned enterprises, supply cannot be channeled into sustainable consumption demand. It is often said that Chinese people like saving instead of consuming. But actually China's household savings rate is much lower than India's. Increase of our savings rate during the past ten years owes not to resident savings rate (it seldom changed from 1993 to 2007) but to increase of enterprise savings and government savings. Besides, the proportion of government consumption is on the rise, and the proportion of resident consumption in decline. If this problem cannot be solved properly, there will arise many difficulties in developing the domestic market.

Second, protection of property rights needs strengthening. Exploring the domestic market can depend not on national monetary policies and fiscal policies but on entrepreneurs' initiative. If property rights cannot be protected effectively – namely, administrative authorities exert superiority over property rights and investment cannot be secured – entrepreneurs will have no initiative in developing the domestic market with more innovative products. It should be noted that integration of the coal industry by confiscation of private enterprises in Shanxi set a bad example. If phenomena of such kind continue to prevail, the consensus on property rights we made during the past thirty years will be overwhelmingly destroyed and entrepreneurs will be discouraged to develop domestic market. This is a problem with the coal industry but one that deserves all of entrepreneurs' attention. China's policy makers should recognize that practices that violate property rights rules and disobey relevant laws will infringe on entrepreneurs' initiative in developing a domestic market as well as interests of the whole country.

Third, the Chinese urban market is separated from its rural market, which prevents formation of a unified domestic market. China is characterized by the institutional separation between urban and rural areas. It is paramount to eliminate urban-rural separation, especially to allow land circulation and abolish the household registration system. Land circulation will create a group of people similar to the middle class. We should thoroughly abolish the household registration system in urban and rural areas. Although we have made progress in reforming the system, the pace needs accelerating. Only when there is no legal distinction between urban and rural residents and no concept of urban household register, can urbanization be actualized soon and the domestic market accounting for 20% of the world population can really be effectively exploited.

Fourth, administration dominates economy. Administrative domination will surely result in local protectionism that hinders formation of a unified market and giving play to regional advantages. It matters too much to development of the domestic market how to eliminate the domination that administrative departments exert upon the economy.

Lastly, enterprises rely too much on export; the export market is highly profitable owing to the undervalued exchange rate of the *renminbi*. Appreciation of the *renminbi* can increase Chinese entrepreneurs' initiative in developing the domestic market. Besides, it can equally create wealth effect, narrow income distribution disparity, and increase consumption demand. If the exchange rate problem cannot be resolved, we will encounter conflicts with not only the United States but with Japan, European countries, and other countries sooner or later. The *renminbi* is linked to the US dollar, which means as the US dollar devalues, the *renminbi* will devalue in contrast to other currencies, and thus other countries will not identify with us. Some people fear devaluation of the *renminbi* will beget loss of China's foreign exchange reserves, but I hold that it is worthy to trade some losses with better economic development, like exchanging a piece of wastepaper for something precious.

On the whole, we can probably do well in exploiting the domestic market only if we promote privatization of state-owned assets and property rights protection, propel integration of urban and rural markets and appreciation of the *renminbi*, and reduce government domination over the economy. Only when we open up the domestic market are we likely to reduce severity of the next crisis.

A return to Adam Smith and a farewell to Keynes[3]

In scientific researches, there is a Whig theory of the history of sciences that denotes that science is always progressive forward and upward, today's is better than yesterday's, and late is better than early. But history has shown it is false, even in circles of natural sciences. For example, it is commonly thought that Copernicus was the first one to propose the heliocentric theory, but actually he wasn't. As early as two or three hundred years B.C., ancient Greek astronomer Aristarchus first put forward the heliocentric theory and held the earth circles around the sun, but at that moment everyone else thought he was wrong. Ptolemaeus' geocentric theory had been prevalent for around one thousand years, and the heliocentric theory wasn't established until Copernicus published *De Revolutionibus Orbium Coelestium* in 1543. So is the case with Adam Smith's and Keynesian economic theory in circles of economics.

China's economic transition, especially transfer of China's economic growth pattern that was highlighted lately, has captured public attention. Let's make a comparative analysis of it from the perspective of Adam Smith's and Keynesian economic theory respectively.

Adam Smith advocates that economists should emphasize wealth creation and economic development. Where does economic development stem from? It stems from increase of productivity, and increase of productivity comes from technological advance and innovation, which rely on division of labor. Division of labor leads to specialization, increase of proficiency, and devotion to research, finally giving birth to invention and creation. The extent of division of labor is dependent on the scale of the market. Expansion of the market will result in deepening labor division, technological advance, and economic development, which can in turn help expand markets through raising income level; thus a virtuous circle will come into being.

If we look at what China underwent during these thirty years from the perspective of Adam Smith's model, the most precious experience we can acquire is making use of the market and expanding markets. In the past three decades, we have achieved development and made fast progress, because the reform fostered our domestic market and opening-up enabled us to exploit China's global market. China's potential for future development still lies in utilizing markets and expanding markets. At the beginning we were great in utilizing the international market but failed to develop the domestic market as well as it should be. Internal trade seemed more difficult than external trade. In fact, China's domestic market possesses tremendous potential. China's population has accounted for 20% of the world population, and China's GDP has ranked second; the economic aggregate of many provinces has surpassed that of many mid-size countries, and the overall total of the thirty-one provinces, municipalities, and autonomous regions all together equal the globe. Therefore, how to develop the domestic market in the future will have a crucial bearing on China's sustainable development.

Unfortunately, we have some conceptual misunderstanding because of the impact of Keynesian economic theory. The fundamental formula of Keynesian economics is that GDP is equal to consumption plus investment plus net exports (we can add government expenditure if necessary). How to raise the GDP according to this formula? As a popular saying goes, economic growth is driven by a "troika", and either of three horses can pull while the other two cannot; when net exports are in decline, we can rely on investment, for example. That is why our government increased a large amount of investment last year. Now there is so much investment that we cannot super-add it; what we should rely on? Consumption. That is the economic growth pattern conceived by a majority of economists.

Adam Smith's theory originates from microeconomics, while Keynesian theory is rooted in macroeconomics. Each of them can give us different understanding of future economic transition.

From the perspective of Adam Smith's theory, for the sake of China's economic growth, we should further open up and develop the domestic market. What's more, we ought to encourage entrepreneurs to create new products and to meet the demands of the market, which is the function of entrepreneurs. But from the perspective of Keynesian theory, economic growth hinges on the increase of aggregate demand, and, especially, it becomes the function of government to stimulate aggregate demand through monetary policies and fiscal policies. For instance, if the demand for computers diminishes, Keynesian theory will suggest government should offer fiscal subsidies or raise money stock to induce people to buy more computers – namely, to encourage everyone to buy one more (or to outdate the older one) even if one computer suffices for everyone. In contrast, Adam Smith's theory suggests increase of demands should rely on producing better quality and cheaper new products and developing new markets. For example, the iPad produced by Apple, which is popular among people, can really create new demands.

In other words, according to Adam Smith's theory, to increase demands means to open up markets and must count on entrepreneurs' innovation. But how to promote entrepreneurs' innovation? By means of motivation mechanism. In particular, only when protection of property rights is secured and transaction cost is low can innovation obtain reasonable reward. But according to the Keynesian view, increase of demands depends not on innovation but on government's stimulating economic policies. However, when entrepreneurs find it is easier to sell off their products under the condition of easy monetary policies and protection of property rights is unsecured, none of them will have initiative in devoting to innovation, because innovation is the product of a long, persistent, and risk-taking undertaking.

Let's give a second thought to investment. In Adam Smith's view, investment is aimed at raising future productivity. To put it simply, the reason why we invest 100 yuan is that we expect to obtain 110 or 120 yuan in return in the future. Investment is carried out for the sake of increasing efficiency; if investment cannot, there is no need to invest. If investment is efficient, a high savings rate is not only not a bad thing but is essential for economic development. From the perspective of Keynesian theory, investing is tantamount to increasing demands; as long as investment is increased, demands can be expanded and the GDP can be created regardless of efficiency. Therefore, the economic growth advocated by Keynesian policies is not only inefficient but wasteful. Even if the GDP is increased, wealth isn't really augmented.

Let's consider trade policies. According to Adam Smith's perspective, the larger a market becomes, the more sophisticated labor division and the more innovation will be; the more innovation there is, the faster the economy will develop. Thus, good trade policies are the ones that reduce trade barriers, expand market freedom, and fight against trade protectionism. But Keynesianism highlights only that net export can increase GDP by means of raising demands. For example, if the export volume of a country is 10 billion dollars, the import volume is 9 billion dollars, and thus the net export 1 billion dollars; the trade makes a positive contribution to increasing the GDP. However, if the export volume of another country is 100 billion dollars, the import volume will be 100.1 billion, and thus the net export is negative; international trade does not raise the GDP but reduces the GDP. How absurd is that! Hence, the worship of Keynesian theory will surely lead to various forms of trade protectionist policies, because Keynesian theory advocates that the GDP can merely be raised by less import volume and more export volume, which is totally opposed by Adam Smith's theory.

Consider ownership structure. What does economic development count on: state-owned enterprises or private enterprises? According to Keynesianism, whatever can increase demands is all right, whether state-owned or private enterprises. When property rights reform and the rule of law aren't accomplished, the best way to raise overall demands is to augment investment of state-owned enterprises. Last year China's stimulative economic policies offered plenty of loans to state-owned enterprises. Indeed, as investment augmented, the pace of economic growth accelerated. But in Adam Smith's view, this practice can make no positive contribution but huge damage to sustainable economic growth.

On one hand, state-owned enterprises lack motivating force of innovation; on the other hand, as far as increase of consumption is concerned, if the proportion of state-owned enterprises in the whole economy is still large, say, over 35%, it is impossible to develop the domestic market, as I argued earlier. During the past ten years, especially during the past several years, the proportion of household income in the national economy was reduced, and the augmented GDP could not really be turned into the purchasing power of ordinary people. Under such circumstances, how can we promote the transition to a more innovation-based economy?

Economists are well aware Keynesianism focuses on short-term problems instead of long-term problems. It is often argued that government cannot care about short-term problems. As a matter of fact, that is the self-consolation of Keynesianists. If a policy is detrimental to the sustainable development of a country, we must keep inquiring into why we should adhere to such a policy. The only reason is political considerations. Politicians usually give priority to short-term interests instead of long-term ones, and so Keynesianism becomes a favored tool for them.

Unfortunately, on some occasions "short-term" problems happen so shortly that decision-makers can barely escape from their bad results. Merely one year ago, in order to deal with the global financial crisis, we were concentrating on how to increase overall demands and in a flurry adopting various stimulative policies to curb deflation, by means of super-adding money, increasing loans, decreasing interest rates, expanding investment, and issuing government subsidies. Lately, the State Council just held a meeting, and what was its major concern? Inflation. It was suggested at the meeting that administrative measures should be taken to stabilize prices if necessary. The measures taken are not much different from the price regulation in the period of planned economy.

In a nutshell, targeting an economic growth rate to 8% will cost us inflation, expansion of state-owned enterprises, as well as possibility of retrogression of institutional reforms. Therefore, I appeal to people again to abandon Keynesian short-term policies and to turn our eyes to the fundamental principle of economics, especially on Adam Smith's idea of the market. China's economy cannot be at the disposal of Keynesianism any more.

Grasp the overall situation and driving forces of China's economy[4]

The global financial crisis occurring between 2008 and 2009 is a major event that today's economists, government leaders, and business leaders still keep in mind. It was usually placed on a par with the Great Depression in the 1930s that changed the historical course of the world. People may not care about the dot-com bubble in 2000, the Asian Financial Storm in 1997, as well as Japan's bubble economy, but cannot forget this severe crisis that exerted great influence upon everyone.

In times of the crisis, the stock market was at stake, a credit crunch occurred, and the confidence index of entrepreneurs declined drastically. In the meantime, industrial production and sales plummeted, and conditions for employment deteriorated sharply; it seemed to be beyond understanding, as if all enterprises made the same mistake at the same time. We all know the role of entrepreneurs is to predict markets and judge what should be done or shouldn't; a successful entrepreneur is more capable of knowing the future development of markets, and an unsuccessful one lacks such a capability. But if most entrepreneurs make mistakes at the same time, that will not be a problem with the quality of entrepreneurs any more.

Entrepreneurs are more skilled than economists at predicting the development trend of a certain market, but it is challenging for them to judge the trend of the whole macro-economy, which plays a vital role in the survival and development of enterprises. This is compared to hanging a picture on a wall: you may find an exact point on the wall, hit the nail on the head, and do a good job of hanging the picture, but if the wall's foundation is unstable and may collapse someday, your effort will be useless no matter how well you do and how hard you hit the nail. Therefore, entrepreneurs ought to value the macro-economic trend the same way as you must attend to the condition of the wall when hanging the picture.

The task of predicting the trend of macro-economy should be carried out by economists, but this crisis indicated economists were not competent. Many people, including the British Queen when visiting London School of Economics, asked, "why can nobody predict this crisis?" Later a group of economists made an apology and admitted current economic theories couldn't predict and judge the arriving time, scale, and severity of financial crises. Thus, this crisis is also the crisis of traditional mainstream economics and has exerted profound influence upon the development of economics.

The crisis also had impact on the course of China's reform. After the crisis, it was thought that the free market failed again. Some people that held extreme opinions questioned, "since the US economy has collapsed and its market economy malfunctioned, why should China adhere to liberalization?" and held that "the reason why no big problem has arisen in China was that China's financial system is not liberalized". These views have posed a challenge to China's future reform. If we think the crisis is the product of malfunction of the market, we shall strengthen government's intervention in economy; if not, we shall adhere to the direction of marketization. Different understandings of the cause of the crisis will give birth to totally different policies.

In view of these considerations, the Eleventh Guanghua New Year Forum held in January 2010 was entitled "China's Economy after the Financial Crisis". We hope to envision prospects for future economic development and industrial trends by means of reflecting on this financial crisis and attempt to enlighten personages of all circles on how to prevent new crises, to conform to changes of industrial pattern, and to search for new footholds in markets.

Till now, perhaps the most severe part of this crisis has passed, but structural problems with the global economy and China's economy have not been solved yet. The foundation for global economic recovery and employment growth is greatly weak, trade protectionism of many countries are emerging, and the exchange rate of the *renminbi* is under heavy criticism and pressure in all directions. When dealing with the global warming, various countries play a complicated game against each other in terms of energy saving and emission reduction and potentiality for economic development, which has had profound impact upon China's future economic policies and current industrial pattern.

After this financial crisis, the major problem confronting China's economy is still how to accelerate structural adjustment and deepen institutional reforms. This is not only the concern of government and scholars, but the concern of industrial circles and ordinary people. At this forum some speakers addressed theme lectures. Their views concerning reforms of state-owned enterprises, private enterprise development, industry restructuring, and domestic market development and the like played a significant role in assisting us to understand the future trend of China's economy.

As far as the exchange rate of the *renminbi* is concerned, appreciation most likely represents the general trend. It is not because others are exerting pressure upon us, but for the sake of a healthier development of China's economy. It was wrong that US politicians politicized this issue, and it was also unjustified that Chinese treated it emotionally.

In 2007 among all economies over the world, only Germany's proportion of export in GDP slightly exceeded China's – namely, Germany's was 39.9% and China's 37.5%; other countries such as the United States, Japan, United Kingdom, France, Italy, Spain, and Canada were not on a par with China in this regard. As far as foreign exchange reserves are concerned, during the process of realizing industrialization (between 1955 and 1975) Japan's and Germany's ratio of foreign exchange reserves to US GDP never exceeded 2%, but China's has reached 12% now. As far as the proportion of foreign exchange reserves in its own GDP is concerned, Germany's and Japan's rarely surpassed 5% during their fast growth period, but ours has exceeded 50%.

During the past twenty years, unit labor cost in China's economy dropped by around 40%, but the exchange rate of the *renminbi* to the US dollar merely rose by about 20%. In the long run, the purchasing power of currencies of China and the United States are, to a great extent, determined by labor productivity; as labor productivity increased, the exchange rate increased. Germany and Japan underwent such a process respectively in the 1960s and 1970s. But China has not finished the process yet.

Now either external conditions or inner conditions suggest that China's export-oriented growth pattern cannot continue. We must open up the domestic market. But if we keep undervaluing the *renminbi*, not only international trade disputes will be aroused but also China's entrepreneurs will be distracted from developing our domestic market. Therefore, the appreciation of the *renminbi* is irresistible, and personages of enterprises and other relevant circles should make preparations for it.

In the long run, the key to China's and global sustainable economic development lies in technological and industrial innovation. What is the direction of innovation? The integration between new energy resources, life science, information technology, biological technology, aerospace materials, and nanotechnology will become the high ground of future industrial innovation and technological innovation. All of these are closely related to the global trend of advocating low-carbon environmental protection. Thus the Eleventh Guanghua New Year Forum invited leaders of National Development and Reform Commission to introduce the United Nations Climate Change conference and China's low-carbon development planning and organized a symposium on New Energy Resources and China's economy, in a bid to assist people from all walks of life to recognize the development trend, to get insights into the current condition of industries, and to take actions as soon as possible to occupy the dominant position in future competition between countries and industries.

The automobile industry is one of China's consumption growth points. In 2009 the production and sales of China's automobiles exceeded 13 million and rose by over 40%. What a tremendous growth speed! It was conservatively estimated by industry delegates attending the forum that the average growth rate of the automobile market would reach 15% at least in the following ten to fifteen years, which will exert profound influence upon China's economic growth and social life. However, it remains a huge challenge how to build independent brands and turn China from "a big country of automobiles" into "a great power of automobiles". In fact, not only the automobile industry but the whole world of industries are confronted with how to turn "made in China" into "created in China".

Whether technological innovation or brand-building, they rely on enterprises eventually. As a matter of fact, the impetus for economic development comes from enterprises, so China's entrepreneurs shoulder a heavy responsibility. In addition to institutional conditions, the emergence and development of entrepreneurs are determined by human entrepreneurship and innovation spirit. According to economist Schumpeter, entrepreneurship is a character of seeking "creative joy and pleasure in action". At this forum, we can see many guests from enterprises represent not only enthusiasm for entrepreneurship but wisdom of entrepreneurship. If such spirit can be carried forward, the future of China's economy will be bright.

During the process of business start-up and innovation, financial support plays a vital role. With marketization reform and formation of competitive mechanism, China's banking has made great progress. Banks have carried out different brand positioning; some of them incline to supply services to middle-size and small-size enterprises, and private enterprises and have begun internationalized operation. Under such circumstances, at the forum leaders of banking such as China Merchants Bank and China Minsheng Bank frankly and sincerely exchanged ideas with audiences from all circles about experience and lessons acquired during the process of internationalization, which not only is contributive to offering beneficial reference for internationalization of other enterprises but shows us the prospects for building first-rate enterprises in the world.

If there is one problem deserving attention, that must be our institutional environments. Many problems with China's macro-economy are underlain by institutional problems such as discrimination between urban and rural areas, monopoly of state-owned industries, and domination of government over investment. If they cannot be solved, the so-called goals of changing economic growth pattern, raising resident income, and expanding domestic demands will be out of our reach. We must recognize that the problems with institutional environments will not only throw cold water on entrepreneurs' initiative in starting up business and innovating, but divert people's enthusiasm to power-based rent-seeking and short-term speculation, which will result in a lot of major potential dangers that have influence upon social stability such as the disparity between the rich and the poor, employment difficulty, and asset price bubble. Therefore, to further reform and build a fair and free market environment is not only the theme repeatedly emphasized by this forum but the key to the sustainable development of China's economy and actualizing the prosperity of the country and happiness of people.

The book is the ideological fruit of the Eleventh Guanghua New Year Forum. Owing to space limitation, what are introduced above cannot cover the abundance of this forum, and I recommend this book to more readers. I am sure every reader that is concerned about China's economic development and industrial development trend will be enlightened about government reforms, industrial patterns, and opportunities for individual entrepreneurship and development.

Last but not least, special thanks go to all attending guest speakers. The success of this forum owes to the fact that they found time in the midst of pressing affairs to attend this forum and exchange ideas with hundreds of audiences. I am also grateful to audience and friends from the media, as well as for painstaking efforts of teachers and students of Guanghua School of Management and colleagues. I am greatly honored to make my personal contribution along with them to exploring China's economic development and growth of enterprises. I expect more friends to join in next Guanghua New Year Forum!

What will China's economic transition hinge on?[5]

The global financial crisis that occurred between 2008 and 2009 has given us three inspirations. First, China plays a more crucial role than we thought. In other words, if China's role had been fully acknowledged by policymakers, the financial crisis would probably not have occurred. Second, China's growth pattern in the past thirty years cannot continue. Third, our inward closed thinking pattern isn't adaptable to today's world any longer.

To understand economic transition requires a return to Adam Smith

The growth pattern of China's economy in the future needs changing. First, export-oriented growth should be changed into more balanced domestic-market-oriented and international-market-oriented growth; second, instead of focusing on coastal areas, we should balance the development of coastal areas, hinterland, the east, and the west; third, in view of our economy's emphasis on investment and low-cost advantages, we ought to rely on innovation and high added value; fourth, we should reduce China's dependence on inclusion of new enterprises and quantitative expansion of enterprises and highlight enterprise merger and reorganization and scale expansion of enterprises.

To understand these changes, we need a somewhat theoretical foundation – namely, the theory of wealth creation proposed by Adam Smith, the founder of economics. Adam Smith holds that creation of social wealth stems from productivity increase. Productivity increase relies on technological advance and innovation, both of which are caused by labor division and specialization, but labor division and specialization are determined by scale expansion of the market. A huge market means more sophisticated labor division; more sophisticated labor division denotes greater technological advance that leads to faster economic development and more wealth accumulation; as a result, scale expansion of the market is propelled in return. This is Adam Smith's economic growth model.

From this perspective, the most important experience for China's economic growth in the past thirty years is that China has done well in utilizing the international market and integrating labor division in value chains with its own advantages, especially with labor advantages, to create marvelous economic wonders.

The domestic market has great potential and the central and western regions are emerging

China has made full use of the international market but paid relatively less attention to the domestic market, so the two markets are unbalanced. For instance, in 2007 China's proportion of export in GDP was 37.5%, surpassing that of any other countries among ten economies all over the world, except for Germany. Moreover, China is a country that falls behind in urbanization, and its rural population accounts for more than a half of the national population, and thus it is abnormal that the proportion of export in GDP was so high. During the past thirty years, our average export growth reached 1.5 times as much as the GDP growth, which was estimated to be difficult to continue.

On the other hand, China has an extremely large domestic market. As far as GDP is concerned, China can be considered as half of "the globe". For example, if regarded as a country, Guangdong province has ranked in eighteenth place, surpassing Indonesia; Hebei's economic scale is larger than Hong Kong's; Beijing's and Liaoning's economic scale are both larger than Singapore's. The population plays an important role in scale of markets. In China, every industry is a huge market, because everyone needs food, accommodation, transportation, study, and entertainment. We can see foot massage is a huge industry, and, besides, there are twelve Chinese educational companies that have got listed in US stock exchanges, which is unimaginable in other countries.

Originally, private equity funds and venture capital seemed to be invested in high-tech industries, but many of them focused now on traditional industries. Owing to incessant advance of urbanization, traditional industries in China still have good prospects. In the following thirty years, China's urban population will increase by thirteen million, equivalent to adding thirteen cities with a population of a million, if 1% of rural population moves into cities annually; as a result, there will be huge demands not all of which are for new high technologies. Therefore, there is still larger room for development of China's traditional industries.

In the meantime, regional economic growth pattern is changing. For instance, during the first ten years after the reform and opening-up, the top four provinces that had fastest economic growth were Guangdong, Zhejiang, Fujian, and Shandong; during the second ten years, the top four were Fujian, Guangdong, Zhejiang, and Shandong; during the third ten years, Inner Mongolia, Shaanxi, Tianjin, and Ningxia ranked at the top; from 2003 to 2008, Inner Mongolia, Henan, Shaanxi, and Shandong occupied the top four. This indicates that as their economies developed, the central and western regions began to give play to their potential advantages including labor cost, natural resources, and especially low land price, which is contributive to development of the central and western regions because the manufacturing industry is in need of plenty of lands.

China is a populous country, but a large population doesn't mean formation of markets; only if we connect these people can we establish markets; thus, transportation plays a vital role. For a long time our transportation had been backward, but in the past twenty years great changes have taken place; in particular, construction of expressways and high-speed rails has laid a solid material foundation for establishment of China's unified market. The remaining problem is transaction costs are too high. For instance, when we enter an expressway, we always encounter a traffic jam at the entrance of a toll station. This is a type of transaction cost. The key to developing a domestic market lies in reducing transaction costs.

Investment-oriented growth is unsustainable, and labor advantages are gradually vanishing

Today's macro-economic policies are based on Keynesianism. Its fundamental formula is: GDP = Consumption + Investment + Net Export. According to the formula, economic growth is driven by such a troika, and either of "three horses" can pull while the other two cannot, which is a totally wrong thinking pattern. For example, investment itself is for the sake of increasing efficiency; if investment is inefficient, there is no need to invest. But from the perspective of Keynesian theory, to invest is to increase demands; as long as investment is increased, GDP can be created, regardless of efficiency. Therefore, under the guidance of this theory, the disastrous consequence of macro-economic polices becomes more and more obvious.

It is ridiculous that China's investment rate last year reached 67% of GDP. What does it mean? Take Hayek's analogy. When a person catches a tiger's tail, the person is confronted with two choices: let go of it and get killed by the tiger, or clench the tail and keep running after the tiger till it is tired to death. The latter choice illustrates the situation with our investment. If government ceases super-adding investment, economic growth will immediately drop; but if government continues super-adding investment, more and more problems will arise in the future. After so much investment these years, what will we do in future? It is impossible to connect every village by high-speed rails. If China's economy declines dramatically in the future, it must be caused by such overinvestment.

Demographic structure has also changed. In 1988 over twenty-five million infants were born; in 2008 annual born infants merely amounted to over fifteen million. In 1990 every one hundred employed people produced 8.5 new employees on average, but in 2007 every one hundred employed people gave birth to only 5 new employees. It can be said that although obviously it remains difficult for college students to get employed in China's society, we, in general, are faced with gradual shortage of labor.

Owing to the one-child policy, many industries will encounter challenges in the future. For example, none will be willing to go to Africa for labor export, because one family has one child. When we travel by plane now, young and beautiful stewardesses will serve you, and when you go to a restaurant, good-looking waitresses will be at your service, but after ten or twenty years, such scenarios will probably vanish. With disappearance of cheap labor advantages, we have to adjust the economic industry structure.

Developing domestic market differs from expanding domestic demands

If we make a good job of developing the domestic market, China's potential for innovation is huge. But it should be noted that developing a domestic market is different from expanding domestic demands. Expanding domestic demands relies on monetary policies and belongs to the government's function or the responsibility of government leaders such as Zhou Xiaochuan, governor of the People's Bank of China, whereas developing domestic market depends on innovation of entrepreneurs such as Ma Yun, Wang Shi, and Liu Chuanzhi.

For example, when the economy is in decline and computers sell poorly, in order to expand domestic demands, government will offer subsidies or increase money supply to encourage everyone to buy more computers. But developing domestic market means earning consumers' recognition through producing better quality and cheaper products the same way as Apple produced the iPad. It holds true for the real estate industry; you must build favorite and affordable houses instead of increasing loans to urge everyone to buy houses. These are two different thinking patterns.

If we intend to expand domestic demands through economic stimulative policies, necessary transitions of growth pattern cannot be carried out. Take innovation, for example: if every product sells well under the condition of easy monetary policies, why do you intend to innovate? Whether China's economic transition can complete is dependent on entrepreneurs. If all of the entrepreneurs complain of less money and ask government to increase money supply, the economic transition will be impossible; but if all of them concentrate on developing markets and try to find every unsatisfied demand, we will have a good prospect.

How to get rid of setbacks? Reforms cannot keep "idling"

As is mentioned above, developing a domestic market is the responsibility of entrepreneurs, but there are many institutional setbacks to be solved.

First, the proportion of state-owned economy in GDP is too big, over 35%. There is no country all over the world that can develop a domestic market under such circumstances. Due to plenty of state-owned enterprises, GDP growth cannot be turned into the purchasing power of consumers, which is the major reason why the proportion of consumption in GDP keeps declining. Only if we can solve problems with state-owned departments and turn state-owned assets into shares of ordinary people or their asset incomes, will there be a good foundation for developing domestic market.

Second, our property rights protection system still needs improving; many entrepreneurs lack confidence in the future, because our government possesses too much administrative power and exerts too much intervention in economic activities. As a result, when people accumulate wealth to a certain extent, every one of them think of applying for green cards and emigrating to foreign countries instead of getting down to innovation and to meet potential market demands. Therefore, entrepreneurs' role in developing the domestic market cannot be given full play.

Besides, severe distortion of the exchange rate of the *renminbi* leads to distortion of resource allocation. We all know the exchange rate is also a price; when the assessed value of the *renminbi* is relatively low, China's entrepreneurs are more willing to undertake export trade rather than develop the domestic market. This is not only the distortion of resource allocation but the distortion of utilizing entrepreneurs' capabilities. It is suggested to charge off the exchange rate by means of inflation, because the *renminbi* doesn't need to appreciate when under the condition of high inflation. I don't think it is a good idea. I prefer to return the exchange rate to its reasonable position.

On the whole, China's economic transition in the future will hinge on developing the domestic market, and the developing domestic market will depend on entrepreneurs instead of easy monetary policies. In other words, we should count on many Liu Chuanzhi's rather than Zhou Xiaochuan's. In order to achieve the transition of growth pattern, we must carry out major institutional reforms including political system reform. In this regard, the biggest challenge is how to maintain elite management during the process of political democratization and to integrate elite management with democratization. To accomplish this challenge, we should, first of all, allow everyone to discuss it and encourage different opinions to probe into it. But unfortunately, it has attracted the attention of merely a minority of people and hasn't been included in the government's agenda. No one discusses how we should move forward, so the prospects for political reform are filled with uncertainty.

Back in the 1980s or 1990s, when carrying out reforms, we did more than we said. Now we say more than we do. Many people are debating over reforms, but no real measures have been taken. I prefer to use a metaphor of "idling", which means stepping on the accelerator but not engaging the gear, so though the engine roars, the car doesn't move. The situation shouldn't go on.

Help entrepreneurs build up confidence in the future[6]

Create a good public opinion environment for entrepreneurs

Now China's economy is faced with the risk of decline, which has various reasons. I think it is not caused by a simple economic cycle, and one of reasons is that under the condition of good economic development of the past, we became overoptimistic and took some inappropriate measures to greatly increase enterprises' costs. For example, Labor Contract Law passed in 2007 rigidified enterprise employment system, and, as a result, plenty of enterprises were unwilling to employ more people and even some enterprises encountered difficulties in operation. Thus, from the second half of 2007, many enterprises began to close and even some South Korean companies took French leave; some enterprises left for the southeastern Asian countries including Vietnam. We shouldn't neglect the impact our policies have exerted on the current crisis; I think at least our policies have aggravated difficulties we are confronted with.

During the past thirty years, China mainly carried out two reforms – price reform and reform of state-owned enterprises. Among other things, without emergence of non-state-owned enterprises, the price reform wouldn't have been so successful; so is the reform of state-owned enterprises, because without non-state-owned enterprises, none would take in the assets and labor released by state-owned enterprises' downsizing for efficiency. However, as long as government published policies, most of them focused on strengthening infrastructural construction and were related more to state-owned enterprises instead of non-state-owned ones.

To tide over current economic difficulties, what is important is to help entrepreneurs build up confidence in the future; thus, they will invest and create employment opportunities. Now I have noticed a bad phenomenon that many entrepreneurs lack confidence, and some of them that hadn't planned to emigrate began to leave for foreign countries. Hence, it plays a vital role in creating a good public opinion environment.

The most important resource allocation is the allocation of people, especially the wisest, because it is the wisest that determine whether people create wealth or distribute wealth and whether the economy stagnates or develops. In my opinion, there are two things suitable for the wisest: one is joining government departments and the other is starting up business. Government redistributes wealth, and businesses create values. So being entrepreneurs is of significance to social development and economic growth.

When we discuss economic achievements during the past thirty years, we cannot forget without the relay-race-like inheritance of entrepreneurs of three generations, China's economy wouldn't have made so many achievements.

According to a simple statistical analysis I made of China's top two hundred richest people, among these three generations, the first-generation entrepreneurs were the ones starting up business before 1988, of whom over 70% changed from "peasants" – namely, 55.3% came from peasants and urban jobless people; the remaining 17.1% were compatriots from Hong Kong and Macao, most of whom actually were also peasants that stole into or emigrated to Hong Kong or Macao in earlier days. At that time, anyone that had a bit of social connections would enter government departments and state-owned enterprises instead of being entrepreneurs to start up business. The second-generation entrepreneurs were the ones between 1988 and 1997 of whom 71.9% came from government officials and managerial personnel of the state economic sector. As far as the third-generation entrepreneurs are concerned, 55% of them were the overseas ones that returned to China – namely, overseas returnee entrepreneurs.

China's economic growth during the first ten years mainly relied on manufacturing and commerce undertaken by peasant entrepreneurs; during the second ten years it was largely dependent on real estate and finance undertaken by those who came out from government; and during the third ten years it relied on high-tech industry mostly undertaken by overseas returnee entrepreneurs.

The first-generation entrepreneurs belonged mostly to disadvantaged groups in society at that time; they did what all of urban people and personnel of state-owned enterprises were unwilling to do and got rich. After the first ten years, our economy grew up and kept growing quite well, which laid a solid foundation for reforms later. But the general opinion now goes that these entrepreneurs are guilty of original sin and earning dirty money. How could they have confidence and a sense of safety? Therefore, government needs to take some measures, like Deng Xiaoping made speeches during his China's South Tour in 1992 to guide everyone to think earning money is glorious. Entrepreneurs not only create social wealth but offer job opportunities. I think, if so, we can overcome sooner or later financial crises we are in the face of, no matter how severe they are.

To make yourself happy, you must make others happy first

At present, we shouldn't think China is supposed to cease liberalization reforms because the US subprime lending crisis triggered the financial crisis. As far as the financial crisis is concerned, I would like to quote the metaphor I used several months ago: we used to be bumping up and down on a tractor, envious of Americans riding in planes, and thus we made up our minds to research on making planes for use; but all of a sudden we find a US plane crashed down, then we feel lucky that we used to ride in a tractor instead of a plane. Is it better to ride in a tractor instead of a plane? Of course not. We should still research building planes for use.

Indeed, there is no institution that can be transplanted simply. But humans have the same nature. It is a universal human nature in any country to pursue happiness. The problem is how to turn the pursuit of individual happiness into the one of making others happy. What is the subtlety of a market economy? That is, it is that you must make others happy first in order to make yourself happy. If an enterprise produces a product that isn't to the liking of consumers, its employer cannot make a profit, which is the regulating principle of a so-called "invisible hand". Such a system is exactly what we are badly in need of – to make yourself happy, you must make others happy first. No matter what measures we take, including American, European, and Chinese ones, and no matter how much all of them probably differ in details, all successful systems must meet the requirement – namely, incentive compatibility, an economic term.

How is human wealth created? It is those real private enterprises that mobilize everyone's initiative and creativity to create huge wealth under the mechanism of incentive compatibility, among other things. US financial innovation is a typical example. US enterprises have taken a lead in the high-tech field in the past thirty years and offered us many good affordable products. Without its relatively free financial system, that would be impossible.

Therefore, China's economic reforms should move forward, and we should continue to expand opening-up as well as offering more freedom to financial enterprises. We cannot think our original system is immune to financial crises. It is just because we have appropriated plenty of resources to tide over these crises. For example, in the past we have spent over 2,000 billion yuan in merely solving bad debts of banks, but in the 1990s annual per capita income of Chinese people was less than 1,000 dollars. Indeed, after we become opener, there will probably arise some crises, but after weighing pros and cons, we should still keep going on.

China's reforms are analogous to drawing white stripes on a horse and then turning such a fake zebra into a real one. Now in China some "horses" have turned into real zebras, but other "horses", including some large state-owned enterprises, are still ones with white stripes. We are done drawing stripes; the next problem is how to turn these white-striped "horses" into real zebras. In order to accomplish that, I feel our reforms in the following thirty years should focus on the transition from economic reform to constitutional reform and political reform. In the future thirty years, we should establish within the first fifteen years an independent judicial system that can offer better protection for the property rights system. Only under such circumstances can the previous thirty-year reform achievements be consolidated. Then during the second fifteen years we can probably set up the democratic election system. Thus, after sixty-year reform, China will become an economically prosperous and democratically developed country.

Notes

1 Based on a speech I made at the 10th Anniversary Forum in May, 2009 held by Shenzhou Branch, Guanghua School of Management. It is included in *China's Economy after the Financial Crisis*, edited by the author.
2 Based on a speech I delivered at the Eleventh Guanghua New Year Forum in January, 2010, and it is included in *China's Economy after the Financial Crisis*, edited by Zhang Weiying.
3 Based on a speech I made at the China Economist Forum 2010 & China Economic Theory Innovation Awarding Ceremony on December 20, 2011.
4 A preface written on April 5, 2010, to *China's Economy after the Financial Crisis*, edited by Zhang Weiying.
5 Based on a speech delivered by me at the Ninth China Business Leaders Annual Conference in 2010.
6 Based on a speech delivered at a seminar on January 15, 2009.

Part four

The prospects for state-owned enterprises

Dominance of state-owned economy leads to unfair competition[1]

An important reason why China's reform was pushed fast in the 1980s was the public debate over practice as the sole criterion for testing truth. The debate was quite important, because it brought about some common ideas and told people what was right and what was wrong, what should be done or shouldn't, thus forming a synergy of promoting reforms.

As China's reform has progressed so far, we need a new ideological emancipation movement in the face of new situations. What I intend to discuss is for what purpose a state exists and for what purpose a government operates. It is ridiculous that some people can do whatever they like in the disguise of protecting state-owned assets, or maintaining and raising value of state-owned assets, but ordinary people think that is all right and proper. As a matter of fact, there is no theory that can offer support for such an idea, whether from the perspective of economics or of political science.

For what purpose do we need a government? In most cases the goal of government is to maximize people's freedom and welfare rather than maximize government's financial income and state-owned assets. Mencius said more than two thousand years ago that "people are on the top of priority, with state following, then comes the monarch". Now many people reverse what Mencius said but give top priority to state-owned assets instead of interests of the populace. If we don't correct this wrong idea in the academic world, in front of government officials, media, and the populace, we can hardly carry out many reforms. Thus, we must reconsider the goal of government's existence. This is the first thing I intend to say.

Second, what role should state-owned enterprises play in order to accomplish such a goal? To put it simply, I think that all enterprises, whether state-owned or foreign-funded or private, should compete equally and that state-owned enterprises should not possess any privilege. But, in fact, it is difficult to make it thus.

When China United Telecommunications Co. Ltd. was founded in 1994, even this newly established state-owned enterprise couldn't easily get access into the telecommunications market, not to mention private enterprises. Thus, in order to give private enterprises equal opportunities to compete, the key lies in taking strict control over conduct of state-owned enterprises. If not, those state-owned enterprises that have already occupied a monopolized position can, by themselves, even without the help of government, exclude from access to the market all rivals that intend to get into or have already entered. Moreover, when they intend to exclude their rivals, they will make it at all costs.

Now state-owned enterprises, especially monopoly ones, make big accounting profits but don't need to pay any dividends to society. In other words, the investment cost of our state-owned enterprises is zero. If you, as a private investor, buy stocks and lend money, you have an expectation about return – for example, 10% annually; if the return cannot meet your expectation, you will be unwilling to invest. But in the case of state-owned enterprises, even if those big groups earn several billion or tens of thousands of billions in profits, none asks them to pay dividends, which is excruciatingly horrible. Because of no fiscal constraints, they can eliminate their rivals at all costs.

Third, what I intend to highlight are problems with the State-Owned Assets Supervision and Administration Commission. It has been two years since the commission was founded, and now we have discovered many problems. What are the goal and function of it on earth? According to a general explanation, its goal is to maximize state-owned assets. If this explanation is correct, we can pose another question: who is responsible for supervising the commission? If its goal is to maximize the assets of a certain owner, for the good of the whole society we must consider who can constrain it; and we even need to question the rationale of its existence.

If you want to merge two large enterprises in Western developed countries, you must accept the inspection of the anti-monopoly law, and it is the court that decides whether you can merge or not. In contrast, the State-Owned Assets Supervision and Administration Commission isn't under such a constraint, and if it wants to merge China Netcom Corporation with China Unicom Co. Ltd., nobody can exert any constraint on it. If both companies are merged, that will surely do good to increasing state-owned assets, because there will be no competition.

However, the purpose of existence of a state should not be to maximize state-owned assets. If existence of a state is for the sake of maximizing state-owned assets, what should government do now? Let state-owned enterprises monopolize all industries including shoe-repairing and vegetable-selling, because it will be easier to increase the value of state-owned assets? But what can the whole society benefit from that? Nothing but damage. Therefore, we must reconsider the role of the commission. Or else, some people in the disguise of protecting state-owned assets or maintaining and raising value of state-owned assets can make whatever policies they like, which will often do great damage to interests of the people all over the country.

What I intend to emphasize is that if there is no big adjustment in government structure, it will be difficult to solve these problems. Why could the reform in the 1980s be promoted fast? Because there was a relatively independent department – namely, the Commission for Restructuring Economic System. This reform commission was not confined by traditional department interests, so it was a force of countervailing other departments. At that time, when some departments such as the Planning Commission, Ministry of Finance, and Ministry of Foreign Trade and Economic Cooperation were about to publish policies, top leaders of central government would listen to opinions of the Commission for Restructuring Economic System. Now this commission disappeared; and basically when every department publishes policies, its officials will present a report, and what top government leaders will do is to merely listen to their report without consulting a countervailing force. As a result, the policies every department makes are to maximize the resources and power it takes control of, which is extremely hazardous to the country's development.

The Development Research Center of the State Council is supposed to conduct independent researches in advance and propose some independent policy proposals. The situation is not so optimistic, however. The center has a budget of merely several million in funds annually. It is said that the center's every department is basically engaged in business-oriented consultancy. It is quite pathetic that as a supreme research institute, it cannot research on policies holistically and focus on national development any more but has become a consulting institute serving a certain enterprise or a certain region.

Lastly, what I must highlight is that these problems reflect an in-depth problem: there is no way to reconcile the role contradiction when government plays a dual role both as an enterprise owner and as a public administrator. In China many ancient theories suggested that government shouldn't get involved in business and held that government would unavoidably compete with people for profits. At present, if government still possesses the ownership of enterprises, fair competition will be impossible. Even if we are lucky enough to have a benevolent regulator, fair competition is still impossible. Suppose the regulator has an ax to grind, fair competition will be completely farfetched. Therefore, the solution still lies in accelerating the reform of state ownership system, especially property rights system reform.

Promoting privatization of state-owned enterprises is more beneficial than turning in more profits[2]

First of all, I highly agree with Professor Jiang Ping's opinion about the reform of state-owned enterprises: the reform of state-owned assets management system should turn from ordinances and policies to laws. In fact, it should hold true for all of reforms. For example, the founding emperor of any dynasty often disseizes the throne "illegally", but, after he sets up a new dynasty, he needs to act in accordance with law. By "illegally" we means the first emperor violates the law of the previous dynasty when he overthrows it. But from the perspective of legitimacy, the overthrow will be probably justified. From the perspective of Confucianism, when a dynasty is too corrupted to make well-being for the populace, it has lost its legitimacy among the people and it should be overthrown. That is what Mencius argued.

Now I think it is time to look at the reform of state-owned enterprises from the perspective of law: who on earth has the right to establish state-owned enterprises and deal with state-owned assets? Take the China Investment Corporation that was newly founded, for example, who has the right to approve of investing 200 billion dollars to establish such a huge corporation? Before it was legally registered, the corporation had already invested 3 billion dollars, and now it has had such great losses. Who will bear the responsibility for this loss? These problems must be considered from the perspective of law.

Looking back on discussions concerning the reform of state-owned enterprises, I find there is a fatal weakness that underlies many problems we are in the face of. What is it? From the beginning, we thought the reform of state-owned enterprises dealt with the relationship between government and enterprises instead of the relationship between government and individual citizens, treating an enterprise itself as a natural person who has inner willpower to make its decisions. Just along with this line, Professor Jiang Yiwei proposed the enterprise-as-basic-unit system, and economists generally advocated strengthening enterprises' decision-making power. The problem with such a thinking pattern lies in that it evades property rights problems by focusing autonomy of enterprises, regardless of ownership as well as property rights problems. Its advocates thought that enterprises should turn into legal persons, and, as long as enterprises changed into independent legal persons, problems with state-owned enterprises would be solved. Whether substitution of taxes for profits or substitution of profits for taxes, they all proposed treating the relationship between government and an enterprise as an interpersonal relationship. In a sense, such a thinking pattern was related to many recurring problems. For instance, Professor Lin Yifu also neglects the property rights problems by highlighting so-called the "regeneration capacity of state-owned enterprises".

Either an enterprise or government is an institutional structure, not a natural person. Enterprises and government departments are run by people, but beneficiaries of and authority exercisers of these institutions are living individuals. An enterprise itself cannot make its own decisions, nor can government; an enterprise itself cannot enjoy, nor can government. All decision-makers are natural persons, and so is the case with all of the enjoyers. How an enterprise acts or makes a decision relies on arrangement of interpersonal relationships. For instance, when we say an enterprise is aimed at maximizing profits, we have actually assumed the enterprise has employees and employers, and employees earn contract income and accept guidance while employers earn residual income and make decisions. In other words, we cannot think that, no matter how interpersonal relations inside enterprises are arranged, they will set a goal of maximizing profits as long as enterprises become legal persons. It holds true for governments. It should not be taken for granted that so-called governments necessarily maximize people's interests. Essentially, how to distribute enterprises' profits or whether profits should be turned over to government involves not the relationship between the state and enterprises but the relationship among natural persons who play different roles in society. These problems we are confronted with are caused by our long avoidance of the property rights problem and deserve our further consideration. As long as we continue to evade the property rights system and focus only on the relationship between government and enterprises regardless of the property rights problem, we are doomed to bring about such a consequence. You just disputed over how much profits state-owned enterprises should turn over to government, but the most important problem is who has authority to decide how much?

Moreover, theoretically, "rent", "tax", and "profit" are three different concepts and represent different institutional arrangements in a market economy. Rent is contract income, tax is legally required income, and profit is residual income. Why are these concepts always interwoven together in our country? To put it simply, because resources are state-owned and enterprises are invested by the state. When the government assumes a triple role as a resources-owner, an enterprise investor, and a public administrator, these three concepts will surely be mingled. The state is analogous to a self-employed person who runs a restaurant. When the person grows vegetables, owns the house, and supplies all services, it seems a bit boring that he or she publically discusses how much house rent he or she obtains, how much wage he or she earns, and how much profit he or she makes. As far as the self-employed person is concerned, distinguishing operating profits from house rents merely involves accounting instead of substantial interests. Once a government becomes an owner of resources, capital, as well as enterprise, no one can enjoy residual income. Thus, the distinction among rent, tax, and profit is only a matter of accounting.

We cannot deny the positive significance of substitution of tax for profit submission and replacement of budget fund allocation by loan granting carried out in the 1980s. But in a sense, these practices can be regarded as virtual games between government and enterprises. In the planned economy, all of enterprises' profits were turned over to government, or, in other words, government levied a 100% income tax on enterprises. After substitution of tax for profit submission, enterprises didn't need to turn over all profits; instead, government left after-tax profits to enterprises management who reinvested some part on behalf of government and distributed the remaining part of profits to enterprises' employees as bonuses. The replacement of budget fund allocation by loan granting was aimed at strengthening accounting check, which was tantamount to entrusting budget financing to state-owned banks. Before the replacement, the capital cost of enterprises was zero, but, after the replacement, banks turned capital funds into loans and were assumed to charge interests. However, the problem is that essentially these loans were still capital funds based on government budget plan. More than a decade ago, we discussed the problem. Actually, management of state-owned enterprises didn't regard loans as debts; in their view, there was no difference between obtaining money from government budget and obtaining money from banks: anyway, it is still the government that decides how much bank loans enterprises can obtain. None of them had an idea of bearing the responsibility for paying back loans. Banks had no concept of risk management either, because they were not a real contracting party of loans. As a result, when loans accumulated to such an extent that enterprises couldn't repay, it is natural that government finance bailed out all the bad debts. The four asset management companies[3] were eventually set up by the government to accomplish the debt-for-equity swap.

This is the virtual game between government and state-owned enterprises in a state-owned economy. Of course, many of China's reforms have undergone a process of turning virtual games into real ones. Without substitution of tax for profit and replacement of fund allocation by loan granting, China's reform would not have gone so far.

At present, state-owned enterprises markedly differ from those in the 1980s. In fact, a part of the income right of state-owned enterprises has been privatized inside enterprises. Whether state-owned enterprises should turn over their profits to government and how many profits they should turn over are essentially a matter of distributing interests between employees of state-owned enterprises and officials of government departments such as the Ministry of Finance and State-Owned Assets Supervision and Administration Commission. If state-owned enterprises don't turn over their profits, it is management of enterprises that exercise the ownership of profits; if their profits are turned over to the State-Owned Assets Supervision and Administration Commission, it is officials of the commission who exercise the ownership; so is the case with officials of the ministry, if profits are turned over to the Ministry of Finance. Different proportions of profits turned over mean different distributions of ownership. Don't think as long as profits are turned over to government, enterprises will be really state-owned and the profits will benefit public interests. It is not as simple as we think. We cannot prove and ensure it will do better to society if enterprises' profits are submitted to government than if they are left to management of enterprises. Or else, is the reform we carried out during the past three decades good-for-nothing? Suppose state-owned enterprises submit all their profits, can all the people surely enjoy profits of Chinese National Petroleum Corp. and China Mobile Ltd.? Not necessarily. To ensure all the people enjoy fruits of state-owned enterprises, how to limit government's power and how to manage fiscal expenditures remain quite major problems. Otherwise, it is probably worse rather than better for the good of social and public interests if tens of hundreds of billions of profits are submitted to government budget.

It should be noted that in a market economy, profit is designed to be a responsibility system, and it is aimed at strengthening motivation and mobilizing people's work incentives, especially giving play to entrepreneurs' initiative in starting up business and innovation, instead of serving as a means of government to obtain fiscal revenue. We should realize entrepreneurs belong to the rarest resources in society. Without the profit system, entrepreneurship cannot be ensured.

It would be more interesting and relevant for us to discuss whether state-owned enterprises should exist at all, whether state-owned enterprises should quit, and how to quit, instead of whether state-owned enterprises should submit their profits to the Ministry of Finance or the State-Owned Assets Supervision and Administration Commission or should leave their profits to themselves. With regard to how state-owned enterprises should quit, we can have different choices. Take Chinese National Petroleum Corp, for example. Since it is a huge company with abundant assets, it should have been a good opportunity for it to quit when getting listed in Hong Kong and the mainland. Companies of this kind have already possessed sufficient cash flow; why are they still allowed to raise funds in stock exchanges? It makes no sense from the perspective of economics; it is quite absurd that a cash-rich enterprise keeps injecting new capital. The correct method is to transfer shares to private investors as government cashes out – namely, selling out hundreds of millions of stocks in Shanghai Stock Exchange and submitting raised funds to government finance as educational funds or social security funds by means of special legislation. If at the beginning we had adopted similar methods to actualize the return of H shares, it would have been far more valuable than raising money from the stock market on one hand and submitting profits to government on the other hand.

As far as China Mobile Communications Corporation and China Telecommunications Corporation are concerned, I think the best way is to turn users into owners. For instance, we can sell a certain proportion of shares to users annually according to users' actual billing, in a bid to dilute state-owned shares step by step till the state merely owns a small proportion of stocks. Under such circumstances, when state-owned enterprises make profits, it should be up to a board of directors and stockholders to decide whether they should reinvest profits or distribute profits among stockholders instead of letting the government decide if they should submit profits to it or keep profits themselves. In a nutshell, I suggest we constantly emphasize promoting privatization of state-owned enterprises, especially major ones. The issue of national security is not an excuse for keeping state ownership dominance. The biggest telecommunications company in South Korea is SK, which is not a state-owned enterprise but a private enterprise. Samsung's revenue accounts for 15% of the GDP, but it is also a private enterprise. However, the national security of South Korea is very assuring and satisfactory.

I read a metaphor in Professor Fang Liufang's article: if we compare state-owned enterprises to an orange, the former Soviet Union and the Eastern Europe slice it into pieces and give a piece to each of their people; in contrast, in China the country owns the orange and allows each of the Chinese to drink its juice by a straw. This is a vivid and insightful metaphor.

In some industries, when state-owned enterprises are too dominant, private enterprises can hardly survive and have to choose to quit. Delong Steel Company, a private enterprise, was sold to Russians (note: they finally failed to strike the deal owing to government's disapproval). It is said Jian Nong Steel Company is also looking for a buyer. It was promising a few years ago that private enterprises might gradually occupy a dominant position, but now in the face of increasing dominance of state-owned enterprises supported by government, they give up and look for buyers. Consequently, all state-owned enterprises come back, which is quite risky. It will be all right if state-owned enterprises can do a better job, but it is not the fact. Most of the profits of state-owned enterprises come from a few large monopolies; a large proportion of their profits are actually rents or probably taxes due, and the remaining part is consumer surplus appropriated by high prices, not economic profits. Profit makes sense only in a competitive market. A competitive market economy is based on the foundation of well-defined private property rights and free contracts. The urgent issue for China is not how to distribute profits of the state-owned enterprises but how to privatize them.

On corporate scandals and corporate governance[4]

In the United States, scandals of companies that are continually revealed recently must have something to do with the economic bubble occurring several years ago. Although those exposed problems are astonishing, any people who are familiar with US economic history will know there is no need to fuss about them, because similar scandals have taken place on many occasions. Thus, I think we needn't overreact to these problems; on the contrary, overreaction will bring about many new problems.

Most scholars will admit that the governance structure of US companies still remains most effective; in spite of some problems, we cannot deny it. Just as a best legal system cannot eradicate crimes, a best corporate governance structure cannot get rid of fraud. I would like to theoretically summarize what a corporate governance structure is as follows.

First, a corporate governance structure involves the relationship between a company's operator and its owner. Since enterprises came into being, human resources have been extremely important, or else, why should we emphasize entrepreneurs? The reason why there is a problem of corporate governance structure is that human resources are a crucial factor. Because there is a distinction between an operator and an owner, there will easily arise conflicts of interests. In the 1980s and 1990s, all the companies in the world emulated US corporate governance structure. For what reason? Because of global competition. Competition can show which structure is more effective. There is a quite simple principle in organizational behavior: if you don't intend to assume any responsibility, you must claim to be responsible for everyone. The stake-holder model cannot solve problems but will lead to the irresponsibility of managers instead.

Second, a corporate governance structure is a contract. On the one hand, we must assume contract signers have sufficient rationality. On the other hand, a contract is a voluntary exchange between individuals. Who will sign a contract that is not beneficial to himself or herself? Moreover, this contract is different from the contract we abide by when buying products. In most cases, when we buy products, the responsibility is obvious, and we can resolve disputes by resorting to the contract law. However, the contract – namely, the corporate governance structure – is very incomplete: stockholders take risks and the manager serves as the agent of stockholders, but the responsibility of the agent can hardly be well defined in the contract, so we have to resort to fiduciary duty. As a result, the duty of loyalty and care in a corporate governance structure comes into being.

Third, a corporate governance structure is an incentive mechanism. In any organization, it is uneasy for everyone to bear the responsibility for their actions, and it is more difficult for a manager to do that. The governance structure is aimed at forcing you to assume responsibilities once you make mistakes and at ensuring you obtain rewards when you do good deeds; therefore, you will be motivated to do things right.

All of these problems can be settled through specific institutional arrangement and social norms. Among other things, the property rights system should play a significant role, because the system per se is the most fundamental incentive mechanism. Without property rights, there will be no possibility of signing contracts, not to mention a governance structure! We are keen on corporate governance structure, but often try to neglect property rights system. That is impossible just like a person wants a baby while avoiding having a sexual life. The property rights system is the foundation of a corporate governance structure. So-called property rights owned by corporates as a legal person are merely a contract arrangement among investors as well as between investors and managers, akin to rights in rem of civil law. A corporate governance structure without the foundation of natural person's property rights is like a contract without signers.

With division of labor, it must be managers instead of stockholders that are engaged in corporate operation, and it is impossible all stockholders participate in operation. Thus, there arises a problem of agent cost.

Distribution of equity is vital. Generally speaking, an enterprise should have a large shareholder, and what if a company consists of minority shareholders? If so, everyone wants to be a "free rider"; the more power directors have, the more powerful general managers will be. An effective governance structure must have relatively centralized shares, with some large shareholders dominating the enterprise. Of course, dominance of large shareholders will also bring about problems – for example, interests of minority stockholders will probably be impaired and how to effectively compensate for that is another problem. In the present, we attribute many problems to dominance of one shareholder, because it is said US companies' equity is dispersed. But I think the major problem with China's corporate governance structure is not definitely so-called "dominance of one shareholder" but dominance of state ownership.

We cannot merely highlight today's US corporate ownership structure. A brief review of US or other developed countries' economic history shows that corporate equity structure has undergone a long-term and significant evolution from centralization to decentralization (diversification). In my view, in China, the judicial system, qualities of court judges, and behavioral norms of the whole society are unable to support a capital market with decentralized equity. Don't think everything will go well once dominance of one shareholder is eliminated. It is like back in 1911 we thought China would realize democracy as long as the emperor was overthrown. The fact is not so simple. Now the problem is that corporate governance structure won't become all right or will even worsen even if all of the large shareholders are eliminated. For instance, if Yonyou Software Co., Ltd., splits Wang Wenjing's equity, it will soon close.

For what reason do I think China's current judicial system and qualities of court judges cannot support a diversified stock market? Why can British and American law make it? Because when many corporate disputes arise, we cannot rely on prescribing solutions before they occur but on judges' judgments after they occur. For example, criteria for directors' and CEO's fiduciary obligations can only be decided by judges rather than be prescribed by law. Common law is quite applicable to these problems, because its norms develop during the process of solving cases. The more the cases are solved, the higher the qualities of judges will grow. Once the criteria are determined, managers will know what they should do or shouldn't, and related lawsuits will decrease. But it will cost a long time instead of several years to establish the criteria. How many court judges in China can judge whether you fulfill fiduciary obligations? If the public lacks confidence in law and judges, how is it possible to carry out a diversified stock market? It is impossible in China, even in countries where civil law is used, such as France and Germany. Therefore, we can see wide diversification of equity mainly takes place in the countries that use common law, and it always takes a long time to make it. The more dispersed equity becomes, the higher the requirement for fiduciary obligations will be, and thus the higher the qualification for judges will be.

Another governance mechanism deserving attention is market competition and reputation. No laws can prescribe all eventualities, and no judges can really judge whether each business behavior is honest. So what can we rely on? On competition. Many enterprises, before getting listed, will disclose their information. They have to, but not necessarily owing to law; even if law doesn't require them to do, they will. Because of competition, they have to do that. Just owing to competition, managers should pay attention to their own reputations in capital market. It is quite understandable that they have the right not to disclose information, but if they don't, no one will buy their stocks.

Lastly, an explicit compensation system also deserves much attention. The biggest difficulty of enterprises is offering managers a long-term incentive, which is far more difficult than offering a short-term incentive. If stock prices can reflect the value of enterprise's return flow in the future, equity option can play the role of long-term incentive. But if stock prices are easily manipulated by managers, equity option will be no use. Why did people falsify accounts? Because they can earn more when stock prices rise up. But this is a short termism; now they are revealed. I think ownership can well serve as a long-term incentive.

There are three questions calling for our consideration in China.

First, a corporate governance structure is mainly business of private individuals instead of government. So, government supervisory authorities should play a marginal role and intervene only when contract disputes arise, just as criminal law should merely punish criminals who have robbed a bank, instead of frisking everyone entering the bank. Since government has assumed so many responsibilities, stock buyers needn't. Now if the stock market goes wrong, government will try its best to rescue it to help investors; as a result, stockholders won't care whether the information disclosed is right or wrong. Given that financial data the government requires are audited by accounting firms and approved by the government, it is natural that the government should be responsible for stockholders. In that case, why should stockholders care about the information? Several years ago it was required by regulations that only listed companies that kept the return rate of capital at or above 10% for at least three consecutive years could issue new stocks. What consequence has resulted? Accounts falsification and enterprises' short termism. How is it possible to ask you to return 10% when you raise 500 million today? The simplest way is to do speculation in stock markets rather than invest in core businesses. The government's real intent is to make listed companies better monitored for the interests of stockholders; good as its intent is, it eventually leads to short termism of listed companies. An investment program that is supposed to make profits five years later will vanish because at that time all the money will have been spent on the stock market or lost.

Before 1933 there was no compulsory requirement for information disclosure in the United States, but information was still disclosed whenever it was necessary. I agree with the principle that you have the right not to disclose information, but you must be responsible for whatever you have disclosed. Just like a US policeman says to a suspect: you have the right to remain silent, but anything you do say may be used against you in a court of law. This principle is much better for interests of investors. In fact, not all information can be disclosed for interests of investors; in some cases, some information such as business secrets must remain hidden. Now our problem is you must disclose information but needn't be responsible for what you disclosed.

Second, the problem with independent directors. The government regulation has a compulsory requirement for certain numbers of independent directors in listed companies. How can government know three or five independent directors are optimal? If an enterprise is really in want of independent directors, its stock holders will elect. How many people can serve as an independent director that acts really independently? Not many, I am afraid. If a college professor serves as an independent director, how much time does he or she have? It is impossible for him or her to well serve as an independent director in several companies when he or she has to devote himself or herself to academic research. Everyone should consider what outcomes will be brought about accordingly by this regulation.

Third, the problem with state-owned enterprises. Now many China's listed companies are state-owned ones, so we tend to regard problems of state-own enterprises as universal problems and set up rules accordingly. For instance, company law prescribes the proportion of intangible assets cannot exceed 20%. Although the prescription that is aimed at preventing state-owned assets from diluting is specially formulated for state-owned enterprises, government intends to apply it to all enterprises, just like giving medicine to others when you are sick. In my opinion, state-owned enterprises should better mind their own business and don't apply your rules to all enterprises. The problem with dominance of one share is that this dominant stockholder is not a real one, but a disguised one.

If China wants to achieve real development and to be competitive globally, private economy is the key. I propose to set up two types of stock exchanges. One is for state-owned enterprises, and the other is for non–state-owned shares and enterprises that have a certain limited proportion of state-owned share (say, less than 10%). In other words, when a state-owned enterprise's proportion of state-owned share drops below 10%, we can allow the enterprise to transfer its ownership and to trade in an ordinary exchange. Let me use a metaphor to make a detailed explanation. A general hospital offers medical services to patients of almost all types of diseases except for two types, mental diseases and infectious diseases. The patients with mental diseases or infectious diseases must be treated exclusively in special hospitals. If we don't separate these patients from others, perhaps other patients will be infected or become mentally ill.

Why not allow users to be shareholders of telecommunications corporations?[5]

Mobile telephone charges are obviously high

Different industries have different pricing guidelines. If an industry's fixed investment is not quite high, its marginal cost is increasing. From the perspective of society, pricing according to marginal cost is optimal, but if an industry's fixed investment is too high, its marginal cost is decreasing; operators or producers cannot recover cost if they set prices according to marginal cost and no one is willing to invest.

If we assume local fixed phone call pricing is reasonable, we can make a preliminary judgment that mobile telephone pricing is much higher. Because the elasticity of demand for local fixed phone calls is relatively low, the demand won't change much as price changes. But the elasticity of demand for mobile phone calls is relatively high; the demand will probably increase by 2 to 3% or even higher as price drops by 1%. Therefore, it is suggested that mobile phone charges should be lower.

The profit rate of the China mobile communication industry is so high that the industry seems profiteering in a certain sense. As far as I know, the cost of mobile communication, in fact, differs slightly from that of fixed phone communication. Under such circumstances, it is obviously unreasonable to set such a high price.

In terms of mobile communication, what most people are concerned with is how to change a two-way charge to a one-way charge. However, this issue itself is not so important. What I intend to say is that we need to worry about the fact that the mobile phone charge set by government is too high, instead of one-way or two-way charge. The profit of mobile communication is probably quite high; there is a need to cut it down. The reason why some local branches of mobile communication reduce prices in disguised form is actually the pressure of intensive competition. This shows that once government liberalizes the price control, competitive prices will be much lower than current ones.

Cancellation of telephone installation fee matters little, and the key lies in designing a reasonable charging plan

In a certain sense, cancellation of telephone installation fees matters little. In the United States, there are probably several hundred charging methods, because there is intensive competition between telephone companies. If your installation fee is high, you must decrease daily use fee. If a user generates bulk calls, it is reasonable to charge a high fee for the installation but a low fee for telephone use. That is called two-part tariff pricing in economics. As far as small users are concerned, there is probably no need to charge them fixed fees, including the fee for installation, and it is more suitable to charge them a high price for each call instead. Take a rich man and a poor man for example. When a rich man often makes phone calls, the optimal method for a telephone company is allowing him to make phone calls as much as he likes, as long as he pays 1000 yuan per month. But for the poor man who is unwilling to pay a monthly fee, the telephone company can charge him 0.5 yuan per call.

Now a more suitable way lies in fostering enough competition to allow enterprises to freely choose what they should do in pricing. Then another problem will arise: why is the mobile phone charge so high? One of the major underlying problems is this: who should determine the pricing guideline, government or enterprises? At present, in China it is government that decides prices. If enterprises can set mobile phone prices, prices will surely duck drastically. If you can have dialogues with China Mobile and China Unicom, two of largest mobile communication companies, you will feel that they will probably cancel the two-way charge system as long as government permits them to set prices. There are two solutions to the two-way charge system. One is drastically decreasing both calling and call-receiving charges. The other is greatly reducing or even probably cancelling the call-receiving charge when the call lasts long enough; in other words, the longer the call is, the less the total charge will be.

Government and enterprises should play their own parts in pricing

When we discuss who should be responsible for pricing, there arises another problem – namely, the split of the telecommunication industry structure. I think the basic principle is clear – that is, as competition becomes sufficient, charges between common users and telephone companies and the fees telephone companies charge retail companies should be open to the market. Government should mostly manage charges among telephone companies – namely, interconnection clearing fees that will probably be in the charge of government within a long time. For example, when you use China Unicom to make a call but the receiver is probably a user of China Mobile, you must call via China Mobile. In this case, the government should take control of how much Unicom should pay for Mobile instead of how much Unicom charges its users, which is the future direction of pricing system.

State-ownership: the deadlock of cost and income

There is a more deep contradiction. If competition is sufficient, the issue of charge can be left to enterprise competition, and there is no need for our government to consider it. However, there is another special condition – that is, all telecommunication companies are state-owned. There is a great distinction between state-owned enterprises and private ones, because state-owned companies are sensitive to the revenue much more than the cost. In other words, these companies merely care about how to make revenue for sharing personal benefits and leave the problem of cost to the government and the state. Thus we are confronted with a dilemma. If the government loosens up all the prices, these telecommunication companies will foster vicious competition. To contend for markets, they are more likely to set prices extremely low, since managerial private benefits (including both control benefits and monetary bonuses) are mainly sensitive to gross revenue and market share. In order to prevent such excessive vicious competition, the government must govern telecommunication charges. Thus, a deadlock of cost and income is reached. To put it simply, on the one hand, it is unreasonable that government is responsible for setting prices; and on the other hand, if enterprises are allowed to set prices freely, prices of telecommunication industry will be thrown into chaos like aviation industry.

Therefore, I think whether we can rationalize China telecommunication prices and whether we can find an effective solution, to a greater extent, depend on property rights system reform of telecommunication enterprises. If the reform still preserves the state-owned system, I think the problem will remain unsolved forever.

Turn users into stockholders of telecommunication companies

With regard to this problem, now there should be some constructive ideas. We all know there are some telecommunication companies that plan to get listed and to solve the ownership problem step by step. In my opinion, since we always feel there is a large contradiction in term of prices between telecommunication companies and consumers, why not integrate property rights system reform with settling the contradiction through turning telecommunication users into stockholders? For example, when a telecommunication company charges a user an installation fee, the company can convert the installation fee into its shares according to a certain proportion. Moreover, a telecommunication company can award a user shares as long as the user pays the phone charge. Of course, there should be some specific rules for defining how much shares a user can obtain when he or she makes a certain quantity of phone calls. I think this is a good way to solve not only the problem of telecommunication property rights but the contradiction between enterprises and users. If users become stockholders, they won't feel so resentful even if telecommunication charges are upward adjusted.

In particular, that will have little interruption upon daily operation of telecommunication enterprises. When they make profits, at present they hand in money to the state; but after users become stockholders, they distribute money to users in the form of dividends. Indeed, that will eventually affect government fiscal revenue. But the fiscal system of a country should not aim at increasing fiscal income; or else, the best way is setting up only one telecommunication company, because one company can monopolize the market and will obtain the utmost income and profit sharing. I suggest government take into consideration the solution. It is time to turn every phone user into a stockholder of telecommunication companies.

Problems with China's medical system are induced by government monopoly[6]

Recently, there have been plenty of debates over China's medical system reform. A prevalent opinion is that we should attribute problems with the medical system to marketization reform. In my view, it is unjustified. Although people always complain that medical care is in short supply on the one hand and medical bills are too expensive on the other hand, the two problems cannot, in fact, coexist in a real market. Marketization will probably bring about expensive medical bills but not the difficulty in seeking medical care. If these two problems arise simultaneously, that indicates we don't really do as market does.

I don't suggest all of the medical services be carried out by means of market. But it is wrong that we attribute all of the current problems with the medical system to marketization reform. If so, that will do no good to our future reform, and we will be at a loss about how to carry on medical system reform. The most important element of markets is free entry, but since the reform and opening-up, the medical sector has been tightly controlled and monopolized by the state. There is no free entry. The second element is free price system. But there is no free price system in the medical services. Not just prices of treatment and medicines are set by government authority, but also especially the salary system of medical personnel is little related to the market, and freedom of their mobility is very low.

What is the fundamental reason for these problems with the medical system? To put it simply, government monopolizes the medical market and forbids others to enter even if it itself fails to do well; as a result, there arises a severe medical supply shortage. Normally, social demands for medical services must grow faster than the economy; but China's medical service supply grows much slower than per capita income. For instance, from 1978 to 2004 the GDP increased by almost ten times, but the number of beds in hospitals merely grew by 60%. Government monopoly has caused a severe medical service supply shortage that begets not only extraordinary increase of medical expenditures but varieties of other problems.

The future medical system reform can be simply summarized by two questions. The first one is, what is the cost-efficient way to obtain a given medical service? The second one is, what level of medical services will we aim at according to our country's economic strength, if we know the answer to the first one? There are two constraints during the process of policy-making: participation constraint and incentive compatibility. If any of the systems we have designed cannot fit the principle of incentive compatibility, it won't be effective.

There is an overriding problem that needs solving first before we carry out the medical system reform. Doctors are whose agent: the government's, pharmaceutical factories', or patients'? Under the previous medical system in the planned economy, doctors are agents of government. During the reform, many doctors become agents of *de facto* pharmaceutical factories instead of patients. I think in a healthy medical market, doctors should be agents of patients and be in patients' shoes, offering services to them and dealing with relations with others.

Furthermore, to carry out the medical system reform, we must open access to hospitals. Now we often discuss public hospitals, private hospitals, profit-seeking hospitals, and non-profit hospitals, so we have four types of hospitals: public non-profit, public profit-seeking, private non-profit, and private profit-seeking. Perhaps a large portion of medical services will be still supplied by government's public hospitals in the future, but we should leave certain room for private ones. Thus, I think the key lies in opening the medical market through allowing non-state-owned and private capital or even foreign funds to run hospitals. Take the United States, for example: non-profit institutions account for only 5% of GDP, but 60% of community hospitals are non-profit. They supply 70% of beds and offer medical services to 70% of hospitalized patients and 30% of nursing services. We can use these figures as reference. Government is obligated to run hospitals and supply fundamental medical care, but it has no authority to exclude individuals and other institutions from running hospitals.

If we really allow private institutions and companies to run hospitals, I think we can solve an important problem concerning transfer payment. People in the high-income bracket can choose to see the doctor in private hospitals and pay bills through business insurance; the saved money can be spent on low-income people who go to public hospitals. As a matter of fact, since ancient times, medical charges have had a function of income redistribution; in the past, village doctors used to charge rich people a high price but offer poor people medical services at a low price or even free of charge. However, if we continue allowing government to monopolize hospitals, we cannot settle this problem. Practices in many countries have proven that universal government subsidies are more beneficial to the rich. If government is reluctant to charge the rich more, it cannot offer assistance to the poor. So is the case with China, not only with its medical system, but also with its educational system. We think we are helping the poor by setting the price low, but the fact is we are subsidizing the rich. Actually it is a win–win game if high-income people spend money in saving time obtaining medical services in private hospitals.

I intend to highlight that all of medical personnel, whether in public or private hospitals, or in profit-seeking or non-profit hospitals, have the right to obtain reasonable compensations in a legal manner. It is inappropriate that now we often regard medical personnel's acceptance of a red envelop filled with cash as an ethical problem. Like all of us, medical personnel have the right to earn reasonable rewards in a legal manner; if they cannot, that will lead to illegal compensations including commission and the "red envelop", which will stain the whole group of medical personnel. If medical personnel can obtain reasonable legal income, the problem of medical personnel acting as agents of pharmaceutical factories will be solved and medical personnel can become real agents of patients.

Another problem to solve is distortion of medical service prices. Prices of treatment and surgical operation are so low that hospitals have to seek compensation in medicine sales – namely, subsidizing medical services with profits from drug sales. We must settle this problem, or there is no way to tackle another problem that hospitals collude with pharmaceutical factories to deceive patients.

On the whole, what I emphasize is that while government ought to run hospitals, it has no right to prevent private and other institutions from running hospitals; government is obligated to pay for some medical services but cannot distort prices; medical personnel are required to abide by professional ethics but also have the right to obtain reasonable rewards in a legal manner. Moreover, I intend to stress that relevant government departments should publish their policies after deep consideration; don't take stopgap measures, and don't haste to publish unfeasible policies.

Three things that must be accomplished by economic reform within the next decade[7]

I think, speaking of macroeconomic management, we are somewhat misled. It seems that as long as we mention macroeconomic management, we merely care about monetary policies or fiscal policies, or to put it simply, about whether we should adopt easier or tighter monetary policies and how much money government should spend. I think real macroeconomic management lies in creating a good institutional environment under which everyone is more motivated to produce, work, and innovate with entrepreneurship given full play to and resources allocated to most efficient sectors. In this sense, I think the best macroeconomic policy is the one that requires government to spend less money rather than spend more money. We rarely see that government can spend money efficiently. In fact, the more money government spends, the less entrepreneurship there will be and the more restriction on the market there will be.

In my view, what matters most to China's economy in the next several years is accomplishing three things.

The first thing is privatization of state-owned enterprises. We can hardly imagine China can establish a real market economy when state-owned enterprises occupy a large proportion and a dominant position. State-owned enterprises have become one of the main obstacles to further development of China's economy in the future. I wish within the next five to ten years, the proportion of state-owned enterprises will drop below about 10% of GDP. It is not an arduous task and merely depends on determination of our political leaders. There are no technical difficulties because plenty of state-owned enterprises, especially the ones owned by the central government, have got listed and government can transfer their shares by means of market to non-state-owned enterprises and individuals, or like what the UK government did under Thatcher's regime, distribute their shares to the populace at discounted prices. I think if our government does so, Chinese residents' wealth can increase drastically. This wealth effect will promote the development of the domestic market, and, what's more, it will bring on more efficient utilization of our whole assets including financial assets. As a result, great quantities of scarce resources and preferential treatment will not be exclusively enjoyed by state-owned enterprises, and some of them including bank loans can be enjoyed by many private enterprises. These resources will be effectively exploited.

The second is privatization of lands. In fact China has plenty of assets that haven't changed into capital – namely, they can be utilized but cannot be transferred freely or used as collaterals against loans for starting up business. The most important part of these assets are lands in the hands of peasants. Every peasant has the right to farm his or her land but doesn't own it, so he or she has no right to transfer it freely. During the process of urbanization, the government carries on urbanization by means of depriving peasants of ownership of lands, which has brought forth many social inequities and social instabilities. If our country can turn lands into peasants' assets, these assets can really become capital. Once peasants have the capital, it will be more convenient for them to move into cities or do other things, and thus we can also prevent unfair treatment to peasants during the process of urbanization – namely, depriving peasants of land at a low cost. If we make it, I think the potential of our domestic markets can be maximized greatly. In other words, we can drastically increase the assets of hundreds of millions of people who will naturally tremendously enhance their consumption.

The third thing we need to carry out is liberalization of finance. Since the 1990s liberalization of finance had begun, but after the Asian financial crisis in the late 1990s and especially the global financial crisis in recent years, it basically ceased. We mistook liberalization of finance for the cause of the

2008 financial crisis, so our policies have been reversed. As a matter of fact, the most important point for China is to marketize the financial industry instead of changing the ways the government manages the economy. We have many misunderstandings. For example, we think our financial order will become disordered without strict regulations of government. But that is not a fact. We can see two hundred years ago there was no central bank, no Banking Regulatory Commission, and no need to be approved by government if you wanted to establish an exchange shop or a money shop. But during the history of over one hundred years, Shanxi Draft Bank operated well and witnessed little fraud, so it enjoyed extremely good credit.

There is another misunderstanding when we speak of financial order. It is totally wrong that we think that merely the order prescribed by government is called order and the order that came into being several thousand years ago is not. Let's see the fundraising case occurring lately. When the public has no real freedom of capital and financial transactions, and thus entrepreneurs cannot raise funds for business development, there will arise illegal and unlawful financing. The most important part of the next economic reform is not focusing on marketization of interest, which also deserves much attention, but opening up the financial market and allowing more people to set up various financial institutions. Only this way can our assets be reasonably utilized and entrepreneurship really be given full play to.

If we can make a good job of these three things – namely, liberalization of state-owned enterprises, of lands, and of finance – China's economy will be embraced by a good future in the next ten or twenty years!

Notes

1 A speech I gave at a seminar held by the Unirule Institute of Economics in 2005.
2 A speech delivered by me at a seminar held by the Unirule Institute of Economics in 2008.
3 They are the China Great Wall Asset Management Co., Ltd., China Huarong Asset Management Co., Ltd., China Orient Asset Management Co., Ltd., and China Cinda Asset Management Co., Ltd., respectively.
4 A speech I gave at the Economic Observer Forum on August 13, 2002.
5 A speech concerning charges and reform of the China telecommunication industry I made at the Forty-Fourth IT Salon. The original version was published on August 9, 2001, in *Market Daily*, sponsored by People's Daily Online.
6 Based on a speech I gave at the Symposium on National Drugs Centralized Bidding and Procurement Policies held by Department of Health Economics and Management, Guanghua School of Management of Peking University on March 10, 2006. It was published in *Health News* (March 16, 2006).
7 Based on a speech I made at the China Development Forum & Economic Summit on March 17, 2012.

Part five

The lifeblood of enterprises

Seek a business model for green economy[1]

As is well-known to us, an ancient Chinese poem goes, "Ducks know first when a river becomes warm in spring". It is a natural phenomenon that ducks can know climate changes. But who is the best forecaster for economic and social changes? Normally, it is the entrepreneur. They should be ones who are most sensitive to the future and most capable of making judgments. Of course, I don't think they never commit mistakes. But on average, they make fewer mistakes than other people. This is the major reason we need entrepreneurs.

If entrepreneurs are less capable of forecasting the future than other people, they will have no value for existence. Now our entrepreneurs highlight green economy, so I am convinced that their judgment is correct. But the problem is that I sense there is a trend – that is, the moment we speak of green economy, we will discuss what government should do accordingly; it seems as if we tend to de-marketize the economy for being a green one. I think a green economy can only be actualized through the market. In fact we have seen when a market stops operating, severe waste will result. For example, after an earthquake took place in Sichuan, the market couldn't operate. Out of love, we donated many supplies, but probably too many instant noodles and drinking water were carried there. We can also see many buildings and facilities that exceed given standards have been reconstructed in earthquake-stricken areas. Is that green? I think that probably deserves much discussion.

What I intend to say is that only by means of market can we achieve sustainable development under any condition. In other words, can our entrepreneurs find a business model for green economy? If we cannot, "green economy" is just a slogan at best, a slogan we can discuss every year but that is not applicable in practice. Essentially what is a business model? Are green companies better in making money than traditional ones? Or furthermore, are our consumers more willing to pay for more environment-friendly and low-carbon products and technologies? I must emphasize the function of price. Without a right price system, we cannot have a green economy.

First of all, price is a signal. For example, who can tell us what we should do and shouldn't and how much green and how much low-carbon we should be? Only price can.

We have no way to believe the criteria determined by a bunch of people sitting inside a room must be the best ones for humans. Let me cite a simple example. As far as a pair of disposable chopsticks and a pair of ordinary ones are concerned, we cannot decide which one is greener. It is said that disposable chopsticks waste too much wood. But the fact is that some trees can be used only for making products such as chopsticks. If these trees are not used to make chopsticks, what can they be used for? Nothing. They will be felled eventually for reforesting. In that case, disposable chopsticks are not less green. Some people believe that ordinary chopsticks are always greener. But they forget that ordinary chopsticks consume lots of laundry powder and disinfectants; if they are not disinfected well, they will spread diseases and cause their users sick and to get hospitalized, which leads to much more waste. Therefore, we cannot judge which one is greener.

Second, price is an incentive mechanism. There is no way to change the nature of people, but we can make use of interests to induce people to make right choices. If we intend to advocate saving water, the most effective or probably only way is raising water price. If we want to save energy, the best way is to increase energy price. If we don't want to raise water price, but in the meantime we want to save water, I think there is no way out.

These are the important functions of price: first, telling us what we should do or shouldn't; second, motivating people to choose right actions.

Advance of a green economy must finally originate from technological innovation. Without technological innovation, we cannot change our growth model thoroughly. Price and profit are the selection criteria and driving force of green technologies and low carbon technologies. For instance, if our petroleum price is extremely high, people will be induced to develop more new energy technologies, and we will not probably need petroleum any more eventually. In fact, in history, people in Western countries used whale oil for illumination. In the nineteenth century, people almost killed out whales, and whale oil became so extremely expensive as to force people to discover petroleum. Now we have used petroleum for over one hundred years, and we think it is exhaustible and not environment-friendly. If we want to develop breakthrough technological alternatives in the future, we need a new business model under which alternatives are more profitable.

Only with the help of market can we find solutions to promoting a green economy. It is vital to define property rights. To have a market, we must define property rights. In the future the low-carbon market or the carbon trading market is likely to be a most potential market when the rights to pollute can be well defined.

Of course, we also have a way to influence the market – namely, by changing preferences of consumers, because preferences can exert influence upon demands. Public opinion and education are able to change people's preferences.

Take how often we should take a shower for example. If we take a shower once every day, we will use more water. It is more environment-friendly that in rural areas we take a shower once every month. Indeed I cannot tell you how often is appropriate, but, as far as water consumption is concerned, the less frequently you take a shower, the greener and the more environment-friendly that will be. But on the other hand, as you bathe less frequently, you will probably be infected with a certain disease that causes you to get hospitalized or leads to other forms of consumption.

Let me cite another example. A large portion of Japanese are Buddhists, so only 3% of leather used in automobiles is animal leather, but 20% of leather used in automobiles in China is cattle hide. If we educate people to feel guilty of using cattle hide, I think more people will not need cattle hide anymore and the price of cattle hide as well as the price of our leather shoes made of cattle hide will drop. Of course, another problem will arise. If the cattle hide price ducks, the cost of beef will drastically rise up, because the cost of raising cattle has to be more shared by beef. Now cattle hide can share a portion of cost, so beef seems to be relatively cheap. Therefore, I also have no idea which outcome is better. Besides, that involves a problem of vegetarianism and meat eating. If all of Chinese are Buddhists, beef consumption will decrease greatly.

I think there are some simple things we can start from now. For example, today we have a green conference, and let's see how much food we wasted and dropped on the table after we had a meal. Today half of food or at least a third of food on the banquet was wasted. I think, if all entrepreneurs start saving food, is it immediately effective?

Furthermore, don't set "green" and "environment-friendly" against "industrial civilization". Around 10000 B.C., there was no industrial civilization, but the global climate grew warmer and the ice sheets melted down. Today, automobiles are considered as the cause of pollution, but, when they were invented, they were contributive to improving the urban environment, because at that moment, the urban environment was quite terrible – say, streets of London were covered with horseshit. There is no industrial civilization in many parts of Africa, but they are obsessed with severe desertification. I would like to specially mention my hometown, the plateau of northern Shaanxi Province. Several hundred years ago, it was rich in vegetation, but later its vegetation was destroyed. Before the reform and opening-up, when I lived in villages, I only noticed most of the mountains were almost bare and few of them were covered with trees, let alone grass. At that moment, there was no industrial civilization, but people were still overexploiting. Today when I went back to Shaan Bei, driving by car via Ordos, Yulin, Yan'an, and Xi'an, I found the afforestation on both sides of expressways became better. Why? Because people in these areas have become rich and don't need to fell trees in mountains, and, thanks to "grain for green" policies, the vegetation recovers quite fast. Without industrial civilization, we would have been confronted with a more terrible environment. As a matter of fact, human beings are quite ignorant; we are unaware what influence our actions will exert upon the outside environment, including climate change and temperature rise. We are ignorant to what extent our actions can influence. At present, we are just assuming.

Of course, we must take more careful measures. However, at the moment we should balance risks and effects. If a measure costs a long time to take effect but implementing it will take a big risk, we'd better prevent it for now. Take burning garbage for example. Several years ago we still considered it to be a method to solve environmental problems; now we hear that burning garbage produces poisonous air, which does great damage to human health. Let's return to what I discussed: experience has proven the market can offer the only best way to remedy mistakes. We have made some mistakes and found the market has enabled us correct them by means of price adjustment and profit, or punishment of loss. Therefore, we should have confidence in the market in this regard.

The good of our offspring is the evitable topic of our conversations. Humans must care about their offspring, and I am sure it holds true for everyone present here. But we are not aware what on earth is beneficial and unbeneficial to our offspring. There was a real story in my hometown. There was a family of a father and two sons. When the father died, he left the same share of land to both sons. For the good of his offspring, the elder son devoted himself to farming and taking care of the land, but the younger one sold out the land and paid money for schooling. Later the younger one managed to become a high-ranking official and came back to buy lots of land, but during the agrarian reform period he got killed because he was a landlord and since then his offspring had been looked down upon. In your view, which way is beneficial to offspring? Now it seems everyone occupies a moral high ground in the guise of "green" and "low carbon", but actually as I just said, we are ignorant of the future of human beings. Of course, our entrepreneurs also try to be politically correct and tend to conform to the mainstream, but different voices and opinions shall be allowed. Many of our business enterprises have vested interests, and so non-governmental/non-profit organizations seem "nobler". However, what I just intend to remind everyone is that any organizations, not just business enterprises, are likely to become a vested interest group. Therefore, at the moment I would like to use history to prove that varieties of voices are always better than one single voice.

The everlasting key to enterprise development lies in incessant innovation[2]

Today, my topic is "built to last" and innovation. All of our entrepreneurs hope to build a time-honored company, but there are few time-honored companies. Why is it so difficult to build an enterprise to last? First, the market environment keeps changing; if you run a restaurant and keep your menu, dish ingredients, and services unchanged for long, I think perhaps less and less guests will frequent your restaurant. In the globalization age, consumers' tastes change much faster than in any age. Second, technology is evolving fast. In the 1990s many people made a fortune by selling Beep Pagers, which are obsolete now.

When I worked in the 1980s, our office used Stone word processors, but several years later, PCs went into offices and households, and Stone word processors became useless. Sony's Walkman once was popular all over the world but is replaced by MP3 now. Third, new rivals enter the market one after another and are destroying old competitive enterprises. None of the enterprises dare to say it has no rival, and even Microsoft is facing the challenge posed by Google. Fourth, enterprises per se are aging, and many successful enterprises are defeated finally by themselves: perhaps because they have too many heritages and too much investment to protect and thus cannot continue innovating by denying themselves; thus, they just vanish.

Surface-level competitiveness relies on deep-level competitiveness

The most important thing for our entrepreneurs is understanding for what purpose enterprises exist. I think what we should keep in mind is the value of enterprises lies in creating value for clients and society. Anytime you intend to achieve sustainable development, you should keep creating value for consumers. To put it simply, we must justify consumers' purchases. Why are they willing to buy my products instead of theirs? As dean of a business school, I always ask myself, why are students more willing to come to Guanghua School of Management? It is impossible to achieve sustainable development if we don't give our clients a strong reason for buying our products instead of rival products.

Then another problem arises. As we usually say, what is your competitiveness? Hereby I share with everyone some ideas of Fujimoto Takahiro, a Japanese professor of management. In *Capability-Building Competition*, he divides enterprise competitiveness into two levels. The first level is surface-level competitiveness – namely, what we can obviously see in the market; the second level is deep-level competitiveness – namely, what are invisible to ordinary clients. As far as the first level is concerned, for example, clients can obviously see whether the price of your products is cheaper and more attractive; what consumers can also see is whether your delivery time is timely and that the advertisement of your product is seductive.

However, in fact, all surface-level competitiveness relies on deep-level competitiveness. The latter is essentially the capacity to create value, which is beyond consumers' judgment, such as your production efficiency, production cycle, rate of qualified products, and development cycle. In other words, can you create more value if you are given the same resources and elements? Before your products go out of the factory, you can have them inspected and leave aside unqualified products, which consumers won't know. But if your rate of qualified products is, say, merely 70% or 80%, that means you are wasting 20% or 30% of resources; thus, you will be hardly competitive in the long run. Deep-level competitiveness stems from the organizational capacity of your enterprise – namely, the capacity to make use of different elements to create value and to increase your efficiency. It is your organizational capacity that determines your deep-level competitiveness and then surface-level competitiveness and business performances, which refer to how much money you have earned and how much market share you have occupied.

During the process of enterprise's operation, there are other important but uncontrollable external factors. For instance, if some changes of macro policies, such as adjustment of interest rate and increase of exchange rate, take place, an export-based enterprise that used to make profits will be in the red now. These factors are beyond our control. Only if we possess deep-level competitiveness can we be adaptable to macroeconomic fluctuations. Take Japanese automobile enterprises for example. When the exchange rate of Yen to the US dollar rose from over 300 yen in the 1970s to 100 yen in the 1990s, why did Japanese auto-mobile enterprises still rank among the top ones in the global market? Because the Toyota-led production model essentially has a much higher production effi-ciency and quicker production cycle than that of US counterparts.

In China, frankly speaking, many enterprises place much emphasis on surface-level things – for example, we are used to waging price wars, packag-ing, and advertising. But these are surface-level, not deep-level, competitiveness, and the former can easily become unsustainable. For example, if we concentrate on making some innovative designs in the exterior of cellphones – say, setting a diamond – our phones will be probably on hot sales merely within a short period, but that won't be sustainable.

A criterion for evaluating deep-level competitiveness

Speaking of deep-level competitiveness, I would like to repeat the charac-teristics I claimed in 2001 when China entered the WTO or the criteria for judging whether an enterprise possesses deep-level competitiveness. They can boil down to four words: unstealable, unpurchaseable, unseparatable, and uncarriable.

First, unstealable. I often advise our entrepreneurs to consider at any time whether there is something unstealable in their enterprise. "Unstealable" is not necessarily in the ordinary sense, although the big problem software enterprises are often confronted with is software theft. If your products can easily be copied and simulated by others, you won't be competitive any longer.

Second, unpurchaseable. You should ask yourself, can your products be pur-chased in the market? Can others do better than you? For example, when your computer company develops chips, can you do better than an independent chip supplier such as Intel Corporation? If you cannot, you won't have a competitive advantage in developing chips. Moreover, talents do not necessarily belong to core competitiveness, because more and more talents enter the market, and, as outstanding as they are, they have their market prices. The problem is, who can afford the highest price for them? Now many Chinese elite talents are hired by some large foreign companies including Microsoft and Google. Why? Because they can afford a higher price. The reason why they can afford it is that the talents can create more value in their companies than in Chinese enterprises. Thus, talents are not necessarily considered as core competitiveness.

Third, unseparatable. You should check whether different people in your enterprise are highly complementary and whether different businesses will become more valuable after they are integrated. Take an enterprise that has four departments or four industries, for example: if every department and every industry is more valuable when it is separated from the enterprise, the enterprise will be unlikely to sustain and will surely disintegrate. Every enterprise is supposed to ask, will its efficiency increase or decrease after it detaches this part of business? If your efficiency increases, you should disintegrate this business.

Fourth, uncarriable. We must ask ourselves whether possessions of our enterprise belong to some certain employees. If these employees leave the enterprise, what will be left to us? If we are left with nothing, for instance, if a client belongs to a client manager – namely, the client will not come to our company when the client manager leaves – we will possess no competiveness.

I think these four words form a criterion for judging and examining whether every enterprise really possesses deep-level competitiveness. Take a KFC outlet, for example: its business won't be affected even if any of KFC employees such as a waiter, head of an outlet, or even CEO leaves. This is its core competitiveness. Here I remember what I talked about with Wang Wenjing, CEO of Yonyou Soft. I asked him, "Do you worry your employees will leave?" He said that he did at the beginning, because he was afraid the employees later would sell the same products as his. However, he doesn't worry about that now; he is sure that even if the employees will sell the same product at a price that is half as much as his price, his clients will not follow the employees. Why? Because Yonyou has already had its own brand and won its clients' trust. In the field of financial management software, it is difficult to compete with a brand-name enterprise, so Yonyou somewhat attributes its survival to establishment of a good brand. As far as many of our enterprises are concerned, their employees can take away their resources and clients, because they have no brands.

Deep-level competitiveness stems from incessant innovation

The deep-level competitiveness I mentioned above is actually a static one. From a dynamic perspective, things are changing. The thing that is unstealable today can be stolen tomorrow; the thing that is unpurchaseable today can be purchased tomorrow; so is the case with unseparatable things and uncarriable things. Why are there so many software outsourcings? Is it because you needn't programming by yourself? No, because software programs are purchasable now. Thus, as an enterprise is concerned, in order to survive, it shall keep creating unstealable, unpurchaseable, unseparatable, and uncarriable things. Every enterprise leader should continuously ask himself or herself, "How long can my competitive advantage sustain? Can I probably survive after I lose my competitive advantage?" Then another problem arises: how to maintain enterprise's sustainable competitiveness.

I think the key to sustainably maintaining unstealable, unpurchaseable, unseparatable, and uncarriable things lies in innovation. In my view, innovation should include business management innovation, which is the theme of today's forum. But as far as an enterprise is concerned, it will be meaningless if you cannot turn business management innovation into products that create value for clients, even though you make a good job of business management innovations. In other words, competiveness relies on whether our products can satisfy clients and whether clients are willing to pay us a higher price. If not, innovation of other kinds will be useless because the existence value of an enterprise is creating value for others instead of perfecting itself and making itself look promising. The nature of the market is whether a product is essentially good or bad is up to clients' assessment instead of its producer's.

It should be noted that the more intense market competition becomes, the faster we will lose a competitive advantage and the more difficult it will be for us to sustain a competitive advantage. Innovation is the key to sustaining core competitiveness. I would like to quote a word of Schumpeter, a US economist. He is the father of innovation theories, and all of the theories concerning enterprise innovation originate from him. What is innovation? He argues that innovation is "creative destruction", meaning you must destroy the past in order to innovate. Innovation in an industry denotes you will destroy the past of successful enterprises. As is well-known to us, many modern technologies stem from destruction of old ones. Computer destroys typewriter, DVD destroys video player, and MP3 replaces Walkman. That is what innovation means.

I think that the most important thing for enterprises to know is that innovation should be an enterprise action instead of a personal action. Don't think innovation is just disclosure of inspiration of some intelligent people. Innovation requires standardized and routinized operational procedures, and innovative capacity of successful enterprises stems from the design of the whole system. Frankly speaking, China's enterprises don't do well in this regard. Now, of all patents we have registered, nearly two thirds are personal patents rather than corporate patents. In contrast, in the United States two thirds of patents are corporate patents. In China, in most cases, innovation involves personal actions instead of corporate actions.

We must recognize that innovation requires steady financial investment, so it really matters whether you are reluctant to spend money. Unfortunately, many of China's enterprises are reluctant to spend money on innovation. We can see most Chinese enterprises generally spend more money in advertising than on research and development. For example, they will not hesitate to pay tens of millions of money for signing an advertising contract with CCTV, but feel short of money if they are asked to invest several million on innovation, research, and development.

We should also realize innovation is a continual persistent process that is not immediately effective; thus, it requires enough patience. Take P & G for example. In the 1950s and the 1960s, P & G developed a kind of disposable baby diaper, and it took a decade to finish the whole process from starting developing it to launching it in the market. It is not because of its product defects but because P & G worked on how to reduce the cost to a certain extent that the ordinary people could afford the diaper – say, each diaper at 3.5 cents. If you keep the cost of one diaper at more than 10 cents, few people will buy your product. That's why P & G spent ten years in decreasing the price of diaper to the level common consumers could accept. Perhaps a lot of innovation will not yield immediate outcomes, but it may lay a foundation for future profitable innovation. It seems quite vital whether we can take a persistent attitude toward innovation.

What I should highlight is that we just mentioned many Chinese enterprises liked to spend money in advertising and in marketing, but now there is another relevant concept of "social responsibilities" that in most cases are related to marketing activities. Marketing activities can merely create surface-level competitiveness but cannot create deep-level competitiveness. When I talked with Mr. Long Yongtu yesterday, we both discussed this problem. It is just like a girl who wants to be liked by others must do some exercises to make her body healthy; if she is only keen on make-up or other surface-level things, no one will like her persistently. The sustainable development of any enterprise in the world cannot rely on advertising, and the sole key lies in innovation.

Innovation is incessant accumulation of knowledge

Next I will discuss knowledge accumulation of enterprises. Without long-term knowledge accumulation, enterprises cannot make a good job of innovation. We can classify knowledge from two perspectives. The first perspective is expressableness of knowledge, and the second is the relationship between different parts of knowledge.

From the first perspective, the academia generally divides knowledge into two types, explicit and implicit or objective and empirical. The former is the one that can be coded and that is easy to transfer and teach. Take a manual, for example: as long as everyone can maneuver a machine by referring to its manual, the manual is filled with explicit knowledge. Implicit knowledge is the one that cannot be accurately expressed verbally and linguistically. It cannot be learned from books but can only be accumulated by experience; to obtain it, you have to experience it continually. Take driving, for example: we cannot learn how to drive a car by only referring to a manual. To drive a car well requires practicing incessantly. That is implicit knowledge, which is empirical.

From the second perspective, we can divide knowledge into substitutive knowledge and complementary knowledge. Substitutive knowledge means when we have knowledge A, we don't need knowledge B, or the value of knowledge A and of knowledge B can be independently accumulated. In other words, if the value of knowledge A is 100 and the value of knowledge B is 100, the value they both created together will be 200. But the value of complementary knowledge cannot be accumulated independently. The overall value of complementary knowledge is more than its sum of its individual values, and perhaps the former is multiplication of the latter.

Therefore, enterprises have four types of accumulative knowledge. The first type is substitutive, explicit knowledge; the second is substitutive, implicit knowledge; the third is complementary, explicit knowledge; and the fourth is complementary, implicit knowledge. As far as enterprises are concerned, every type is important, but what plays the role in determining competitiveness is not explicit knowledge and substitutive knowledge but implicit knowledge and complementary knowledge or complementary, implicit knowledge. What enterprises really desire to accumulate is complementary, implicit knowledge, so we must ask ourselves how much knowledge we have accumulated in this regard. Here what I intend to emphasize is how much a successful enterprise differs from an unsuccessful one in knowledge accumulation. Probably no more than 5%! Because in an enterprise a large amount of knowledge that is commonly used by everyone is like an admission ticket, and, without an admission ticket, you will have no admission qualification, but an admission ticket doesn't mean you will succeed. It is 5% or even 2% and 3% of knowledge that determines your success. That knowledge is included in complementary, implicit knowledge. Because it is complementary, according to my criterion, it is unseparatable and uncarriable. An employee who possesses complementary knowledge is unwilling to leave his or her enterprise, because he or she cannot transplant his or her efficiency to another enterprise; because it is implicit, it is not easy to be stolen, simulated, and copied by other enterprises. If we call up the best employees of the best enterprises in China and organize them into a new enterprise, its efficiency will not surely be higher than that of the previous one, because most of the implicit knowledge the employees obtained by empirical accumulation has vanished. Thus, do our enterprises have the incentive and patience to constantly accumulate complementary knowledge?

Take Panasonic, for example. We all know Panasonic is an excellent company. In the 1980s it was about to launch a household auto electric toaster. In order to make a hit, it must ensure the bread its new product toasted is much better than the bread bought in marketplaces; or else, its product had no value. They spent much time in solving the quality problem but failed; the bread they toasted was not always satisfactory, and they couldn't figure out why its color and flavor were not good. When they learnt of Osaka International Hotel making the best quality bread in Osaka, they sent a development team of eight researchers to learn toasting bread from the chef in the hotel for two months. They finally realized the quality of toasted bread was determined by the process of kneading dough. They managed to master this implicit knowledge and to apply it to the design of toasters; in the end, the new toaster was a hit and became the most profitable appliance of Panasonic. Likewise, the reason why the quality of jiaozi (dumpling) produced by a jiaozi machine sold in the market is worse than that of handmade jiaozi is that the producer of jiaozi machines doesn't master the implicit knowledge of making jiaozi.

In many enterprises such as software enterprises, the knowledge possessed by sales personnel, financial personnel, and technicians should be extremely complementary and almost implicit. If our technicians don't know some basic knowledge of enterprise management, they cannot understand what sales personnel are talking about and what financial personnel are thinking of; if so, I doubt they can make satisfactory ERP software. Therefore, establishing complementary implicit knowledge is highly vital for such enterprises as Yonyou.

Indeed, enterprises' competitiveness should be eventually embodied by profits. But where does real profit come from? It actually comes from your innovation, product innovation, and technique innovation. Innovation is not technological invention but means that you make use of the same resources to create a product that consumers are willing to pay a higher price for or that you make use of less resources to produce the same quality product with a lower cost. Innovation must undergo the test of the market and examination of consumers, just like P & G produced the baby diaper I mentioned above. Of course, innovation of any enterprise is faced with uncertainty; without uncertainty, there will be no risk, and innovation will not make profits. In a word, profit stems from innovation and uncertainty. Only innovation of the most far-sighted entrepreneurs can become the growth point of enterprises' profits.

On this occasion, I think it is necessary to repeat what I said about Chinese enterprise innovation in some place. I highlight innovation and uncertainty. As a matter of fact, our Chinese enterprises are also busy with innovation and dealing with uncertainty. Thus, what difference is there between Chinese enterprises and Western enterprises? The difference is that Western enterprises are mainly confronted with uncertainty of the market and of technologies, while our Chinese enterprises spend too much energy and time in coping with uncertainty of policies and policy changes. In other words, innovation of Western enterprises largely involves products, technologies, and business models – namely, how to create more value for consumers – while Chinese enterprises spend much time on so-called "institutional" innovation (namely, how to carry out property rights reform, whether bonuses can be distributed, and whether stock options should be implemented, regardless of product innovation). In the long run, that is not feasible in the age of globalization and competition, because what consumers care about is the value you have created for them but not how busy you are. Of course, after China's reform was carried out during the past several years, especially after entering the WTO, Chinese business environment has been remarkably improved; now Chinese enterprises can spend more time and energy in studying uncertainty of the market and making product innovation.

To be a jujube instead of being a peach tree

When I was a child, I heard a saying in my hometown: "A jujube is not dead even if it seems to have no sign of life for three years. A peach tree is not alive even if it seems to thrive for four years". When a jujube doesn't grow leaves and dates for three years, you think it is dead, but it isn't actually; it will probably thrive in the fourth year. When you grow a peach tree and you see its leaves flourish for four successive years, you think it is alive, but you probably find it dies in the fifth year. Why? Because both trees have different roots. The root of jujube grows quite deep, so it dies uneasily; in contrast, the root of peach tree grows shallowly, and it hardly survives once the outside climate changes. I wish all of Chinese enterprises were jujubes rather than peach trees. We should think long-term and strike our roots deep to build real deep-level competitiveness instead of seeking short-term interests and caring about ostentation. Now enterprises pay more attention to risk control; as a matter of fact, building deep-level competitiveness is the best risk control. Any successful enterprise in the world will encounter crises, and only enterprises that have undergone the ordeal of crises and the trial of death can be considered as mature ones. Therefore, don't feel frustrated even in the face of difficulties in business. It is time that you build a great enterprise, because these difficulties are the propelling force for constant innovation and for building core competitiveness.

How private enterprises grow bigger and stronger[3]

Today my topic is about how private enterprises grow bigger and stronger, and my speech is targeted at those who have an ambition to make an enterprise into a cause. I believe most of private entrepreneurs present here have the ambition.

First of all, we can see in the past twenty years private enterprises experienced fast development. Some enterprises closed, and some thrived. According to the rankings made by the National Enterprise Association of China's top five hundred strongest enterprises in 2005, private enterprises account for 15.8%, compared to merely 3.8% in 2002. This is a great change, and I expect the proportion will increase year by year.

We can see that among the top five hundred strongest enterprises the efficiency indexes of private enterprises are higher than those of state-owned enterprises, which makes us feel gratified. We hope to make enterprises stronger, and we have thousands of reasons to do that. But why should we merely care about these major enterprises? We all know that medium-sized and small enterprises often outnumber large ones in any country and the proportion of large enterprises is merely a few percent, even less than 1%; why should we value them? What do they mean to society at large?

A large enterprise is actually a wholesale contractor. Merely 10–30% of its sales income is incremental value it creates. If we say 20% of sales income comes from its incremental value, the GDP created by China's top five hundred strongest enterprises is about 17%. We value large enterprises because they are leading enterprises, and what's important is that they lead the direction of industrial development and set technical standards. Besides, they determine global allocation of social resources including design, production, and sales. These large enterprises all over the world, like the top strongest ones, are more influential than many countries. They design products in places where there are best design talents, produce products in places where the cost is lowest, and sell products in places where there is the biggest market. Large enterprises are leaders of technological advances: 80% of research and development in the world and 71% of technological innovation are conducted by the world's top five hundred strongest enterprises, and 62% of technological transfers are also carried out among them.

Today I also intend to emphasize a view that has been my concern – namely, large enterprises play a significant role because they serve as a keeper of market order. That is to say, whether market order in a society is good depends on whether there are sufficient large enterprises and whether these enterprises can, on behalf of consumers, assume the responsibility for supervising producers in all of the value chains. Profit comes from responsibility, and large enterprises, to a larger extent, make profits by assuming supervising responsibility. From this point of view, the reason why the market in our country is in chaos is that there are no sufficient large (private) enterprises that are willing to bear the responsibility for upholding our market order.

In industrial value chains, the added value of large enterprises merely accounts for about 20%, but the proportion of their profits is much higher than that. Why? The most important reason is they have assumed supervising responsibility in place of consumers. Only they are capable of assuming the responsibility, so they can make profits. The proportion of service industry in value chains is extremely high and increasingly high. Why? Our consumers are distant from production, and we don't know where the goods we bought today are produced, so why should we trust them? The enterprise that finally sells products for us is willing to assume responsibility, so we like to pay the enterprise for that. That is why we value large enterprises.

How can we build a large enterprise? First, I will explain the experience of developed countries, and I summarize the following factors.

First, core technologies. We can see Microsoft and Intel thrive on core technologies. Once a company possesses core technologies, other companies will cooperate with it and become its suppliers, so it can grow bigger.

Second, low cost advantages. When you have cost advantages, you can grow bigger, especially in terms of manufacturing, but service industry is not the case.

Third, a supply chain management capability. How is your management capability from raw materials to processing to sales? How do Cisco, Dell, and Walmart that produce nothing become the largest global companies? It is the supply chain management capability. Dell can do a good job of managing all technological procedures for producing computers; thus it can supply you with computers in a timely manner when you order computers from it. Likewise, Cisco and Walmart are not producers either, but both of them value chain management.

Take Lenovo and Dell, for example. The profit rate of sales income of Lenovo is 10% and that of Dell reaches 30%. Dell creates value by means of outsourcing while Lenovo produces many of its own products.

Fourth, brand. Brand stands for a responsibility. Consumers are highly ignorant; and because they are ignorant, they are willing to pay reliable enterprises but unwilling to pay unreliable ones. We know some service companies and automobile companies such as Nike, P & G, and BMW belong to such reliable ones.

Fifth, monopoly of resources. There are two types of resources, natural resources and market resources such as capital and credit. If these market resources are monopolized, we have to obtain loans from banks. If we can obtain loans, we can build an enterprise into a bigger one; if not, we cannot make our enterprise grow bigger. Besides, there is industrial regulation. If government exerts strong regulation upon admission to industries, only enterprises that can obtain admission to industries can grow bigger.

If I have to sequence the above five factors in order of importance, I cannot say which one is the most important. But I think the first four factors are the most important core ones for growing enterprises in the competitive market. These four factors are correlated and influence each other. If you have core technologies, you will likely possess cost advantages; and after you have cost advantages, you will have a supply chain management capability and then brand. So, they are not isolated from each other.

How can China's top five hundred strongest enterprises grow so big? First and foremost, monopoly of resources. We can see 47.4% of profits made by these five hundred companies come from ten companies involving petroleum, chemical engineering, and telecommunications, all of which are monopoly enterprises and none of which is private. This indicates a big problem – that is, building a stronger enterprise in China requires monopoly. But I don't think private enterprises ought to do it like this.

Second, scale economy. Among China's top five hundred strongest enterprises, our manufacturing enterprises account for 56%, but many of them thrive on a cheap, low-cost scale economy.

Third, brand. There are four Chinese brands ranking among the World Top 500 Strongest Brands: Haier, Lenovo, CCTV, and Changhong. Many Chinese enterprises grow bigger but not owing to their brands.

Fourth, a supply chain management capability. Our enterprises do badly in this regard.

Last, core technologies. Few Chinese enterprises dare to say they thrive on core technologies. As far as China's top five hundred strongest enterprises are concerned, the proportion of research and development in sales income is merely 1.05%, and only 106 enterprises spend more than 1% on research and development; and a third of total research and development expenditure comes from ten companies. This is a striking contrast to the situation of Western countries.

According to international statistics of the proportion of national research and development expenditure in GDP, China is at the bottom, merely more than 0.5% but less than 1%, while Japan is at the top, followed by the United States, Germany, Britain, and Russia. We can also see it is good news that we are ascending recently.

After reviewing the contrast between China and Western countries, to admit it or not, we have to possess consciousness of urgency. Since competition is globalized, can our advantage of resources monopoly defeat others' core technologies? Can our low-cost advantages defeat others' brand advantages? Can our production capacity win over others' supply chain management capabilities? My answer is no! I am sure that when the market is open, our service industry will encounter bigger threats.

Besides resources monopoly enterprises, manufacturing enterprises are most likely to rank among the world's top five hundred strongest enterprises, and service enterprises will be promising in the foreseeable future. From the perspective of world labor division, we tend to work at the bottom of value chains because the top has been occupied. As a result, amid world labor division, the gap between the volume we produced and the value we created is widening; we have to pay plenty of transportation costs, but we obtain little added value. Moreover, we should worry about whether there will be a lot of international or domestic foreign-funded enterprises based in China that rank among the largest Chinese enterprises. Currently these foreign-owned enterprises are not considered as Chinese enterprises when we make the ranking. That deserves much attention from all of us.

For the sake of China, who will bear the responsibility of making large enterprises? I think without resource monopoly, our state-owned enterprises cannot grow bigger; they can impossibly grow bigger by merely relying on either their technologies or their brands. However, there are still some industries in which state-owned enterprises can continue to survive, such as tangible assets-intensive industries, resource monopoly industries, political-goal-oriented industries, and those where demands change slowly or technologies advance stagnantly. State-owned enterprises can plunge into these industries and can survive regardless of efficiency.

As far as enterprises that possess real international competitiveness are concerned, China's future depends on private enterprises. I am pondering over what we have done, and it is a vital problem how our private enterprises make their efforts. Here I propose several suggestions for your reference.

In my view, private enterprises must enhance research and development and emphasize developing core technologies and independent intellectual property rights. They used to take whatever from others and produce and sell them, but it is useless selling products without making profits. It deserves our reflection that currently many Chinese enterprises spend much more money in advertising than on research and development and pay too much more money for eating, drinking, and entertainment than for training employees. If we invest the money spent on eating, drinking, and entertainment into employee training and the money paid for advertising into research and development, long-term profits will be made.

There are diverse ways of building brands, including independent brands and international brands. In order to do that, we must do a good job of human resources preparation. Because we are going to carry out internationalization, it will seem impetuous if we don't make good preparations in human resources reserves.

In addition, we should improve supply chain management capabilities, which I intend to reiterate to the service industry. I worry about whether we can compete with Walmart and whether there will be any local Chinese enterprise engaged in chain-store retail business in China ten years later. Of course, we can get aided by many new technologies that are at our disposal to achieve the goal.

However, in order to make it, we must learn to cooperate and share value with others. Last year I also said that many Chinese enterprises preferred to pocket all profits without sharing. If there is no cooperation and value share among different enterprises, no enterprise will grow bigger and stronger.

Moreover, we must be cautious of traps in capital operation. If we don't have core competitiveness but become obsessed in capital operation, many private enterprises will be misled.

Lastly, the responsibility of government is paramount. Government should offer private enterprises bigger room for survival and more opportunities for competition and turn its speeches into actions. Many private enterprises don't feel safe, because they always think they tread as if on thin ice. We should be aware that macroeconomic regulation becomes deprivation of private capital, which is prevalent in many government departments and local governments. In a Chinese movie *A World without Thieves*, Wang Li (played by Rene Liu) deliberately seduced General Manager Liu (played by Fu Biao), and then Wang Bo (played by Andy Lau) as partner of Wang Li blackmailed Liu for that and drove his BMW away. Does it hold true for government? Government first entices private enterprises to make investment, and several years later it will take enterprises away. It is pathetic that such things keep occurring and that many private enterprises are ruined.

Indeed, there has been something wrong with some private enterprises. Some public media probably intended to use these examples to smear all private enterprises, which does much damage to the group of our entrepreneurs. What I am worried about is that if nothing changes, most of the enterprises occupying the Chinese market in the future will be foreign enterprises instead of Chinese ones. When our state-owned banks and large monopoly petroleum companies want to get listed in stock exchanges after reorganization, foreign companies are invited into investment as strategic investors, and Chinese private enterprises are not allowed to do so. Why not allow our private enterprises to hold some shares? If things continue this way, I am afraid many private enterprises that are most likely to succeed will flee away and they would rather sell their shares to foreigners than get fleeced. What good will that do to our country?

As I once said, the attitude we take toward private enterprises is a patriotic problem. If we don't want to sell the whole country to foreigners, we must provide private enterprises with a good enough environment and equal opportunities for access to markets.

Where is the room for local enterprises?[4]

Brand sensitivity and cultural sensitivity can serve as an analysis framework for simply explaining development prospects of Chinese and foreign enterprises engaged in different industries.

After China entered the WTO at the end of 2001, the academia and circles of enterprises cast their anxiety upon the prospects of Chinese enterprises. More than five years passed and facts prove that Chinese enterprises have done a much better job than many scholars and entrepreneurs had expected, which can be indicated by the following two indexes. The first index is amount of exports. China's amount of exports rose from 266.1 billion US dollars in 2001 to 969.1 billion US dollars in 2006. It is after entering the WTO that China has made such an achievement. The second is national foreign exchange reserve. Our country's foreign exchange reserve has surpassed 1,000 billion US dollars and will exceed 1,400 billion US dollars this year. We could not make it without the competitiveness of Chinese enterprises. We all know this has brought about many problems – for example, appreciation of the *renminbi* has become an international issue.

Under such circumstances, we have observed that Chinese and foreign enterprises engaged in different industries in China's markets perform differently. Take two industries – namely, mobile phone manufacturing and Internet, for example.

In 1998 there was no Chinese brand in the cellphone market, but in 2003 Chinese brands reached their golden age and accounted for 58% of the market share, and since then they have been in decline. Last year they merely accounted for 29% of the market share and are expected to continue decreasing this year. Foreign brands including Nokia, Motorola, and Samsung are dominating China's mobile phone market. Nokia has occupied 30% of the market share and Motorola 21%. Three or four foreign enterprises have basically divided the majority of China's market. Let's see the list of the top fifteen most popular brands. Nokia, Sony Ericsson, Motorola, and Samsung are at the top of the list. Among Chinese brands, Lenovo ranks the first place.

But the situation with another industry – namely, search engines and the like – is probably different. Statistics show that in 2006 in the search engine market, Baidu, a Chinese local enterprise, occupied 62.1% of the market share, Google 25.3%, and Yahoo! and other engines altogether less than 8%. Another market survey indicates that Baidu reached 66.3%, Google merely 18.1%, and Yahoo! 6%. Both surveys are indicative that a Chinese enterprise takes a lead in the search engine market. Furthermore, in 2004 there was a little difference among Baidu, Google, and Yahoo!. Baidu's market share is highest, 32–33%, and Google's and Yahoo!'s are both more than 20%. In 2006 there was a big difference: Baidu occupied 66%, Google and Yahoo! merely less than 20% or even less than 10%.

Besides search engines, let's see instant messengers. QQ occupied 78.7% of the market share, and MSN, the largest foreign brand, has accounted for 11.5%; other Chinese messengers such as NetEase POPO made up a certain proportion. Generally speaking, Chinese enterprises have taken a lead in the industry. Take C2C e-commercial business for example. Although Taobao is a latecomer, it has made up more than 60% of the market share. Each net has merely made up 29% after it was bought by eBay. In addition, other Chinese brands such as paipai also have accounted for a certain proportion. Thus, Chinese brands occupy a dominant position.

Let's see the online payment system. The largest payment system is Alipay, which occupied 42.9% of the market share, followed by Chinapay, accounting for 21%, and PayPal, a foreign brand, merely 17%. Chinese enterprises have still dominated the market. A global view indicates the top four most popular websites in China and Russia are domestic websites, and in Britain and France the top four are American websites. In South Korea the top three are Korean websites, and the fourth is Yahoo!. In Japan, the first two of the top four influential websites are American ones, and the rest are Japanese ones.

What is the reason why Chinese enterprises perform differently in different industries? Is it related to enterprises or industries? In early days experts in strategic management emphasized how an enterprise chose an appropriate industry, but, in the past decades, they tended to highlight whether you possessed core resources and core competitiveness, regardless of what industry you are engaged in. I am sure in the aforementioned examples, Chinese enterprises operate differently both for enterprise and for industry reasons. In other words, it really matters whether an enterprise itself develops well and whether the industry it engaged in flourishes.

Next I will propose an analysis framework for explaining such phenomena. We can look at an industry from two perspectives, brand sensitivity and cultural sensitivity. Brand sensitivity mainly comes from asymmetry of product and service information, which is related to complexity of technologies. To put it simply, the more complex technologies a product adopts, the more sensitive people are to its brand. It also has some bearing on household income level. The higher the income level of consumers is, the more sensitive consumers are to its brand. Cultural sensitivity stems from whether consumer products are group consumer products. Group consumer products mean how much satisfaction people can obtain from consumption relies on not only whether they can consume but on who other consumers are and whether these products can be enjoyed by many people. For example, the value of news is determined not only by its contents but by whether people are interested in similar news. Only when most of the people you are acquainted with show an interest in the news will it be a delight in your mind.

If we categorize industries from these two perspectives, there will be four types of industry. The first type is industries with high brand sensitivity and high cultural sensitivity, the second type is industries with high brand sensitivity and low cultural sensitivity, the third is industries with low brand sensitivity and high cultural sensitivity, and the fourth is industries with low brand sensitivity and low cultural sensitivity. Thus, that's why in different industries Chinese enterprises and foreign enterprises perform differently. Chinese enterprises know China better but lack brands in contrast with foreign enterprises. Chinese enterprises are still younger than foreign ones and in need of international reputations.

We can see, in the first type of industry, it will be difficult for foreign well-known brand-name enterprises to succeed because they have difficulty in having a full understanding of Chinese culture and consumers, which gives Chinese enterprises (latecomers, though) some certain opportunities and much time to emerge. Thus some Chinese brands will take a lead in these industries. But in the second type of industries, Western well-known enterprises will easily occupy the Chinese market, leaving few opportunities to Chinese enterprises. As far as the third type of industry is concerned, foreign enterprises can hardly enter Chinese market because of high cultural sensitivity; in contrast, owing to low brand sensitivity, Chinese enterprises can probably have chances to develop, but there won't be a group of enterprises dividing the market, nor will there be a dominant brand. In the fourth type of industry, both Chinese and foreign enterprises are likely to succeed, and in the meantime there will be no leading brand.

Now we can explain the phenomena mentioned above. The Internet industry is an industry with high brand sensitivity and cultural sensitivity, so every country can foster its own brands, like QQ, Baidu, and Sina in China, and Google in the United States. The mobile phone manufacturing industry belongs to the second type of industry in which Chinese enterprises have few opportunities to develop, and foreign brands can easily surpass Chinese ones. As for the third type, I haven't found an exact sample. Maybe it holds true for the industry of TV series. It has high cultural sensitivity, but we have few brands. Plenty of TV series emerge in China annually, but we have no idea where they are produced. The industry of components belongs to the fourth type. Take OME for example. Both foreign-funded enterprises and Chinese enterprises can do well in this industry but cannot easily obtain great market shares.

We must acknowledge culture per se is of variety and changeable. The United States, France, and Russia are culturally different from each other, though they are Western countries. After carrying out the socialist planned economy for several years, Russia has a great cultural difference from the United States. Thus, it is challenging for US companies to succeed (in the Internet industry, for instance) in Russia. However, British culture is quite similar to US culture, so is the case with France. Though French people have strong resistance to English, their cultural thinking is similar to Americans; thus American enterprises are successful in France. Take South Korea and Japan, for example. Japan is a highly open society, and Japanese culture (it is unique, though) mainly originates from foreign countries. As a result, in Japan foreign brands will be likely to dominate the market. In contrast, South Korea is partially open, and its culture partially comes from outside; thus foreign brands cannot easily obtain a leading position.

This is the analysis framework I propose. I expect it will be contributive to analyzing what Chinese enterprises should do and how they go global. When some Chinese enterprises including search engine enterprises that have obtained success in the domestic market decide to go global, they should be cautious because they won't necessarily succeed in other marketplaces. For example, if Baidu starts business in Europe or the United States, it deserves their careful consideration of how likely they will be to succeed. In industries where US enterprises have difficulty in succeeding in China, it is uneasy for Chinese enterprises to obtain success in the United States.

Management in the age of innovation[5]

The age we live in is called High-Tech Age, Information Age, or Age of Knowledge-Based Economy; as a matter of fact, all of them can be collectively referred to as Age of Innovation, which is mainly characterized by ever-changing science and technology. Therefore, persistent innovation has become the foundation stone of enterprise development.

In this ever-changing age, entrepreneurs and managers, as the subject of creating social wealth, are required to comprehend the essence of innovation and to keep transcending themselves, for the purpose of promoting persistent prosperity of enterprises.

First of all, ideologically we should fully recognize that innovation is not only the obligation of technicians but the fundamental function of entrepreneurs and that innovation per se shall be a practical and profitable action rather than a theoretical and imaginary one. Take Microsoft, for example. Microsoft is a leading company noted for innovation. In fact, its most successful innovations don't only lie in science and technology, since many successful inventions of science and technology used by it are not made by Microsoft. The key to its success lies in that Bill Gates created the concept of the software industry as he started his company. Without Microsoft, there would be no software industry in the world. It was Bill Gates who separated software from hardware and created a brand-new industry. Therefore, apparently the core of Microsoft's innovation is creation of a new business model, not merely advances of science and technology.

Second, the Age of Innovation has imposed concrete requirements on entrepreneurs' capabilities. The major concern for enterprise development has been what capabilities entrepreneurs and managers must possess in order to propel an enterprise's persistent innovation. As a matter of fact, entrepreneurs and managers are not required to be sci-tech experts, but they must possess a capability of seeing the future through clouds and have a thorough understanding of the development trend, future prospects, and applications of science and technology. The better a person's capability of foreseeing the future, the more likely he or she will be an entrepreneur and succeed. Bill Gates is a typical example. When computers were the size of a large room, Bill had foreseen the future of desktop personal computers. It was his great foresight that created success of Microsoft.

Creative destruction is possibly the most ill-accepted innovation. Schumpeter is an Austro-born American economist who is considered to be the father of innovation and originates many theories of enterprise innovation. He once said, "Innovation is creative destruction". In other words, innovation means destroying the past, the past of successful enterprises in industries. As we all know, many modern technologies have destroyed the past. For instance, Sony's Walkman revolutionized phonographs and tape-recorders, and DVD revolutionized video recorders, which led to the destruction of the industry in question. From today's perspective, these destructive innovations are self-evident, but still few companies can make them. For example, Sony has made few innovations in MP3 and MP4 because it didn't want to destroy the success of Walkman, although it was fully capable of taking the lead in the industry of portable audio products. In the early 1990s Microsoft didn't expect good prospects for the Internet because of Microsoft's special preference to personal computers. Fortunately, Microsoft eventually had the backbone to deny its previous wrong judgment.

With regard to understanding of innovation, more importantly, I think, we should recognize innovation is an action conducted by an enterprise instead of an individual. We should not hold that innovation depends on a burst of inspiration from some clever minds, but, in fact, it should be made by means of a standardized and routinized procedure. As to a successful enterprise, its innovative capability lies in the design of its holistic mechanism for fostering innovation. In this regard, Chinese enterprises still have a long way to go. In China, most innovations are created by personal actions, and nearly two thirds of patents are personal, not enterprise ones. In the United States, two thirds of patents are enterprise ones. One of the main reasons is that many Chinese enterprises are unwilling to invest in innovation. They lack a profound understanding of innovation.

Besides, what we must emphasize is that innovation is an incessant and persistent process. In other words, in order to carry out innovation, entrepreneurs and managers must possess enough patience and a long-term vision, because innovations are not instantly achievable nor do they exert an immediate impact on development of enterprises. In the 1960s P & G initiated disposable diapers, but it took a decade to go through the whole process from the beginning of their development to their release in the market. It was not because of technological problems but because it simply cost ten years to achieve the price level accepted by the market.

There are many innovations that are not instantly profitable, but they may provide enterprises with the foundation for future development; and therefore, it matters whether we are persistent in making innovation. The authors of this book take advantage of their ample innovation experience and entrepreneurship experience to tell readers of a series of setbacks during the innovation process and share with readers their success and joys after accomplishing entrepreneurship and innovation. They exhort readers to possess long-term vision and perseverance instead of impatience and impetuousness – that is, never attempt to innovate a technology or product within a short time that can occupy the large part of the market, let alone the whole market.

Innovation matters a lot to enterprises, and, under the conditions of economic globalization, innovation plays a significant role in sustainable development of enterprises. The overall policies of opening-up and reform have offered our enterprises a ticket to participate in the world competition, but whether we can rank among the world's top enterprises depends on whether our enterprises can forge the core competitiveness through technological and business innovation. However, sustainable technological and business innovation demands the collective efforts of the whole society, not merely investment of individual enterprises. As a popular saying goes, everyone bears their share of responsibility for promoting innovation. That is one of the purposes of publishing this book.

In order to build our society into an innovation-based society, first of all we must have freedom of thought, which is dependent on changing the mode of our preliminary education; second, we must foster some core values such as innovation risks, protection of intellectual property rights, and free competition. It is with regard to these topics that authors of this book share experience, exchange ideas, and elaborate theories. In particular, they expect this book to arouse readers' in-depth contemplation of changing our society into a real favorable society for innovation in a bid to better and extend our road of innovation.

Two essential capabilities an enterprise must foster[6]

Though all of you present are leaders of China's entrepreneurs, I venture to say, according to the research I have carried out for many years, the key to success lies in fostering two capabilities: I term the first one as a capability of creating value and the second one as a capability of assuming responsibility.

What on earth do enterprises compete with each other for? In fact, they compete for who can create more surplus value for consumers. By "surplus value" we mean balance between maximal value of a product or service for consumers and the price that an enterprise actually charges for its product or service, which is also called consumer surplus. Competition among enterprises is for the sake of creating the biggest surplus value for consumers, not for the sake of creating the biggest absolute value for consumers.

Take two enterprises, for example. Suppose the first enterprise's product creates the absolute value of 9 for consumers, and its cost is 6; and the second enterprise creates the absolute value of 8, and its cost is 4. As a result, it must be the second one that defeats the first one. The achievement China has made in the past thirty years is creating more consumer surplus for world consumers. The quality of our products is probably not better than that of US products, but some US enterprises cannot contend with ours; why? Because our cost is much lower, and we can leave more surplus to US consumers.

What should we keep in mind is an enterprise must emphasize creating value, which is also my understanding of market. What is a market? A market is a system in which others (i.e., consumers) instead of you have the final say. The job of entrepreneurs is serving consumers, and so entrepreneurs are actually servants. In the history of human beings for a long time, basically it was less intelligent people that served more intelligent ones. Only in a market economy do more intelligent people serve less intelligent ones. Entrepreneurs should remember that consumers are not grateful to the past. No matter how good your products used to be, they will leave you immediately as soon as your products are not so good as available alternatives. Only when your products remain good quality will you survive; otherwise, you will be finished.

Generally speaking, the more clients you serve, the more you are capable of making money. In other words, a market economy is the one benefiting the populace. You cannot make a fortune if you serve only a small number of clients. Therefore, we must bear in mind that the success of a new product depends on how big its market will be.

We must prioritize creating value because consumers are real bosses of enterprises. However, consumers often don't know what they really want. The paramount task of entrepreneurs is guessing out what consumers are in need of. In this sense, entrepreneurs can be classified into three types.

The first type of entrepreneurs can meet the needs that consumers themselves don't figure out. Take Steve Jobs, for example. He doesn't do market research, but he can produce goods to meet the needs of consumers, which they are unaware of. He is considered as one of the first-class entrepreneurs. The first-class entrepreneurs can create industries that haven't existed before.

The second type of entrepreneurs can meet the needs that have already existed in the market, such as building houses, running restaurants, and producing automobiles. Entrepreneurs of this kind focus on how they can surpass others. For instance, everyone is fond of Sichuan cuisine, but South Beauty has upgraded Sichuan cuisine to some extent.

Entrepreneurs of the third type focus on "make to order" (MOT) – namely, producing what clients design. What they should do is merely finishing clients' orders according to requirements, so is the case with OEM.

I think most of China's entrepreneurs belong to the second and third type and few belong to the first type. What we produce are almost the goods that have already existed in the market. If we are short of the first type of entrepreneurs, we can hardly create new industries. I hope we can make progress in this regard. This is the first capability I said, a capability of creating value.

The second capability is the one of assuming responsibility. Many cases that happened recently indicate some Chinese enterprises are not capable of assuming responsibility. The Melamine Milk scandal, Shuanghui's clenbuterol-tainted pork, and the problem with Alibaba's suppliers are typical examples. The market grows bigger and bigger; how to make trades? They rely on joint responsibility. How could Chinese emperors rule such a big country, without phone, e-mail, and Enterprise Resource Planning (ERP)? They adopted collective punishment formulated by Shang Yang (390–338 B.C., an important statesman of the State of Qin during the Warring States period of Chinese history). At that time, once an individual committed a crime, all of his or her relatives would be executed; and as a result, people had to supervise each other because as long as a person dared to rebel against rulers, others might get killed. However, enterprises' joint responsibility is different from collective punishment. The former is based on contracts instead of blood relationships and regional relationships. Everyone joins in an enterprise voluntarily, but as soon as he or she joins in, there will be a joint responsibility.

How can enterprises' joint responsibility be effective? That's the main reason why we need entrepreneurs and bosses. What is a boss? As I said many times, a boss is the one that has to be responsible for all the faults if he or she cannot find others' faults. What is an employee? An employee is the one that is faultless if others cannot find his or her fault. Everyone present here is private entrepreneurs; I think all of you must be aware of that. Take running a restaurant, for example. If a consumer suffers from diarrhea and gets hospitalized after he or she eats the food served by the restaurant, the restaurant owner will be responsible for it even if the owner is travelling abroad at the moment. The boss must assume the joint responsibility on behalf of all of employees.

Besides, an employer shall assume joint responsibilities for upstream enterprises. Take an Audi automobile, for example. Though the engine and most of the components are not produced by Audi, if the automobile goes wrong when a consumer drives it, for example, a bearing breaks down or steel material is unqualified, the consumer will hold Audi accountable. Audi shall assume the joint responsibility. Indeed Audi must have a set of responsibility presumption systems in a bid to ensure every link to function well. That is a capability of assuming responsibility I talked about. Suppose you run a restaurant and recruit a waiter; you will require him to make a physical examination even if no law prescribes you to do so; because if the waiter has an infectious disease and then infects your guests, you will have to bear consequences.

In the present, dairy companies develop fast, but their capability of assuming responsibility has not been established. That is the reason why consumers don't trust our products. We have to work hard on this problem. One of my students runs a dairy company, and his business goes smoothly for these years. I asked him why there was no problem with his dairy product. He said he had taken preventive measures. He had bought a milking machine and asked dairy farmers to bring cows to the company and use the machine to milk cows at 3 p.m. every day. Thus he thought it was unlikely that melamine could be added. But what if melamine is added to feedstuffs? If so, a milking machine will be useless. Therefore, establishing trust in society is paramount.

Profit stems from a capability of assuming responsibility. Only when an enterprise fosters a capability of assuming responsibility can it make a fortune.

Take China Guardian Auctions, for example. What if one of the items it has auctioned is a forgery? If so, Chen Dongsheng, president of Guardian Auctions, doesn't have a legal liability for compensation, because there is no related legal provisions. But he cannot avoid responsibility for his market reputation. Once an auction house's reputation is destroyed by selling forgery, no one will entrust it with authentic items. In fact, an auction house is a trading platform, and it cannot make a profit unless it is capable of assuming responsibilities for buyers. Without such a capability, it will probably be finished. Likewise, Ma Yun, president of Alibaba, shall assume responsibilities for tens of thousands of sellers in his e-business platform. If a fake product is sold through Alibaba, its reputation will be damaged; if it cannot foster a capability of assuming responsibility, its value of trading platform will diminish drastically, and it will be confronted with a bleak prospect. Of course, I believe enterprises tend to draw lessons from mistakes.

It should be noted that in the future China will be quite different from what it was. One reason is changes of China's labor supply will take place. For a long time, labor wage was kept at the same low level. In the past few years, it has risen, and in the future it will continue to rise up drastically. For example, in Beijing the salary of a nanny was 480 yuan monthly in 2002 and reaches 2400 yuan monthly this year, five times as much as nine years ago. When its cost keep increasing, how much surplus can an enterprise leave to consumers? Thus competition is growing intensive; only if you leave more surplus to consumers will consumers buy your products. That's why I suggest innovation is first and foremost. If we don't innovate and don't improve the capability of creating value as well as capability of assuming responsibility, we cannot survive in the future market. Although in the past we didn't create much overall value, but because our cost was low, we could survive by means of leaving much surplus to consumers. If you don't increase overall value in the future to rival US or European products, your money-making capability will be reduced greatly.

What I should remind you is that China's labor cost determines global labor cost. If labor wage of China doesn't increase, global labor cost won't rise. Once China's labor cost begins to rise, global labor cost will go up. What consequence will result? In contrast with the past thirty years, the proportion of labor in national income will rise, but the proportion of capital will drop within next thirty years. If you don't enhance your capability of creating value, you will be hopeless. Of course the capability of creating value is related to the capability of assuming responsibility. Only if an enterprise fosters both of them can it have a good prospect for development.

Lastly I would like to give some advice. What I just talked about is the logic of the market; as a matter of fact, there is another logic, the gangster logic. What's the difference between the logic of the market and gangster logic? The logic of the market means you cannot make a profit unless you create value for others, while the gangster logic means you can make a profit by means of robbing others of belongings. Frankly speaking, some of Chinese enterprises earn money by relying on the gangster logic rather than the logic of the market.

State-owned enterprises are typical examples. They allow nobody but themselves to go in for business, like gangsters. Now I am quite worried that private enterprises will commit the same mistake. Because government takes control of too many resources, private enterprises cannot make profits through creating value for others. It is risky that they are induced to make money by fostering good relations with officials of government departments or even by colluding with state-owned enterprises to impart interests of rivals and consumers.

Entrepreneurs shall face up to the market and cater for consumers' needs instead of relying on government and fawning on government officials. In particular, our private enterprises should learn to make profits in accordance with the real logic of the market rather than rob wealth in accordance with gangster logic.

Entrepreneurs with thinking power look further[7]

Part I

I am somewhat one of the earliest people that appealed to everyone to emphasize the group of China's entrepreneurs. It was as early as September 1984 that I published an article entitled "The Age Is in Need of Innovative Entrepreneurs" in *Dushu* (*Reading*, literally). Before that, discussions concerning economic reform in circles of economists largely revolved around income distribution and how to expand the decision-making power of enterprises; and entrepreneurs, the subject in market operation, had been neglected. My article was probably the first one published in China to publicize the role of entrepreneurs, and so it had exerted much influence after it was published. In this article, I put forward three views: first, entrepreneurs are the kings of economic growth; second, innovation is the fundamental function of entrepreneurs; and third, an adventurous spirit is one of basic qualities of entrepreneurs.

If we look at human history in the long run, we can find in the past two hundred years that there have been great differences among different economies; there has been much disparity between the rich and the poor; and there have arisen developed countries, underdeveloped countries, and developing countries. Given these obvious differences, we should also observe what the most famous and successful people in a country were doing: where they were starting up and doing businesses, the country flourished economically and became developed; where they were in government or military departments, the country was surely stagnant economically and remained underdeveloped. In fact, that has involved a problem of human resource allocation. To put it simply, a country's economic growth relies on the market, and the core driving force and organizer is entrepreneurs. Thus, the emergence of entrepreneurs is the growth of a country's economy. In retrospect, as China carried out the reform and opening-up in the past thirty years, more and more outstanding talents left government departments to start up business. Of course, at the beginning the first group of Chinese entrepreneurs came from the countryside. At present, more and more high-caliber talents such as doctors and postgraduates choose to start up business or join in enterprises. As a matter of fact, this is tremendous progress of the times, and human resources have been allocated and utilized efficiently. The process of China's reform and opening-up and the fast growth of China's economy is also that of China's entrepreneurs growing from a premature phase to be mature.

In the past thirty years, great changes have taken place in the external living conditions. First of all, our economic system is approaching a market economy. This means the environment for starting up business is becoming better, and competition in both the domestic market and the international market is intensifying, especially after China entered the WTO. Take entrepreneurs of the 1980s, for example. At that time they were undereducated and were at the bottom of society. They had nothing but an adventurous spirit. Because everything was in shortage at that time, they could make money as long as they were bold enough to do businesses. However, from the 1990s till now, the situation has changed. To be a successful entrepreneur, boldness is not sufficient. Broader vision, knowledge of the future, and understanding of clients' needs become more significant. In particular, the globalization has turned the whole world into a unified platform for competition. If any enterprise, whether from the East or the West, from a developed country or a developing country, intends to succeed in the globalized market, the key lies in mastering the market itself.

It can be said that Chinese entrepreneurs have made great progress in these decades. Few enterprises that emerged in the 1990s can rest easy, because new ones keep rising, and many enterprises are dying. After thirty years, it is only those surviving enterprises that dominate the market today. These enterprises have survived an intensive market competition and elimination process, and now they become more competitive. We can see successful Chinese entrepreneurs are fast learners and quite adaptable to changes of the environment. Among them there are some outstanding ones that can adapt to changes of the whole international environment and can succeed not only in China but in the world, such as Ren Zhengfei, president of Huawei, and Liu Chuanzhi, president of Lenovo. However, most of our enterprises succeed in the domestic market but lack the competence of participating in international competition. Their future is confronted with great challenges.

Part II

I always keep my eyes on Chinese entrepreneurs. But my attention is natural and totally independent, and it is just a responsibility of a scholar, unintentional and uncomplicated.

I am a scholar and professor and work on campus. The foremost thing for a scholar is remaining highly sensitive to practical problems in society and in the meantime being critical of society, government, and entrepreneurs. Either my critical views or constructive suggestions are for the sake of promoting social advance. Therefore, on the one hand, we should see Chinese entrepreneurs are always facing difficult living conditions and should appeal to everyone to change policies, laws, other systems, and cultural environments that are unfavorable to growth of enterprises and entrepreneurs. On the other hand, we have to admit that the whole community of entrepreneurs has many defects during its growth. The community of entrepreneurs consists of individuals, and every one of them will commit mistakes or even a crime. Thus, we are supposed to constructively and kindly warn them and continue reminding them of keeping in mind that their value lies in creating value for society and consumers and that they must be constantly innovative rather than be self-satisfied with being a stick-in-the-mud. Technological advance, enterprise expansion, and industrial restructuring are all actually products of enterprises' incessant innovation.

In reality, entrepreneurs will err and face many temptations. For instance, many people cannot resist the temptation of immediate short-term profits and are busy in making a fortune but regardless of long-term goals. As a result, plenty of enterprises have vanished after their transient golden age. At the moment, scholars are obligated to remind these entrepreneurs of what mission and what conception an enterprise shall have. Only when they adhere to this mission and this conception, can they build a sustainable enterprise. Let me give a simple example. Now the real estate industry and stock speculation are extremely profitable, and so many enterprises are allured into the real estate industry and stock speculation. But Liu Chuanzhihas managed to stand his ground. He is clearly aware that his enterprise lives on selling computers and is engaged in the high-tech industry, which is the mission and responsibility of his enterprise. However, many of his contemporary peers just vanished from our sight shortly after a flash in the pan, because they failed to resist temptations. There are some temptations that will probably lead to more disastrous consequences. In essence, enterprises are obligated to create value, but some of them are tempted into redistributing others' value, which we call rent-seeking; it will distract entrepreneurs' energy and time. At the moment, we need to remind them that they ought to spend their energy and time creating value instead of distributing others' value.

Indeed, if the social system and legal system are sound and well-developed, the only way of achieving success and earning money for entrepreneurs lies in creating value for others. Only if consumers recognize and buy your products can you make profits and your enterprise develop. If the systems are defective and full of many loopholes, especially when government takes control of many resources and powers, probably some people think the best way of earning money is fostering good connections with government instead of creating value for consumers, which is an unhealthy phenomenon. However, in China individual actions involve not only individual ideals and ideas but social environments; at times, it is difficult to clearly tell what is right from what is wrong. We must look at entrepreneurs' actions in the context of China's reform. When government plays a dominant role in many areas, entrepreneurs have no choice but to spend much more energy dealing with the government, or they won't survive. I keep reminding people where the border between enterprises and government is. In this regard, I wrote related papers and articles long ago, and for ten years I have been discussing that. Actually it was and is a big hot potato for entrepreneurs how to deal with the government. But luckily we are approaching marketization. In early days an individual's success was more dependent on his or her relationship to the government; as time goes by, the government's powers are decreasing. Now you may think you can succeed as long as you can foster good connections, but the fact is not necessarily so; in most cases it is the opposite. Therefore, you must concentrate your energy on making good products and satisfying clients. You cannot survive if only government is satisfactory.

Chinese scholars and intellectuals researching on entrepreneurs are confronted with a quite complex group. Now several million people can be called or claim to be entrepreneurs, but their qualities vary from one to another. Different people will encounter different problems. For example, when Li Dongsheng's TCL was going global, the biggest problem it faced was how to establish a cross-cultural enterprise and then manage it effectively. However, as far as a local real estate enterprise is concerned, the challenge is indeed how to obtain land from government. Thus, when we communicate with entrepreneurs, first of all we should understand what they think, value, and desire. The same thing will probably bring about different problems under different situations. In my view, Chinese scholars have made greater progress in understanding the group of entrepreneurs. But some people still feel intellectuals and entrepreneurs cannot understand each other, which I don't agree to.

In China the entrepreneurs had been despised in the past, especially during the period of a planned economy. In this regard, the purpose of our carrying out reforms is, in fact, to change such a situation. We intend to create a group of entrepreneurs for the sake of society and nation instead of themselves. Therefore, problems of entrepreneurs are not individual ones but nation-wide ones. It is crucial for our country how to induce more outstanding talents to start up enterprises. A successful entrepreneur must successfully create wealth and value for society. As to public opinion about entrepreneurs, it is always either good or bad, especially when Chinese government has quite complicated relationships with enterprises. Of course, it should be said that in a relatively developed, healthy, and democratic society, people are more inclined to be good at appreciating others and to gratefully and positively judge a person's contribution instead of criticizing individual actions so as to criticize the group as a whole. Indeed in our society there is a prevalent practice – namely, people seem to feel like envying and defaming others. But we should notice greater progress has been made. Back to twenty-five years ago when I wrote the first article on entrepreneurship, "entrepreneur" was basically a derogatory term, whereas now we at least don't regard it as such a term any more. In particular, many people are willing to call themselves entrepreneur, which is indicative of big progress.

Part III

Must the group as such be insightful or have so-called strong thinking power? I think it depends on what enterprise they are engaged in. For instance, running a small restaurant might not require any insightful thought, as long as customers are well served and satisfied. But running a world-class enterprise or a competitive enterprise in the global market, to a greater extent, is dependent on an entrepreneur's judgments and anticipation of the future. Because clients are from all parts of the world and their interests and tastes differ from each other, it becomes quite significant how to grasp the future. If a person wants to grasp the future, a great deal of thought training is essential.

It can be said there are plenty of entrepreneurs with thoughts, such as some members of China Entrepreneurs Forum and council members I contacted. Their thoughts displayed their judgments of the whole macro-economy. In particular, some of their views clearly expressed judgments of industrial development tendency, and some were indicative of their high inner humane qualities and management wisdom as well as such ideas as how to understand China's special development pattern and how Chinese enterprises grow in a world dominated by Western enterprises. However, in the face of China's challenging circumstances, mere thoughts don't necessarily lead to success. In any case solid work is necessary. Entrepreneurs can have solid thoughts, but they aren't thinkers after all; they are obligated to run enterprises. Sometimes we can see some entrepreneurs are good talkers but probably bad doers.

Chinese entrepreneurs have many deep-rooted thinking patterns related with Chinese traditional culture. In particular, I think, many of their ideas about managing people inherit Chinese traditions, whereas their ideas of managing things are mainly borrowed from Western countries. All of these ideas, Eastern or Western, are necessary. It must be acknowledged that, after having been accumulated for several hundred years, Western management ideas give expression to general characters of human beings. Don't think Chinese are essentially different from Westerners; there is no essential difference between us and them. Only because there is no essential difference can we observe that they were developed, but we were backward and that we have been trying to catch up with them for thirty years. If there was an essential difference, it would be impossible to explain these problems and make any comparison between us and them. Therefore, outstanding Chinese entrepreneurs must excel in integrating Chinese traditional culture, humanistic spirit, and managerial wisdom with fruits of modern Western management science and management practices.

As a matter of fact, every country has its own feature. The growth course of China's enterprises is quite short, so it is a great challenge for them to adapt to so many changes within as a short period as twenty or thirty years. It can be said that in the past many Chinese enterprises were basically related with circumstances and plenty of leaders spent too much energy dealing with changes of economic policy and institution, whereas now they are required to do well in bold operation, institutional innovation, and grasping development tendency of market and technology. I observe that when Western entrepreneurs get together, they are concerned about changes of technology and industry and how to do their job well; in contrast, when Chinese entrepreneurs have meetings, most of their topics revolve about policy problems as well as complaints such as unequal treatments private enterprises received, no access to loans, and no guarantee of property rights security. It is difficult to judge which one is right or wrong, and that is actually a process of people interacting with environments. To survive, you must adapt to environments you are situated in, but to develop, you must surpass environments and look much further.

Entrepreneurs cannot be passively adaptable to environments. They must do their utmost to change environments. A simple example is Vanke Real Estate Corporation. Why has Vanke been so successful compared with other real estate companies? At the beginning it didn't obtain a low-price land advantage from the government, so it had to lay emphasis on how to satisfy clients well. It could make profits only when it sold high for it couldn't buy low. How to sell high and satisfy buyers in the meantime? Create high value! Vanke spent much energy designing houses and satisfying buyers. In contrast, some other entrepreneurs who could buy land at a low price paid little attention to satisfying clients; they may make a fortune temporarily but will eventually vanish when competition is intensified. It is the favorable advantage that some enterprises have acquired that has destroyed themselves, because as environments change they are unable to adapt to them. In my view, this is equally the Achilles heel of Chinese entrepreneurs. To be an insightful entrepreneur, you must notice and overcome such a weakness.

Notes

1 A speech delivered at the Annual Summit of China Green Companies 2010, in April 2010.
2 On September 1, 2007, the annual Summit of Enterprise Operation and Management Innovation & Connecting World Class Management: China's Advantages and China's Models was held in Beijing by Yonyou Software. This is a speech I delivered at the summit.
3 Based on a speech I delivered at the Non-public Economic Development Forum of China 2005.
4 Based on a speech delivered at China's "Future Stars" Enterprises Annual Meeting on June 30, 2007.
5 A preface to *Innovation Wins the World*, edited by Zhang Yaqin and Zhang Weiying.
6 A speech delivered at the Summit of China Entrepreneurs Forum in Langfang, Hebeion, September 16, 2011.
7 Published on page 51 of *Economic Observer* on November 23, 2009.

Part six

Choices for the future

What should China's reform focus on in the following thirty years?[1]

A basic judgment of China's reform

If we look at China's reform within a span of sixty years, the reform in the past thirty years focused on economic systems and the emphasis in thirty years to come should be laid on political systems. China's economic system reform mainly revolves around four aspects: first, price liberalization; second, enterprise privatization (including establishment of new private enterprises and privatization of state-owned enterprises); third, decentralization; fourth, opening-up and internationalization.

In 2009, I made a judgment: with regard to economic reform, we had settled nearly all the economic problems and were solely left with technical problems. Some people probably have some misunderstandings about this judgment and think there is still a long road ahead for economic reform. Though I cannot agree to it more, I esteem that economic reform, including the future reform of state-owned enterprises, is left with technical problems. Take the reform of state-owned enterprises. In the 1980s and 1990s we were confronted with guidance problems, but in the future our reform will concentrate on technical problems, such as how to reduce state-owned shares. In my opinion, these technical problems can be solved without being discussed in Party Congresses. In the past year we witnessed that some new phenomena called "as the state advances, the private sector retreats" have reversed the reform carried out in the past several years. However, I am more optimistic. Within a span of sixty years the proportion of state-owned enterprises is expected to drop to no more than 10% by 2040, while it still accounts now for more than 35%. What does 10% mean? Before Margaret Thatcher, former UK prime minister, carried out privatization of UK state-owned enterprises, the proportion of British state-owned enterprises in the GDP was just 10%. Considering current situations, it will be a great change if the proportion of state-owned enterprises in the GDP drops from 35% to about 10%.

The measures we adopted to cope with the global financial crisis will probably foster bad debts of state-owned enterprises soon after several years.

Therefore, we will possibly require a new round of debt restructuring, just like what we did in the 1990s, which will impose pressure on the reform of some state-owned enterprises.

Besides, there is a major problem – namely, social system reform. Our government will spend a large amount of money on medical care, social security, and education. However, our future normal budget revenues are unable to afford these expenditures. A feasible way is to resell, sell off, and cash in state-owned shares, which can supply some financial support for social system reform. Hence, I optimistically believe that the proportion of state-owned enterprises in the GDP will drop to less than 10%. These problems can be tackled by technological means instead of being officially discussed in Party Congresses.

Emphasis should be laid on political system reform in the thirty years to come

First of all, it is a much more appropriate reform procedure that economic marketization comes before political democratization. As a matter of fact, since Deng Xiaoping started reform, we have been emphasizing political system reform; notwithstanding, till now the pace of political system reform has been relatively slow. I esteem this is right. Why must economic marketization come before political democratization? We must first clearly define what should be done by market and what should be done by government. Many people misunderstand democratization as if political democratization could solve problems concerning economy as well as education and social equity. Actually, democratization is a compromise and a political means for solving collective choice issues, not the best choice for every issue. So if we can cope with problems by appealing to market, we should not turn to democracy. What is the difference between market and democracy in the way of dealing with problems? A simple example can be illustrative. For example, assume that we want to have a lunch. Market means that every one of us carrying along money directly goes to a restaurant we like and orders whatever we like, whereas democracy denotes that we make a decision of where to go and what to eat collectively by voting – for example, a simple majority of people can decide what we will eat. Therefore, democracy is a compromise and will inevitably deprive a group of people of their rights and sacrifice efficiency.

To carry out democratization, marketization becomes more significant. Marketization is liberalization. If people, before economic marketization is completed, dream of political democratization that can bring out satisfactory effects, problems that can be better solved by individuals' appealing to market will be imposed on government. People will repose all their hopes on democratization and reform of government governance. However, historical experience indicates it cannot be unsuccessful. All those countries, whose economies are marketized, are destined to experience a lengthy and torturous process when they carry out democratization. In contrast, democratization would be easier after economic liberalization is accomplished. As is known to us, India is characterized by the fact that its democratization came before marketization, while our Taiwan and Hong Kong are successful examples of prioritizing economic marketization over political democratization. If government dominates too many resources, democratized politics cannot tackle corruption problems. For example, India is a highly corrupt country. Likewise, many democratic countries are equally quite corrupt. The reason is that they didn't undergo a marketizing process and their governments directly took control of plenty of resources to carry out democratization.

Second, democratization must be based on the foundation of citizens' fundamental consciousness of responsibility. But what is the basis for citizens' fundamental consciousness of responsibility? The middle class. As a matter of fact, human development in the past two hundred years is a process of the middle class continually emerging. Now it is noted that globalization is globalization of the middle class. Why? Because we all know democracy emphasizes that the individual must exercise a right and the exercise will consequently impose influence upon many people, unlike a person's wrong decision on buying stocks that only influences himself or herself. In other words, any of your decisions will produce a far-reaching effect, such as voting to elect someone as a leader or voting to decide whether a law should be passed. We can suppose what will happen to the population that is polarized by two extremes of the wealth distribution – namely, the richest on one side and the poorest on the other. The poor are unlikely to have any responsibility and are easier to be bribed and manipulated by a minority of people when voting in elections. The rich are immune to these restrictions because they are in possession of money and power and even can hire mafias to work for them. Therefore, neither the rich nor the poor would bear much more responsibility for society. In contrast, the middle-class people are rich enough to assume certain social responsibility on one hand, because they possess houses and cars and don't like social turmoil; but on the other hand, they are not rich enough to bully others at will. Therefore, among all these strata the middle class is the one with strongest responsibility consciousness. If the middle class is not dominant, a democratized society will probably become a society of mobs and be, in reality, manipulated by a minority of people. Only when the middle class is dominant will democratization possibly become a process that guarantees social liberty and equity.

It holds true for human history. Indeed, the United Kingdom started democratization quite earlier, but it was a progressive course after the rule of law was established. Initially the UK government merely allowed people who owned land to participate in elections, and those who didn't as well as women weren't allowed to vote. Of course, in order to carry out democratization today, these restrictions are not applicable. But we must consider some underlying reasons – why can some people vote and the others cannot? Even today when we carry out democratization or in democratic elections, not everyone has the right to vote. Only people above the age of eighteen can vote. The reason is also understandable. It is appropriate to permit an individual to vote only when he or she demonstrates enough responsibility through his or her behaviors and has responsibility consciousness of voting consequence and a capability of bearing responsibility. Things will surely go wrong if those who are not capable of bearing responsibility are allowed to vote.

So is the case with India's democratization problems. India abounds in plenty of poor classes, but middle-class people are scare, so it is a minority of people that manipulate a majority to carry out democratization. In 1990 I attended an international meeting held in Britain, and all of the attenders including journalists, politicians, and scholars of various countries applauded the reform of the Soviet Union and East Europe because at that time East Europe started democratization shortly after the Soviet Union Russia collapsed and Yeltsin came into power. None of attenders thought highly of China's reform and they even figured China's reform had failed because the 1989 disturbance just happened. I advised the host to arrange a seminar on China's reform. At the seminar I voiced some of my opinions. A Canadian reporter said to me, "I have written down all of what you said and if twenty years later your words are proven to be right, I will write a related article". The period from 1990 to 2010 is just twenty years. Facts have proven my judgment is right; I will discuss this with the reporter this year.

I still remember I drew a diagram like the Taiji Diagram to express the relativity between economic reform and political reform. China's reform doesn't merely mean economic reform. Economic reform occupied a large proportion in the first thirty years and gradually became less important in the second thirty years, while political reform took up less proportion in the first thirty years and progressively became dominant in the second thirty years. Indeed, in the end both economic reform and political reform are basically accomplished, and we will live in a market-based democratic society.

What is the core challenge of political system reform?

How can elite politics and elite management be integrated with democratization? China must prevent democratization from turning into gangster democracy, violent politics, and finally autocratic democracy. Why is it vital to develop the middle class in China? As is mentioned previously, if there isn't a strong responsible middle class with consciousness of citizenship, democratic politics, whether by electing or by voting, will lead to gangster management instead of elite management. Therefore, we should not rush into carrying out China's political democratization and economic marketization, because both of them are progressive processes that cannot be accomplished overnight.

Moreover, during the reform, a rule-of-law society must be established. The key lies in setting up authority of law and of courts. For example, when we elect a governor or a county mayor, it matters very much whether the election result is recognized by both winner and loser. If the result is controversial (even a US presidency election is sometimes controversial), an authoritative institution is needed to conduct arbitration. If authority of courts isn't established, everyone will stand their ground and disputes will still remain. If authority of courts is established, a court can decide who is winner and everyone must acknowledge the court' decision even if you are unhappy with it. A lot of similar problems also happen in Taiwan, and we can see courts' authority plays a vital role.

However, unfortunately, lots of our practices are weakening instead of strengthening authority of law and courts, which presents an extreme risk for our future reform. Many civil mass unrests were resulted in by people's seeking legal protection. Theoretically, when an individual's right is infringed, he or she can appeal to judicial decision and seek legal protection. Take house demolition and relocation, for example. What right do you have to demolish my house? How do the demolished protect their rights from infringement? These disputes between both parties are supposed to be judged by courts. But many practices are weakening authority of law, and in the meantime they are strengthening the administrative coordination by authority of government departments. Many individual cases evolved into mass unrests one after another owing to that people dealt with them in a non-legal way, which is extremely dangerous. Plenty of government departments have been oblivious of that.

In the present, we can see many disputes are solved by means of petitioning, appealing to government's coordination, and buying off, which will result in major events sooner or later. If courts settle, through legal means, civil disputes such as house demolition, and relocation compensation, you can refuse to accept as final, but once courts make a final decision by law, you have to obey it. If so, no major social disturbances will arise. Thus, I intend to note that this problem hasn't been fully realized by government. If government relies on itself to resolve these social contradictions and conflicts, social unrests, even turmoil, will probably be aroused. What is important is that only by appealing to the authority of courts and judicature can social issues be translated into various concrete cases and individual problems, which will guarantee social stability.

With regard to how to tackle other problems afterward, I think it is advisable to discuss them publicly in detail. Unfortunately, public discussion of this kind is not allowed under current circumstances. In the past, we held some grand public or closed meetings to discuss such issues as economic reform, price reform, and ownership reform; in contrast, overwhelming as political system reform is, we cannot discuss it freely in public, nor can we establish institutions to research on related problems.

It is quite troublesome that political system reform has always been a catchword after such a lengthy economic reform. I think it is advisable to research such models of democratization as Taiwan's and Hong Kong's. As a matter of fact, the pattern we adopted to deal with the issue of Hong Kong is equally contributive to solving many problems confronting political system reform in Mainland China. I think it is an effective way of guaranteeing elite politics and elite management to take advantage of functional organization-based election to complete transition. My view is not necessarily right, but I think we ought to discuss it. In particular, it should be discussable what procedures are more suitable for electing leaders and superior officials of governments at different levels. We are supposed to research on these problems such as how to safeguard social stability and take on elite politics and elite management during the democratizing process. If we cannot reach basic consensus on these problems, we will be thrown into an unfavorable situation.

The last act of China's two-hundred-year historical revolution

We anticipate China's reform will basically complete after thirty years from now, or by 2040. I agree with Chinese historian Tang Degang's view that there are two major structural revolutions in China's history. The first revolution is the change from feudalism to autocratic monarch, lasting two or three hundred years (from the reign of Duke Xiao of Qin to the reign of Emperor Wu in the Han Dynasty). After Emperor Wu, the imperial political system as a whole was stabilized, and how to manage it became a top priority. The second revolution is from autocratic monarch to establishment of democratic society and civil society, which also cost about two hundred years to complete. The period from the beginning of the Opium War in 1840 to 2040 just spans two hundred years. The past thirty years and the following thirty years will probably be the last act of China's two-hundred-year historical revolution. Since 1840 we have been seeking solutions to China's transformation by means of the Westernization Movement, the Hundred Days' Reform, the Revolution of 1911, the New Culture Movement, the Socialist Reformation, and the Reform and Opening-up. Finally, Deng Xiaoping helped us find a good road to prospering our economy. In the thirty years to come, we will need to find an effective way of carrying out political system reform.

Maybe this topic strays from my point. But if all of us adopt a historical perspective, years passed in a flash and these past happenings seem to be recent. For example, in 1776 the War of Independence broke in America; in 1865 black slaves were liberated; and one hundred years later – namely, in 1965 – US black people earned the equal right to vote. How long it is! However, then just over forty years later, a first black president was elected. That is really short! With regard to the climate issue under the spotlight, it was also in the 1960s that it began to attract attention from a small group of people; now it is on the top of the political agenda. Therefore, history is lengthy, but in retrospect it seems to happen in a flash. I have a bold prediction that China's second major historical transformation, economic or political, will basically be accomplished by 2040. Of course, accomplishment of China's historical transformation won't mean we will have nothing to do further. We will still be busy with consolidation of a democratic society. However, once the institutional framework is set up within next thirty years, what will remain are technical problems or routine management problems.

The ideas of politicians[2]

First of all, I intend to discuss the ideas of and sense of historical responsibility of the ruling party and its leaders. The reason why *The Resolution on Certain*

Questions in the History of Chinese Communist Party since the Founding of the People's Republic of China (*The Resolution* for short) came into being in 1981 is that the then leaders, including Deng Xiaoping and Hu Yaobang, had a right idea and vision about how to reform the country's system and to build it into a better one. Ideas direct actions, and actions call for qualified doers. Once I read a story about Deng Xiaoping. In 1977 Deng decided to restore the National College Entrance Examination, but the head of the Ministry of Education seemed to somewhat disagree with his decision and told him the exam was too complicated to be restored that year. Deng just replied, "It is up to you. Do it if you can; or I will let a more capable one do it". Then the problem was settled. Have there been similar examples today? No. I happen to know another story. In 1988 Shen Zulun was the governor of Zhejiang Province. The central leadership of the Chinese Communist Party made a decision to appoint him as Party Secretary of Zhejiang Province, which was an important promotion in China's official rank. However, Shen said, "I am fitter to be a governor rather than a party secretary. Please let me be a governor and choose a more suitable one for party secretary". Can we still possibly see such examples today? No. Indeed, at that time there was a group of doers full of ideas.

These days our country's disposition has altered, and our country seems to be in sub-health status. Some of us are solely keen on being government officials instead of doing practical things and care about gains and losses instead of what is right and what is wrong. I feel politicians should be much different from civil servants. Politicians are supposed to have conceptions, ideals, and ambitions and intend to earn a niche at the temple of fame. Civil servants are required to follow rules and make no mistakes. Experience of various countries has shown politicians cannot be cultivated in an orderly way from among civil servants and eminent politicians always appear out of the blue. However, the big problem with our system is that leaders of governments at various levels are mostly selected from among civil servants whose thoughts and conceptions probably lose individuality and become formularized after a great deal of cultivation. The problem is so crucial that if we cannot tackle it, in the future China will be confronted with big trouble – that is to say, when facing major crises, we can hardly make decisions according to our ideas, which is quite risky.

Second, I think we must give a re-understanding of history. Most of the history we have seen from official textbooks is not real or even falsified. After the global financial crisis we suddenly saw China's international status was quite high, and last year China's GDP ranked the second place in the world, surpassing Japan's. However, if we have a close look at the real history, we will find at least before the financial crisis, China's status didn't surpass its global status in 1945. Recently Zhu Min was appointed vice president of IMF, which was considered as a symbol of raising China's position. But long before the financial crisis China had already been one of four founders of the United Nations, a founder of many international organizations including the WTO's predecessor GATT as well as a member of G4. By 1943 all the unequal treaties those

Western imperialist countries imposed upon us had been annulled. In contrast, now our country hasn't been a member of G8 yet.

I intend to say the picture of our history has been extremely distorted. It is quite pathetic that people's understanding of history is distorted. If we don't thoroughly deny the Cultural Revolution, the spirit of Chinese people will not be purified and the shackles imposed on Chinese will never be broken. But to deny the Cultural Revolution thoroughly, you must tell the truth and allow facts to be published and known to everyone. However, I think it isn't justifiable that the problem remains unsolved even after thirty years since *The Resolution* was published. Though we felt excited about commemorating the Thirtieth Anniversary of the Publication of *The Resolution*, I think we weren't in a good mood.

Third, I figure the most vital thing we need to do is to implement the Constitution. In principle, a constitution is the fundamental law of a country and the most significant law. However, in our country the least important law is the Constitution. For example, in China you can cite any other legal provision in a lawsuit, but you are not allowed to cite articles of the Constitution. After I carefully reviewed our Constitution, I found few of the articles had ever been implemented and some of them were merely nominally implemented. Many of our written legal articles are good, but the problem is that they haven't been put into effect. If our descendants write history according to written versions of documents, the history will be distorted. If we spend ten years or twenty years implementing the Constitution, I think China will really become a country under the rule of law. Therefore, I appeal to carrying out a campaign of implementing the Constitution.

Lastly, the problem of ends and means. One of the errors we human beings make easiest is that we mistake a means for an end. For instance, earning money is supposed to be a means for living a happier life; however, many people are so obsessed with earning money that they gradually regard it as their end. Do we make errors of such kind in many aspects? Yes. Both the ruling of Communist Party and socialism are supposed to be means that make people happy, instead of an end. If they are means, you can judge advantages and disadvantages of different means according to the given end. However, if we mistake a means for an end, we cannot adopt one means to assess another means. For example, if travel is an end, you can judge which is better, by train or by plane. If you regard traveling by train as an end, all other transportation means will be less satisfactory in comparison. Therefore, in my view the problem of ends and means is a crucial one for us to discuss the future reform.

The rise of China relies on transformation of Chinese government[3]

Nowadays we have encountered some interesting phenomena. When we attended some international conferences, we found one of the most debated topics was China's economy, but I seldom noticed Chinese entrepreneurs and scholars appeared at these meetings. We can see products made in China are ubiquitous all over the world, but few of them belong to Chinese brands or brand products of Chinese enterprises. Recently the exchange rate of the *renminbi* (RMB) against the US dollar has become a hot issue, but on newspapers and TV programs all over the world, you cannot acquire a daily quotation of the exchange rate of the RMB against even major foreign currencies. I am really greatly confused about whether the RMB is important or not.

In the past twenty-five years China's economy has experienced quite fast development. In my view, the rise of China doesn't merely refer to the rise of China's economy, but has at least three connotations: first, the rise of China's economy; second, the rise of Chinese enterprises and entrepreneurs; third, the rise of Chinese culture. Currently it should be said that the rise of China's economy is much faster than the rise of Chinese entrepreneurs, which is far faster than that of Chinese culture in the world. Even if China's economy will surpass America's in 2050 just as Mr. Hu Zuliu just envisioned, I don't think our country is a powerful country standing rock-firm in the world if Chinese culture doesn't have a proper place in the world. Of course, the road to the rise of culture is still long and tortuous. There is a need for us to review what we have done in the past more than one hundred years. We must admit some of what we have done has ruined Chinese traditional culture, which resulted in plenty of problems we encounter today. Before we intend to rejuvenate Chinese culture, there are a number of problems to be tackled.

In retrospect, why is the rise of China's economy far faster than that of Chinese entrepreneurs? I think one of the main reasons has some bearing on government conducts. It can be said 50% of exported Chinese manufacturing products are exported by foreign enterprises, and Chinese entrepreneurs occupy an inferior status in the world. In contrast, India's economy is less developed, but Indian entrepreneurs enjoy a higher international status. It is difficult to say how many Chinese enterprises and how many Chinese entrepreneurs enjoy a respectful position the world over; besides, China's economy hasn't received a general recognition. Our state-owned enterprises stand at the commanding point of China's economy and are declining, whereas our Chinese private enterprises still occupy an inferior position. Why? I feel there is much to do with our government's conduct and its operating pattern. I believe there are six considerations in transformation and transition of Chinese government.

First of all, how can our government change from an unlimited and all-function one into a limited one? Our government is still in charge of too many things. In the past several years, the central government and local governments have been streamlining administrative approvals, but a closer look indicates many administrative approvals are maintained under other names and real rent-intensive approvals are not streamlined, though some government departments claim to reduce the quantity of approvals.

Second, how can we turn an offline government into an online one? For such a purpose, we should appeal to current network technologies. Recently when I attended the Cisco Public Management Summit during Nobel Week,

I was told a piece of important news that governments of various countries were strengthening E-government to enhance service efficiency and quality. Chinese government has made great progress in E-government. Though lots of governments in the world have reached the third or fourth stage of E-government and begun to provide services, most of the governments in China are still in the first stage – that is to say, they seldom offer services to local people but lay emphasis on uploading information to the Internet, including government files, activities of government leaders, and leaders' speeches.

Third, how can a government change from a local monopolist into a global competitor? We have noticed under a long-term closed economy the government serves as a monopolist, because no one can compete with it. Now the globalization confronts our government with a big conceptual change – namely, government isn't a monopolist any more. Because talents are on the move and capital is on the move, in the process of globalization our government becomes one of many competitors such as the US government and British government. Thus, our government is required to change its attitude and to earnestly increase the government's competitiveness, especially its global competitiveness from the perspective of a competitor.

Fourth, what's the most important is how a government can turn into a rule follower from a rule maker. Our government used to make rules and wasn't accustomed to obeying rules. At present, in the process of globalization a government is supposed not only to make rules but to abide by rules. In China the departments responsible for making rules are usually the ones that break rules. Take traffic rules, for example; do you know whose vehicles usually disregard traffic rules? Police vehicles, military vehicles, as well as government's vehicles. Currently government officials are hardly concerned about the interest of the people. As a matter of fact, we should see in a country under the rule of law most of the rules are made on government and for preventing the government from abusing its powers. Once, I explained many laws were designed for restricting discretional power. In fact, as far as penalty measurement is concerned, all people are equal before the law; but considering efficiency or fairness, it is wrong. The reason why we advocate all people are equal before the law is that we intend to prevent law enforcers from abusing their powers. If an individual makes a mistake, we should take measures suited to each individual. For example, a person who is in good health should be flogged forty strokes and a person of poor health twenty strokes. If both of them are given forty strokes of flogging respectively, it is unfair because the stronger one will stand it but the weaker one won't survive it. However, without equal punishment, someone who should be flogged forty strokes is more likely to be sentenced to twenty strokes or will be spared from being flogged under the excuse of poor health if the judge is bribed. If so, lots of problems concerning judge's abuse of powers will be aroused. That's why we insist law should be universal for all.

Fifth, how can a government change into a provider of social services from a social controller? Herein what I intend to highlight is problems concerning information supply. Many government departments hold a great deal of information, which is supposed to be used for the society and should be offered to enterprises, researchers, and the common people free of charge or at an appropriate price. However, many departments have monopolized information of such kind just for controlling people, even for making profits. We all know in modern society information is power and monopoly of information means monopoly of power. That is why they are unwilling to supply the information to enterprises and the common people. Therefore, a big change should take place in this regard.

Sixth, how can we turn our government from a self-centered one into a customer-oriented one? Government should regard the common people as clients the same way as enterprises treat clients as God. In a customer-centered and people-oriented government, what should be done depends on the interest of the people instead of the interest of government. We ought to introduce Customer Relationship Management (CRM) into government administration including the design of the government's website. Take the design of foreign governments' websites for example. When you enter their websites, you can sign up as a local resident or a guest. According to the demands of different customers, they will guide you step by step and offer you services suited for you. But it isn't the case for our governments' websites. Many of them including the website of the Planning Commission and of the Personnel Bureau aren't appropriate, because they are mere introductions to themselves.

Some fundamental changes have taken place in the relationship between government and citizens, which is caused by plenty of factors. One of the major factors is change of tax system. We know under the planned economy our government didn't tax individuals but gave us salaries after it obtained profits from state-owned enterprises. As a result, we used to think that every penny we earned was paid by government, so we should be grateful for each salary increase. However, the situation has changed. Now government begins to tax individuals. Although some of us are not used to taxation and unwilling to pay taxes, we should recognize that government raising revenue through taxation plays a vital role in improving government's services. Because when we pay taxes, everyone's consciousness of citizenship will be enhanced, and we will naturally demand that since government taxes us, it should offer better services to us. Let me take an analogy to make my point. When you are invited to a friend's home for dinner, you won't complain even if dishes taste bad and instead you will say "thank you", "the dinner is quite delicious and wonderful", and the like. But when you dine in a restaurant, you will complain if dishes are terrible. That is the difference. In the past it seemed like government fed us, but actually it used our money to feed us; and we felt grateful because we didn't realize it. Therefore, how government serves the people has become a crucial problem when taxes are levied on us. Or else, I think the people will have lots of complaints.

If we can do better in these six aspects, I esteem China's economy will have good development, and real world-class Chinese enterprises and entrepreneurs will eventually rise in the world.

The future world pattern hinges on China's reforms[4]

In the following twenty to thirty years, the United States will still hold the leading position. This, as a matter of fact, is equally in the interest of China, because China hasn't been qualified in all aspects for leading the world and cannot afford the huge price of assuming an international leadership responsibility.

In modern history, the United States has been the country with the greatest leadership, because it has exuberant social vitality and is capable of self-correcting and self-restoring. On the other hand, America, as a melting pot, attracts outstanding talents from all the parts of the world; such a characteristic has laid the foundation for its strength and prosperity.

On many occasions I recommended two books for US politicians. The first one is *An Inquiry into the Nature and Causes of the Wealth of Nations* by Adam Smith. It was published in the same year when America's War of Independence occurred. In principle, for more than two hundred years Adam Smith's idea has been spreading over the world. The reason why US politicians ought to read the book is that nowadays the United States is inclined for protectionism. No country with a closed mind instead of an open one can lead the world, and a closed world leader isn't legitimate. The second book is *Tao Te Ching* by Lao-tze. The United States used to lead countries with the same or similar values, whereas it begins to lead the world consisting of countries with plural or even different values. Under such condition, America ought to know, "What makes a great state is its being a low-lying and down-flowing stream"; in other words, adopting a low profile is the key to leading the world. However, at present, the US government is characterized by hegemony. It emphasizes freedom and democracy domestically but adopts autocratic foreign policies. Currently no other countries can challenge US leadership, but its leadership pattern needs to be changed. What China cannot accept is not US leadership but its leadership style.

In the past two hundred years the world has experienced an overwhelming change from the Great Divergence to the Great Convergence. Statistics have indicated that two hundred years ago the correlation coefficient of a country's population and GDP was 1, whereas it decreased drastically after the nineteenth century and reached the lowest level in the 1970s (the Great Divergence), and then dropped to around 0.55 at the beginning of the twenty-first century (the Great Convergence). It has exerted overwhelming impact on the world pattern of international relations whether the Great Convergence can continue.

In my view, the world pattern and the position of the United States, to a large extent, hinge on what China will do. If China keeps making mistakes, America's position will be strengthened. I used to take an optimist attitude toward China's development, but in the past two or three years my attitude has become discreet. It is because, first of all, some things that we previously considered as irreversible have begun to reverse, such as reversion of economic system, a new return to price regulation, and a planning system resulted from more and more government intervention and "as the state advances, the private sector retreats". In particular, the whole country's disposition has changed; for example, as far as government officials are concerned, in the 1980s they competed for earnestness and adventurousness, whereas at present they indulge in idle talks and cautiousness.

China has turned economic transformation into a matter of macro-economy, a matter of monetary policies as well as a matter of fiscal stimulus. However, the key to economic transformation lies in opening up the market and entrepreneurship. As for domestic markets, in recent years China has made its greatest achievements in transportation development. By drastically reducing transportation costs, China has fostered favorable conditions for unifying markets. However, the overriding problem is extremely high transaction costs. Chinese institutional weaknesses give birth to high transaction costs; and as a result, entrepreneurship cannot be given full play to, and eventually economic transformation cannot be completed. Besides, China's inclination to nationalism is overwhelmingly influential. Nowadays, state-owned enterprises have become a crucial factor in the Sino–US relationship. From a long-term perspective of international strategies, to maintain the state-ownership of state-owned enterprises is not beneficial and will bring about negative impact on China's globalization.

China's future development hinges on, to a large extent, political system reform. The major difference between China and India in development pattern is that India carried out political system democratization first and then economic liberalization while China did so vice versa. I feel that though chronologically China's development pattern is much better, it will surely be confronted with a huge risk, because political system reform is definitely unavoidable. In contrast, India has gone through such a reform.

I insist that in the following thirty years, China needs first to lay emphasis on judicial reform and establishment of a society under the rule of law within the first fifteen years and then focus on democratization reform in the second fifteen years. Putting judicial reform before democratization reform is quite vital, because the rule of law is the basis for social stability. In the long run China ought to explore a new path, and such an exploration can probably be enlightened by Hong Kong's, Taiwan's, and Vietnam's experience, which deserve our research. China can begin political reform first in functional groups and inner-party democracy. Perhaps, within thirty years, China can gradually complete the transition toward democratization.

There are plenty of conflicts in the Sino–US relationship, and they are mainly categorized into two types. The first type is interest conflict. Both countries contend with each other for interests including geopolitical advantages and resources. The other type is ideological conflict. The Sino–US relationship always revolves around both types of conflict. For example, the Taiwan issue is an issue of interest. The United States often fights for interests internationally under the banner of values.

However, occasionally, the United States is faced up with inner conflicts between interest demands and values demands. For instance, in the Middle East the rulers supported by America such as Mubarak are dictators whose values are against America's. Once these countries go wrong, the conflicts between interest and values become obvious. According to my observation, to deal with latest Middle East issues, the United States eventually subordinated interests to values instead of flagrantly supporting those dictators. America's inner conflicts will make trouble for the whole international community and affect the Sino-US relationship.

As far as interest conflicts are concerned, in principle, US entrepreneurs, economists, as well as political leaders are convinced that the economic interest brought about by win-win cooperation is much bigger than that in mutual conflicts. Thus, when it comes to economic interest, the United States and China mainly seek cooperation. The main conflicts come from differences of politics and core values. How can these conflicts be solved? Some solutions that can easily resolve international conflicts are hardly well acknowledged by domestic people.

In this regard, solutions to many Sino-US conflicts rely eventually on establishment of democracy through China's political system reform. The process of China's democratization is quite vital and risky, because China will be quite likely to either fulfill the rule of law and democracy as expected or worsen the current situation.

At present, we are confronted with two huge challenges, populism (including socialist egalitarianism) and nationalism respectively. After the country's several-decade development, authority of China's leaders can hardly be legitimated by seizing state power and consolidated by economic reform alone. The only way of reestablishing legitimacy is to promote political system reform. However, it is quite risky to promote the reform, if the leadership lacks political courage as well as sufficient decisiveness and authority, just by resorting to nationalism and populism for legitimacy. In that case, retrogression instead of large-scale reforms would probably take place. Imaginably, when subordinate leaders are acting wildly in defiance of the law and public interests and superior leaders don't have sufficient authority to take control, retrogression will be prevalent. When nationalism is mixed with populism, it becomes more difficult to carry out any rational act in China. When encountering problems currently we tend to make moral judgment, by appealing to popular opinion instead of logic of the market and spirit of the rule of law, and then disregard legitimacy of methods that we should adopt to solve problems. In brief, political system reform will be the decisive factor upon China's future development.

All in all, in the following ten years, either change of or maintenance of China's political system will bring crucial influence on China's future. As far as the United States is concerned, it is hardly to challenge its leadership in the years to come. Possibly China's economy will surpass America's in the future, but that doesn't mean China will be able to challenge the United States and be competent for leading the world. In 1890 America's economy surpassed the United Kingdom's, but America's leadership was not established until after World War II.

When dealing with economic problems, US leaders are too political and Chinese leaders too emotional, thus causing many troublesome situations. Take appreciation of the *renminbi*. It is unclear what good it does to the United States, but there are at least two anticipatory consequences the appreciation will bring about. First, American consumers will pay higher prices, and the United States will encounter faster price inflation; second, the appreciation will exert huge impact on profit structure of large international companies, especially transnational corporations and brand-name corporations, because they are situated in oligopoly markets where abundant profits can be earned and the appreciation will grab a portion of these profits.

In terms of international relations, in contrast to the United States supported by many open allies in the world, China doesn't have any open and staunch ally the world over; and hence it is difficult for China to challenge America's leadership.

I am convinced that it is ideas and thoughts that can determine history in the long run, but I hold both an optimistic and a pessimistic attitude. What I feel pessimistic about is transmission of ideas and thoughts is quite time-consuming; what I feel optimistic about is ideas and thoughts are still changing unnoticeably. Youths differ from the older generation of people in ideas. Currently in China there is control of speech on the one hand; on the other hand, transmission of information is really fast, and new ideas are being created continuously, which beyond all the government control.

For a long time, the connection between China and the United States was merely a governmental one, but now there are a lot of connections made by some non-governmental groups such as enterprises, scholars, and media, whose influence has been emphasized by the United States government. All of these groups are influencing how the world views China as well as the Sino-US relationship. In the future these non-governmental diplomatic forces will be the second channel of international exchange.

If a country is compared to an enterprise, from the perspective of the evolution theory, any country will surely encounter an opposing force when it evolves to some extent; similarly, no tree in the world can grow into the sky unrestrictedly! I feel the United States is unlikely to decline, but its international position will begin to decline in contrast to its glorious history. If China can keep promoting marketization reform and steadily carrying out political system reform, and can adopt appropriate diplomatic strategies, one-player domination of the United States will not probably continue for long. If China embarks on a wrong path, however, change of China's position and of America's position will become subtle.

Entrepreneurs and Taiwan's democratization[5]

Although I have been to Taiwan several times, I only have but a general knowledge of Taiwan. Both aforementioned papers have given a comprehensive and valuable introduction to related issues, which has benefited me a lot. In my view, it is appropriate that liberalization of economy comes before democratization of politics. It holds true for many countries and regions all over the world, of course, but not for all. For instance, in India democratization of politics came first. As far as Taiwan is concerned, its economic liberalization came first; and then the rise of the middle class naturally promoted political democratization. Generally speaking, Taiwan's relative success of its political transition is attributed to its early economic liberalization to some extent.

Taiwan's bureaucracy has played multiple roles in the transition; in particular, it gives room for entrepreneurs' survival. Any industrial policy or leaders' ideas that are unable to motivate entrepreneurship will not succeed easily. Apparently, Taiwan's economic success is underlain by non-governmental entrepreneurship. Here arises a significant question: why did few Chinese engage in enterprises in the past? Evidently, it is not because Chinese people lacked entrepreneurship but that the Chinese government was too powerful. In a long time the Chinese Imperial Examination System opened the doors of the bureaucratic system to the whole society, so that most talents swarmed into the bureaucracy. The temptation of being government officials frustrated people's will of being entrepreneurs. However, when Chinese people go abroad where they are excluded from government, they will choose to be entrepreneurs. Hong Kong is a typical example. Because Hong Kong had been under British control for so long, it was politically closed to local Chinese. They had no entry into government, so they had no choice but to go in for businesses. Eventually they prompted economic development of Hong Kong. Taiwan is another example. When KMT moved to Taiwan, they transplanted their political system. The local talents were denied the opportunity of moving upward – that is, being members of the bureaucracy, so they moved downward by starting up enterprises. Taiwan's manufacturing is outstanding, because manufacturing is the best industry for competitive entrepreneurship. In a word, I think the most influential factor of Taiwan's success lies in giving full play to entrepreneurship of local entrepreneurs.

The other crucial factor is making full use of the international market. Taiwan's market is quite small, but making use of the international market can bring about many favorable conditions. Besides, closedness of Mainland China's economy and politics at that time also gave opportunities to Taiwan, especially during and after the Korean War. Of course, if Mainland China's market had been open, a huge market between Taiwan and Mainland China would have taken shape if there were no political barriers. If so, perhaps we wouldn't have an opportunity to discuss Taiwan's experience today at all.

The development of entrepreneurship also plays an irreplaceable role in the democratization of Taiwan. When the demand of entrepreneurs for democratization grows to some extent, it cannot be suppressed but be met.

Next I will discuss what some of you mentioned in the morning. As far as I am concerned, it is quite vital that democracy is not about encouraging government to do good deeds but preventing it from doing wrongs. If democracy is expected to play a positive role, government shall have limited scope of authority and limited control of resources. If government exerts control over allocation of a quantity of resources, little room will be left to the market. In such a case, democracy won't assure a good government, nor will it prevent corruption, no matter how well-developed it is. Experience of many developing countries including India has proven that.

To a large extent democracy enables ordinary people to curb governmental actions; however, the society needs to operate after all, and thus elite management is required. In particular, our Chinese culture is traditionally a system of elite management conducted by either emperors or scholar-bureaucrats. When KMT moved to Taiwan, they also adopted elite management. If Mainland China pursues democratization in the future, we will be confronted with a quite important problem: how to integrate democracy with elite management? If we fail to solve it, democratization will become populization, because populism conforms to some aspects of human nature: everyone is inclined to profit at others' expense and gain without pains. That is the reason why populism is prevalent. It poses us a great challenge as to how to solve the problem!

In an enterprise, there is a board of directors and a board of shareholders. The latter differs from the former in terms of operating procedures and electoral rules. Shareholders take a vote for the sake of their own interests, while directors make decisions for the sake of holistic interests of the enterprise as required by fiduciary duty, instead of personal interests. Democratic election is akin to an election of a board of directors, so is the way of government leaders exercising its authority to a board of directors. For instance, in a presidential election, I as a citizen have a right to vote for whomever I like in term of my own interests. However, once the president takes office, he cannot merely represent voters who voted for him. Take the American president, for example. Though not all Americans vote for him, once he becomes president, at least he shall publicly claim to represent the entire country instead of those who voted for him. I have no idea of the philosophy of the Legislative Council, but I think it is more or less similar to that of a board of directors. In this regard, I should consult all of you. I am aware that we research on Taiwan-related issues because we are concerned with the future change of mainland instead of Taiwan per se. Taiwan's electoral system cannot be replicated in the mainland in the early stages. I attach importance to the voting systems of functional organizations in Hong Kong, which I think can be used for reference in our future democratization. Of course, the first and foremost thing is judicial independence. Without an independent judicial system, democratization is likely to lead to a civil war.

I am afraid the issue of Foxconn is not a micro-mechanism issue but a macrosystem one. As far as I know, Foxconn has built many entertainment facilities for their employees and given employees good salaries. However, under current circumstances in China, because of the household registration system, a worker is considered as a working tool instead of a human with emotions. This problem is beyond the capability of a single enterprise. The reason why I mention this is that whenever a problem arises, government often guides the public opinion against enterprises and entrepreneurs. Take inflation for instance; as a matter of fact, inflation is caused by the government, but the government diverts the public attention to enterprises by means of price fixing.

When we discuss problems concerning democracy, economic liberalization should be given top priority, because political democratization cannot work out these problems. The economic market remarkably differs from the political market. The former is easy to understand. To put it simply, an enterprise has to produce products that cater for consumers' needs; if consumers don't buy its products, it will not survive. In contrast, government is immune to this supply-demand rule, because the source of government's income is tax that is coercive. Whether the ordinary people are content with governmental services or not, government has income. Therefore, budget constraint becomes of importance to political democracy. With regard to tax, many people hold a holistic view that government's tax is never too much, and even the common people think so. However, if we want to curb government, generally speaking, another type of tax shall be reduced once a new type of tax is increased. If government's income is too much, democracy cannot prevent government from abusing its power.

Our government tends to snowball all its budgets incessantly. However, we must recognize that the common people will not feel secured if the government's power is not curbed first. Why are so many rich people in Mainland China eager to emigrate? Because the more property they possess, the less sense of security they have. This problem cannot be resolved merely by voting. What we are in want of is a society in which wealth keeps growing and individuals are granted a quantity of rights. This is what I elaborated above – that is, liberalization of economy comes before the democratization of politics. Besides, the private property system is extremely significant. When you own a house, you will be more or less motivated to protest if your house is coercively taken away by government. In this regard, development of real estate plays a crucial role in future democratization.

The Constitution of Mainland China has stipulated freedom of speech and other types of freedom in paper, but it hasn't been implemented yet. Actually, many of our political frameworks needn't be undone, and the problem lies in how to realize them in the future. We can borrow good ideas from our Constitution and learn from Taiwan's exemplary experience how to materialize them.

Notes

1 A speech the author gave in a symposium in 2010.
2 A speech delivered at the Forum for Commemorating the Thirtieth Anniversary of the Publication of *the Resolution on Certain Questions in the History of Chinese Communist Party since the Founding of the People's Republic of China.*
3 Based on a speech delivered at the 2004 Observer Forum.
4 A speech delivered at a seminar on Sino-US Relations held by *International Economic Review*, Institute of World Economics and Politics, Chinese Academy of Social Sciences. The original version was published in the fifth and sixtieth 2011 issue of *International Economic Review.*
5 A speech delivered at a seminar on political transition of Taiwan sponsored by Boyuan Foundation in 2011.

Index

For Product Safety Concerns and Information please contact our EU
representative GPSR@taylorandfrancis.com
Taylor & Francis Verlag GmbH, Kaufingerstraße 24, 80331 München, Germany

www.ingramcontent.com/pod-product-compliance
Ingram Content Group UK Ltd.
Pitfield, Milton Keynes, MK11 3LW, UK
UKHW020949180425
457613UK00019B/603